our funding, employment, and research direction still coming directly from the CIA and US military. No one genuinely concerned with the integrity of the discipline can afford to ignore this important book."

— David Graeber, Goldsmiths, University of London. Author of
Fragments of an Anarchist Anthropology

"[David Price is] the foremost authority on the ways in which anthropology has been used by the military."

— Jeremy Keenan, *Time Higher Education Supplement*

"A clarity of political principle has motivated David Price's work over the past twenty years. Price has been a determined—if sometimes lonely—voice highlighting the risks of anthropological collaboration, both covert and overt, with military and intelligence agencies. Price is partially motivated by frustration at what he sees as the silences surrounding military involvements, and how a lack of institutional and disciplinary memory has political consequences, most vividly seen in the increasingly open role played by anthropologists in combat operations in Iraq and Afghanistan."

— David Mills, University of Oxford.
Journal of the Royal Anthropological Institute

"David Price is a cartographer of covert power. He maps in topographic detail how deeply the CIA and other intelligence agencies have infiltrated American campuses, recruiting students, administrators and academics to work for the dark side. This meticulously researched book reveals how the discipline of anthropology has been perverted into a virtual "smart bomb" to be inflicted on indigenous populations who stand in the path of the imperial machine. *Weaponizing Anthropology* is a required field guide for how to spot a spook in the post-9/11 world."

— Jeffrey St. Clair, co-editor *CounterPunch*,
author of *Born Under a Bad Sky*

WEAPONIZING ANTHROPOLOGY

First published by
CounterPunch
and AK Press 2011

CounterPunch
PO Box 228
Petrolia, California
95558

AK Press
674-A 23rd St
Oakland, California
94612-1163

ISBN 978-1-84935-063-1

A catalog record for this book is available
from the Library of Congress.

Library of Congress Control Number:
2011920476

Design and typography by
Tiffany Wardle de Sousa.

Silhouette of Predator from a
photograph by Ryo Chijiiwa.

Typeset in Minion Pro, designed by
Robert Slimbach for Adobe Systems Inc.
and Hypatia Sans Pro, designed by
Thomas Phinney for Adobe Systems Inc.

Printed and bound in Canada.

WEAPONIZING ANTHROPOLOGY

SOCIAL SCIENCE IN SERVICE OF THE MILITARIZED STATE

DAVID H. PRICE

CounterPunch
PETROLIA

For Laura Nader, who teaches anthropologists to study up and confront power; and who taught me that critics have to work harder than those aligned with power.

Learn from me, if not by my precepts, at least by my example, how dangerous is the acquirement of knowledge.

—Victor Frankenstein

It is the nature of knowledge to escape the bonds of its creator; to believe otherwise is to persist in a supreme naivety about the nature of knowledge production and distribution.

—Montgomery McFate, 2007

If [Human Terrain Teams are] going to inform how targeting is done—whether that targeting is bad guys, development or governance—how our information is used is how it's going to be used… All I'm concerned about is pushing our information to as many soldiers as possible. The reality is there are people out there who are looking for bad guys to kill…I'd rather they did not operate in a vacuum.

—Human Terrain social scientist, Audrey Roberts quoted in the *Dallas Daily News*, April 8, 2009

TABLE OF CONTENTS

INTRODUCTION   Anthropology's Military Shadow **1**

PART I   POLITICS, ETHICS, AND THE MILITARY
INTELLIGENCE COMPLEX'S QUIET
TRIUMPHAL RETURN TO CAMPUS

CHAPTER ONE   War is a Force that Gives Anthropology Ethics . . .   **11**

CHAPTER TWO   The CIA's University Spies: PRISP, ICSP, NSEP,
and the Big Payback **33**

CHAPTER THREE   Social Science in Harness: The Gravitational
Distortions of the Minerva Initiative **59**

CHAPTER FOUR   Silent Coup: How the CIA Welcomed Itself
Back onto American University Campuses
without Public Protest **67**

PART II   MANUALS: DECONSTRUCTING THE
TEXTS OF CULTURAL WARFARE

CHAPTER FIVE   The Leaky Ship of Human Terrain Systems **95**

CHAPTER SIX   Commandeering Scholarship: The New
Counterinsurgency Manual, Anthropology,
and Academic Pillaging **113**

·   CHAPTER SEVEN   The Military Leveraging of Cultural
Knowledge: The 2004 Stryker Report
Evaluating Iraq Failures **133**

CHAPTER EIGHT   Rendering Cultural Complexities as
Stereotype: Anthropological Reflections
on the *Special Forces Advisor Guide* **139**

PART III   COUTERINSURGENCY THEORIES,
FANTASIES, AND HARSH REALITIES

CHAPTER NINE   Human Terrain Dissenter: Inside Human
Terrain Team Training's Heart of Darkness **155**

CHAPTER TEN   Going Native: Hollywood's
Human Terrain Avatars **173**

CHAPTER ELEVEN   Problems of Counterinsurgent Anthropological
Theory: or, By the Time a Military Relies
on Counterinsurgency for Foreign Victories
it has Already Lost **179**

CHAPTER TWELVE   Working for Robots: Human Terrain,
Anthropologists and the War in Afghanistan **193**

References Cited **203**

Index **213**

ANTHROPOLOGY'S MILITARY SHADOW

Just as it was becoming passé to remark on anthropology's status as colonialism's wanton stepchild, George Bush's Terror War rediscovered old militarized uses for culture, and invigorated new modernist dreams of harnessing anthropology and culture for the domination of others. Because I began in the early 1990s using the Freedom of Information Act, interviews, and archival research to document American anthropologists' interactions with military and intelligence agencies, by the time the post-9/11 push by the Pentagon and CIA to again use anthropological knowledge as tools for intelligence, warfare and counterinsurgency, I had a decent head start on documenting and thinking about some of this history. By the time America got its terror war on, I had already documented the details of how this worked in the past, and had thought about the core of the ethical, political and theoretical fundamentals of a critical approach to questions relating to the weaponization of anthropology.

But beyond my work on the ways that McCarthyism limited critical political debates in the 1950s, this head start offered little preparation for the wave of American jingoistic support for all things military and CIA as the nation willfully forgot the CIA's past involvement in torture, illegal arms deals, assassinations, undermining foreign democratic movements not to its liking, and embraced new forms of militarization as if this past had nothing to do with the rise of anti-American militarism around the globe.

Today's weaponization of anthropology and other social sciences has been a long time coming, and post-9/11 America's climate of fear coupled with reductions in traditional academic funding provided the conditions of a sort of perfect storm for the militarization of the discipline and the academy as a whole. While all societies have links between the production and use of knowledge and larger economic and political structures,

1

in the United States, the structural desires and holes that anthropological knowledge are desired to fill have been apparent for at least the past century.

Anthropology has always been funded to ask certain types of questions, or to know certain types of things: sometimes this has meant that there were more funds available to study the languages and cultures of specific geographic regions, in other times this meant entire theoretical approaches were fundable (like the simplistic culture and personality studies of the post war period, used to study our enemies at a distance), while others (critical Marxism, ca. 1952), were not. But even while the directions taken by anthropologists were frequently steered in general directions by the selective availability of funds, this arrangement allowed for some great variations in approaches or areas of study. But the post-9/11 world brought new variations on these old themes where a new form of the National Security State now wanted to cherry-pick individuals early in their careers and secretly place them in departments even while they maintained secret relationships and contacts with the CIA and other agencies. As the chapters on Minerva and the Pat Roberts Intelligence Scholars Programs argue, these new initiatives are built out of a recognition that military and intelligence agencies are ill-prepared to confront the issues and problems raised first by Bush's Terror Wars, and then Obama's Counterinsurgency Wars. Instead of freely funding social scientists to conduct research of their own choosing, the government now funds academics to think in increasingly narrow institutional ways—ways that are institutionally linked to the damaging narrow ways that the Pentagon, CIA and State already approach these problems.

As others have pointed out, while World War I was the Chemist's War and World War II the Physicists War, the current wars with their heavy reliance on the cultural knowledge needed for counterinsurgency and occupation are envisioned by many Pentagon strategists as the Anthropologists Wars; yet many in Washington seemed truly surprised at the push-back from anthropologists upon news of the formation of Human Terrain Teams and other efforts to adapt anthropology for counterinsurgency and asymmetrical warfare.

As military campaigns shift away from wars between states, to wars of quick conquest and grueling endless occupations of regions identified with ethnic or "tribal" groups rather than national boundaries, the needs for anthropological knowledge and skill sets grow. The needs for on-the-ground cultural knowledge, linguistic competence, knowledge of local customs, traditional symbols and culture history loom large, but so far, the American military clearly misunderstands just how much difference cultural competence could make in hiding the nakedness of American mercenary ventures. But the military also misunderstand what elements of anthropology they can and can't meaningfully use. Much of this confusion is exacerbated by the anthropologists who often misrepresent the discipline and its skill sets as they sell their wares to an eager military hungry for answers.

There is an inherent irony in the military's recurrent desires to acquire and weaponize anthropology. The military does not understand that anthropology is not just a product: when practiced ethically, anthropology can be transformative. Anthropologists can come to have rich understandings not only of the people they live with but of the larger processes governing the warfare that desires to consume anthropological knowledge; and the intellectual, personal and professional loyalties of anthropologists engaged in such transformative processes therefore often tie them to the communities they study.

It is because of these inherent relationships that the military can't easily have anthropology for counterinsurgency. I don't mean "can't" in some sort of defiant way—I mean that (despite a history of efforts to harness anthropology for such ends) the processes of using anthropology to subvert political movements is very unanthropological. While the military can hire people with anthropology degrees, read our work, steal it without attribution (as they did in their new COIN manual), republish our writings in classified forms, and use our methods…they can and *have* done all of these things: but they are getting something less than anthropology. Given the inherent sympathies that emerge from anthropologists' process of participant observation one of two things will happen: either these counterinsurgent-anthropologists will psychologically dissociate themselves from their betrayal of those they study for counterinsurgency—telling themselves that they are "protectors" not subvertors; or the process of ethnographic identification will lead them to redirect their own loyalties from those of their military masters to those they study. One outcome is something less than anthropology, the other something more than the military bargains for.

It's not that we live in a universe where those who live with the "others" anthropologists study are transformed in ways that make it impossible for anthropologists to betray them or their interests (as if knowing such interests were somehow objectively clear); but it also isn't that we live in a universe where something like this can't happen. Perhaps this explains why even under current conditions in which anthropology graduate students sometimes graduate with debt loads that used to be associated with Medical School, there still remains only a small handful of anthropologists succumbing to the outrageous fortunes being paid to those who will overlook the obvious ethical and political problems of working for Human Terrain Teams. Today, out of the over four hundred Human Terrain System's employees, less than eight have advanced anthropology degrees.

There are good logistical reasons why military commanders want the sort of cultural information that anthropologists possess about the cultures they study—but when faced with conflicting duties pitting the claimed needs of nation against professional standards of conduct, anthropologists must stand upon clearly thought-out ethical standards that clarify why the satisfaction of these needs lies beyond our disciplinary limits. These lessons were learned though anthropological experiences in past wars, but naïve anthropologists striking avante-garde poses dismiss the past, acting as if their individual goodwill could overcome this history on the fly.

The chapters in this book make passing references to the history of anthropologists' interactions with military and intelligence agencies, this is because my analysis of the contemporary expansion of military and intelligence agencies onto our campuses is deeply informed by my academic research and writings on the history of these interactions. I find extraordinary continuities of roles, status, and economic contingencies between the military and academy as many of the present efforts to use anthropology for conquest mirror specific failed efforts to use and abuse American anthropology during the Second World War and the Vietnam War with little realization of these continuities of failure. Beyond this historical background, I also draw upon my anthropological interest in studying relationships between cultural economic systems and cultural ideological systems of knowledge. Though it counters the predominant postmodern fashion of rejecting meta narrative explanations: the political economy of American academia needs to be critically examined as linked to the dominant militarized economy that supports American society. These chapters chronicle a dramatic shift in the production of academic knowledge, as military and intelligence sectors are now impatient to receive the broad range of social science knowledge that has long served them as they now take active measures to more directly harness the production of knowledge to more exactly fit their intelligence and training needs.

* * *

The book is organized in three sections: the first section describes the ethical and political problems of anthropologists, and other social scientists' engagements with military and intelligence agencies and accounts of recent innovations (programs like the Minerva Consortium, the Pat Roberts Intelligence Scholarship Program and the Intelligence Community Centers of Academic Excellence) designed to enmesh the military industrial state with anthropology and other social sciences. The second section critically examines a series of leaked and publically available military documents; using these texts to understand how the new military and intelligence initiatives seek to harness social science for their own ends in current and future military missions. These leaked manuals demonstrate how the military dreams that culture can be (has been) conceived of as an identifiable and controllable commodity that can be used (to quote the 2004 Stryker Report Evaluating Iraqi Failures) as a "lever" to be used to move (enemy, occupied, resistant) populations by smart military or intelligence agencies. Missing from these manuals is any sort of understanding of the complexities of culture that fill anthropologists writings, these complexities are instead edited out, leaving uncomplicated heuristic narratives that create fictions more than they simplify. Finally, the third section considers a variety of contemporary uses of social science theory and data in support of counterinsurgency operations in the so called "war on terror," including the training and policies of Human Terrain Teams for use in Iraq and Afghanistan.

To clear up some possible confusion about the title, from 2005-2007, *Weaponizing Anthropology* was the working title of my book that became *Anthropological Intelligence* (Price 2008), and any published references to the title *Weaponizing Anthropology* from the 2005-2007 period refer to that re-titled book.

In the weeks after 9/11 I published my first piece in *CounterPunch,* and Alexander Cockburn and Jeffrey St. Clair are the people most responsible for allowing me to develop the essays that form the heart of this collection. Without *CounterPunch*, I would not have had the support or venue to develop these critiques, and even if I did, other editors would have pushed me to ease the directness of my critique, urging obscurantist prose in the name of "nuance." The work benefitted from exchanges with the following colleagues and friends: John Allison, Thomas Anson, Julian Assange, Catherine Besteman, Andy Bickford, Jeff Birkenstein, Jason Collins, Tony Cortese, Daniel Domscheit-Berg, Greg Feldman, Maximilian Forte, Roberto González, Linda Green, Hugh Gusterson, Gustaaf Houtman, Jean Jackson, Bea Jauregui, John D. Kelly, Kanhong Lin, Brian Loschiavo, Catherine Lutz, Stephen Mead, Sean T. Mitchell, Hayder Al-Mohammad, Laura Nader, Steve Niva, David Patton, Midge Price, Milo Price, Nora Price, Lisa Queen, Eric Ross, Marshall Sahlins, Schuyler Schild, Daniel Segal, Roger Snider, David Vine, Jeremy Walton, Michele Weisler, and Cathy Wilson.

The initial sources for chapters are as follows: Chapter One: is based on a paper I presented on February 9, 2009 at Pitzer College as part of Pitzer's Interpreting War and Conflict series; Chapter Two: *CP* 2005 12(1):1-6; *CP* 2005 12(5):3-4.; *CP* 2008 15(15):6-8; Chapter Three *CP* online 6/25/08; Chapter Four *CP* 2010 17(2):1-5; Chapter Five: elements from *CP* online 12/12/08 and *CP* online 2009 4/7/09; Chapter Six: *CP* 2007 14(18):1-6; Chapter Seven *CP* online 4/18/08 & Keynote Address, War and Social Sciences Symposium, University of Arizona, 1/24/09; Chapter Eight: is expanded and reprinted with permission and is based on my 2010 article "The Army's Take on Culture" *Anthropology Now* 12(1):57-63 and incorporates material from a October 1, 2009, presentation at Syracuse University's Anthropology Department on "Structural Limits of Anthropological Engagements with the Military,"; Chapter Nine: *CP* online 2010 2/15/10; Chapter Ten: *CP* online 2009 12/23/09; Chapter Eleven: paper presented on April 24, 2009 at the University of Chicago Anthropology Department's conference on Reconsidering American Power; Chapter Twelve: *CP* 2009 16(17):1, 4-6.

PART I POLITICS, ETHICS, AND THE MILITARY INTELLIGENCE COMPLEX'S QUIET TRIUMPHAL RETURN TO CAMPUS

CHAPTER ONE

WAR IS A FORCE THAT GIVES ANTHROPOLOGY ETHICS

Try to learn to let what is unfair teach you.
—David Foster Wallace, *Infinite Jest*

Anthropology has always fed between the lines of war. Whether these wars rage hot in the immediate foreground of fieldwork settings or influence the background of funding opportunities, wars and the political concerns of "National Security" have long influenced the development of anthropological theory and practice. Since the 1960s, anthropologists have become increasingly conscious of the ways that knowledge honed from fieldwork was historically used by colonial and military powers against the populations anthropologists share lives with and study. American anthropology's efforts to grapple with the political and ethical problems associated with warfare have been episodic, occasionally heroic, sometimes timid, and often embarrassingly linked to the whims of market forces as funding sources have recurrently situated individual anthropologists between the needs-of and duties-to those they study.

Although anthropologists have historically lent their skills to a range of military and colonial campaigns, the last hundred years has not been without moments of progress, minor enlightenments, and tangible contributions to social justice movements. During the past half-century, even while the need for anthropologically informed military maneuvers has increased, the fundamental ethical, moral and political issues raised by these activities have periodically forced the discipline to not only critically confront ethical and political questions about what anthropology is and what it is good for, but historically for American anthropology, it has been the abuses of anthropological knowledge in times of war that forced the discipline, in episodic spasms, to develop professional ethics codes.

In a world of political power struggles and military might, knowledge of other cultures has long been recognized as possessing a strategic value. Long before there was even a formal academic discipline of anthropology, politicians and militaries had uses for understanding the language and culture of their enemies. Because of the structural needs of occupations after conquests, basic forms of counterinsurgency have been around far longer than David Galula, Edward Lansdale, Sir Richard Thompson and contemporary counterinsurgency gurus. Sun Tzu understood the dangers of occupations and acknowledged that insurgencies at times lead wise leaders to abandon some occupations. Alexander the Great encouraged his mercenary armies to intermarry with locals, providing them with financial incentives to put down local roots in ways that stabilized the empire, and plenty of other conquerors have understood the basic principles of population centric dominance. The Greek occupation of Ptolemaic Egypt became a sort of historical high water mark in the cynicism of military occupations, as the Greek occupiers calculatingly merged their religious views with local Egyptian beliefs in ways that eased the political scene, allowing the export of goods and profits back to the empire's core.

But counterinsurgency isn't just concerned with occupations through forms of indirect rule. At times, counterinsurgency campaigns undermine traditional power structures and traditional economic systems, asserting external economic forces on indigenous political economies. There is nothing modern in recognizing that if one can get enemy populations to give up their traditional means of economic independence and make them dependent upon occupiers for the health or economic well-being, one can undermine traditional systems of governance and dominate these populations. These are standard counterinsurgency tactics, and the elements of these tactics can be seen in the Vietnam War's failed Strategic Hamlets Program as well as contemporary economic reformation projects in Afghanistan undermining poppy production and other elements of the traditional local economy.

To provide but a single pre-anthropology example of historical forms of intercultural counterinsurgency, consider American President Thomas Jefferson's secret briefing to Congress of January 18, 1803 in which, while secretly asking for $2,500 to fund the Lewis and Clark Expedition, Jefferson described plans to undertake what would later become a staple tactic of Twentieth Century counterinsurgency: undermining the traditional economic systems of enemies and then entrapping them in aggressive market-based economies in which they will have difficulty competing on an equal basis. President Jefferson advised congress that:

> The Indian tribes residing within the limits of the U.S. have for a considerable time been growing more & more uneasy at the constant diminution of the territory they occupy, altho' effected by their own voluntary sales; and the policy has long been gaining strength with them of refusing absolutely all further sale on any conditions, insomuch that, at this time, it hazards their friendship, and excites dangerous jealousies [and] perturbations in their minds to make any overture for the purchase of the smallest portions of their land. A very few tribes only are not yet obstinately in these dispositions. In order peaceably to counteract this policy of theirs, and to provide an extension of territory which the rapid increase of our numbers will call for, two measures are deemed expedient. First, to encourage them to abandon hunting, to apply to the raising stock, to agriculture and domestic manufacture, and thereby prove to themselves that less land & labor will maintain them in this, better than in their former mode of living. The extensive forests necessary in the hunting life will then become useless, & they will see advantage in exchanging them for the means of improving their farms, & of increasing their domestic comforts. Secondly to multiply trading houses among them & place within their reach those things which will contribute more to their domestic comfort then the profession of extensive, but uncultivated wilds, experience & reflection will develop to them the wisdom of exchanging what they can spare & we want, for what we can spare and they want. (Jefferson to Congress 1/18/1803)

Jefferson's counterinsurgency operation recognized that the US government could provide economic incentives for Indians to become more dependent on raising stock, and therefore "abandoning hunting," which would open more lands for the US government to claim. This planned destruction of the Indian's reliance on their traditional economy would necessarily erode cultural cohesion. With time, and a certain amount of armed counterinsurgency, as the forests became "useless" to these displaced peoples, they became increasingly dependent as marginal players trapped as latecomers cornered at the edge of a market economy. The lure of increased "domestic comforts," in modern times promised by an assortment of economic hitmen, remains a central carrot from Jefferson's time to the present, and those pitching these schemes are seldom held accountable for their failures. Jefferson's approach contained seeds of the standard tactics of population dislocation and population control.

We are left to wonder how much smoother Jefferson's counterinsurgency campaign might have been had President Jefferson dispatched a squadron of applied anthropologists to soften the blow of conquest, offering microloans, helping to relocate settlements, and getting to know the names, lineages and traditional songs of those succumbing to the needs of the Republic. On one level Lewis and Clark's role as agents in this American expansion westward made them like members of a first generation of development anthropologists selling the promises of modernization to those who would be displaced and damaged by the "progress" to come.

The early formalization of anthropology as a discipline occurred in the mid- to late-nineteenth century in a political economy where a mixture of colonialist gentlemen explorers, missionaries, functionaries at colonial outposts, dilettantes and occasional savants slowly came to understand the ways of the "others" that lived within and at the edges of Empire's borders. Early anthropologists filled that complex hole of empire's knowledge base with a useful understanding of culture that was both enlightened and mercenary. Anthropology's roots grew in the soils of established military might in lands conquered by European powers, often some years after military forces laid conquest. The arrival of anthropologists often followed a progression of arrivals that flowed from infantries, to plantation or mining engineers, missionaries, then finally: anthropologists—these at times being self styled ethnographers working as colonial administrators in the hinterlands of empire. As the British, Dutch, French, and German, etc. empires spread around the globe, national traditions of ethnology and anthropology emerged. The needs of colonialism often required some knowledge of the occupied populations they sought to manage, and anthropology was born. As

Talal Asad observed almost forty years ago, "anthropologists can claim to have contributed to the cultural heritage of the societies they study by a sympathetic recording of indigenous forms of life that would otherwise be lost to posterity. But they have also contributed, sometimes indirectly, towards maintaining the structure of power represented by the colonial system" (Asad 1973:17).

The early American history of ethnological studies of Native Americans cannot be told as separate from a shameful history of conquest and genocide; and while many early American ethnographers did not conceptualize their work as being part of a larger history of conquest, the federal agencies which most often employed them (e.g., the Bureau of American Ethnology, Bureau of Ethnology) were organized under the Department of Interior which at times had direct commerce with the U.S. Army; agencies relocating, undermining and controlling Indian populations. Disciplinary ancestors like Major John Wesley Powell often mixed the tasks of cataloging the geography and exploitable natural resources on empire's frontier in ways that added the ethnographic details of the peoples inhabiting these environments as curiosities rather than integrated natural features.

While anthropologists trace their intellectual roots back in a great variety of directions, I remain struck by the importance of the American tradition quietly launched by James Mooney in the late 19th century. Mooney began his work for the U.S. Bureau of Ethnology even as the Department of Interior and U.S. Army were engaged in actions and policies designed to enact physical and cultural genocide against the native Indian people that Mooney was assigned to study. James Mooney first arrived on the Sioux reservation in 1891 just days after the Seventh Calvary had slaughtered Sioux men, women and children at Wounded Knee. An arrival that forced Mooney to confront the political forces framing and funding his research and to become aware that ethnography is not a neutral act. Recording and reporting cultural information under such circumstances risked making these populations vulnerable. Mooney understood early on that there was no political neutrality for ethnography.

There were mixed motivations guiding Mooney's bosses at the Department of Interior's Bureau of Ethnology as they sought to make native peoples legible during a period of conquest, but the details of Mooney's work went against these colonial administrative demands as he produced rich ethnographic reports that instead of providing military and administrative enemies with cultural tools for conquest through counterinsurgency, provided narratives establishing the full humanity, equality, and cultural richness of these peoples who were treated by others as sub-humans without proper culture. Mooney's detailed work on the Ghost Dance, Peyote Sacraments, and the Sun Dance earned him administrative and Congressional enemies—as well as congressional investigations and sanctions; and though Mooney suffered these hardships he did not betray his work or those he studied (Moses 1984).

Mooney had no professional ethical statements to guide him beyond his own religious and personal understanding of what individuals owed to others; yet while employed by a government actively working to undermine American Indian culture, he chose not to create forms of counterinsurgency or psychological operations directed against those he studied. Though never articulated as a litanized code of ethics, Mooney's work reveals his ethical commitment to those he lived with and studied—and while the idiosyncratic nature of this understanding was largely personal, it was also professional—even if it would remain uncodified and professionally un-recognized for decades.

I do not fully understand how Mooney came to such an enlightened understanding of his ethical duties to the Indians who allowed him to live amongst them, but I would like to think it was at least in part a result of the simple and profound act this very act of sharing his life through fieldwork's core performance of participant observation. Shared knowledge, shared meals, shared lives should (yet, always doesn't) imply if not shared loyalties and trust, then at a minimum: shared internalized understandings.

The American anthropological tradition is not unique in having its disciplinary roots firmly planted in a history of studying populations of others whom governments and other sponsors wished to conquer or shape in ways that would be today loosely recognized as counterinsurgency. The history of early anthropology establishes how British, French, Dutch, and German anthropological traditions were linked with colonial desires in Africa, Asia, Indonesia and elsewhere. While global colonial campaigns set a stage that made the sort of prolonged travel, or work at colonial outposts that birthed Nineteenth and early Twentieth Century anthropology, the social relations of European military dominance influenced the forms of often racialized cultural evolutionary theory that emerged in this colonial context. European and American expansions brought occupations, and ethnology became first a curiosity and then a tool of managers ever concerned with the prospect of native insurgency movements.

In the early Twentieth Century, anthropology programs grew and spread to a number of American universities. At Columbia University, Franz Boas cast a great shadow, teaching a core group of students (including folks like Margaret Mead, Alfred Kroeber, Ruth Benedict, Ashley Montagu, etc.) an American form of cultural relativism that championed racial equality, rejected notions of cultural evolution and valued all cultures equally. His insistence of intense linguistic study of the complexity and beauty of Indian languages inevitably taught lessons of respect for these others. By contemporary standards Boas had serious ethical shortcomings. His scandalous involvement in grave robbing, and lying to an Inuit child about the death and burial of his father, testify to this, but Boas' recognition of the equality of cultures and his insistence that anthropologists should undertake fieldwork, sharing their lives with those they studied, shaped the lives and sensibilities of American anthropologists in ways that warfare would inevitably twist and test.

As the United States waged foreign wars throughout the Twentieth Century, some anthropologists were forced to consider the inherent obligations they had to those they studied. The end of the First World War brought American anthropology a seminal moment raising core questions about anthropologists' ethical discomfort in using their discipline to further warfare. In 1919 Franz Boas published a letter under the title "Scientists as Spies" in *The Nation* denouncing four anthropologists for having "prostituted science" during the war when they pretended to conduct archaeological research in order to undertake espionage in

Central America for the Office of Naval Intelligence. Boas wrote that these spy-anthropologists "have not only shaken the belief in the truthfulness of science, but they have also done the greatest possible disservice to scientific inquiry. In consequence of their acts every nation will look with distrust upon the visiting foreign investigator who wants to do honest work, suspecting sinister designs. Such action has raised a new barrier against the development of international friendly cooperation" (Boas 1919). Two weeks after his letter was published, Boas was censured by the American Anthropological Association (AAA). The irony of the AAA's 1919 vote to censure Boas was that the Association accused *him* of abusing his position for political ends. This was not a moment when the discipline was interested in questioning its relationship to the larger economic and political world in which it was enmeshed, much less to develop ethical codes or principles championing disclosure of sponsorship, or obtaining voluntary informed consent. Boas' censure sent clear messages to any anthropologists interested in questioning who or what anthropology should serve.

Before the Second World War, there was a surprising lack of formal or informal concern with basic political or ethical questions relating to anthropology. Even basic practices such as using pseudonyms to protect research participants was so foreign that when Margaret Mead and her then husband Reo Fortune both studied the same Omaha Indian community, Mead's book used a "pseudonym of the Antler Tribe, to shield the feelings of the individuals and to give no affront to the tribal pride" (Mead 1932:16), while her husband's book fully identified the same town as Macy, Nebraska, its real name. Issues of power differentials between researchers and "research subjects" were seldom discussed in ethnographies, even by anthropologists who held otherwise progressive political views. Many anthropologists adopted a research stance that valued the discovery of scientific truths over concerns for the well-being of those they studied.

Without even a loose set of ethical standards, it was easy for anthropologists to be swayed to set aside even basic standards of decency in the quest of gaining new knowledge. A list of abusive anthropological practices during these early years would be a long one. The looting of sacred objects for museums and private collections was widespread, voluntary informed consent was rare, Boas and others secretly looted native grave sites, Leslie White bribed members of an Acoma Pueblo village to disclose sacred secrets, John Peabody Harrington once sent an emergency telegram demanding that a dying Indian elder (who had served as a linguistic informant) be dosed with opium to keep him alive until Harrington could travel to his side in order to complete a word list he had begun compiling, and so on.

While anthropologists' interactions with warfare would eventually cause them to establish (and later revise) American anthropology's formal ethics codes, it was the more mundane interactions with research participants and communities that showed most anthropologists the need for ethical standards. Because Pre-World War II anthropology was a minor discipline with a few scattered university departments and museum anthropologists mostly collecting artifacts and cultural data, not as part of large coordinated projects, but as individual efforts to collect cultural information for its own sake, it is easy to understand how these codes did not develop or become formalized in the first half of the Twentieth Century. Anthropologists were free agents, collecting information that interested them, often using their own funds to finance their fieldwork. Before the war, there was not much systemic appreciation of the uses to which anthropology could be put, or of the impacts anthropologists left simply by conducting fieldwork. But like many other elements of American life, the war changed all that.

Like other Americans, American anthropologists enlisted and served in a wide variety of capacities during the Second World War. Anthropologist Murray Wax recalled that at Berkeley, "after Pearl Harbor, Alfred Kroeber came to the departmental common room and encouraged the students and junior faculty by declaring, 'We will show them what anthropology can do!' Indeed, anthropologists recruited themselves" (Wax 2002:2). Suddenly anthropologists weren't just useless campus nerds; the military soon realized that they needed pieces of anthropology's skill set: things like language skills, customs, geographical knowledge of the others who were now enemies. In this war social scientists were harnessed at new levels as intelligence analysts, propagandists, guerilla insurgents, language instructors, jungle survival specialists, saboteurs, foot soldiers, officers, and spies.

Given anthropology's geographical, cultural and linguistic expertise, anthropologists had vital sources of information for commanders and American troops fighting their way northward from New Guinea, through Micronesia towards the Japanese homeland—and throughout Africa, southern and eastern Asia and Europe. Anthropologists scouted for the needed natural resources like petroleum, magnesium, tin, and rubber in Central and South America—sometimes lying about their intentions while posing as fieldworkers; at least one of the spies that Boas had criticized during World War One, reprised his role of archaeologist spy in Peru (Price 2000). Some anthropologists formed secret and quasi-secret agencies like the Ethnogeographic Board (meeting in the Smithsonian's castle) and the "M-Project" (secretly meeting in the Library of Congress to generate fantastical scenarios for relocating refugees at the war's end), while others worked in the War Relocation Authority camps detaining Japanese American citizens (Price 2008).

American anthropologists weren't the only anthropologists contributing to the global war. British, German, French, Japanese, and anthropologists from other nations contributed their cultural, geographical and linguistic knowledge to their nations during the war. In *From Racism to Genocide: Anthropology in the Third Reich*, Gretchen Schafft broke a deep silence surrounding the details of Nazi anthropologists, documenting how anthropometric research, measuring Germans and others, was adapted and used to justify Nazi policies (Schafft 2007). Schafft raised serious questions not only about the political contexts determining the uses and abuses of anthropology, but she documents anthropology's own blind-spots. Schafft's research into Joseph Mengele's formal anthropological training, reveals that the anthropologist with the highest name recognition in all of history was not Margaret Mead, but was instead Joseph Mengele. That most anthropologists have no idea that Mengele was formally trained in anthropology is a small but significant monument to the ways that the discipline has divorced itself from its historical interactions with power.

American anthropologists at times also worked on disturbing war projects. One OSS study sought to identify specific biological differences among the Japanese that could be exploited with biological weapons. Another OSS project was designed to destroy food sources for the Japanese homeland, hoping to use ethnographic knowledge to refine techniques of terror. Some anthropological projects used newly developed applied anthropological methods to manipulate studied populations (at home and abroad) in ways that troubled some of these anthropologists at the time and at times subverted democratic movements. These applications of wartime anthropology with few limits led anthropologist Laura Thompson to publicly write of these concerns in 1944, asking what would become of such an anthropology without limits, and wanting to know "are practical social scientists to become technicians for hire to the highest bidder?" (1944:12).

It was the Nuremberg Trials after the war that provided anthropology and all the human and social sciences the basis of their modern ethic codes. The Nuremburg Code insisted that scientists studying human beings (in war *and* peace) must obtain voluntary informed consent, must avoid causing mental and physical suffering, must protect research subjects, must use qualified personnel, and must give research subjects the power to end the studies when risks appear. While it was Nazi atrocities, many of which were conducted not simply as acts of cruelty, but to gain valuable information to assist their war effort (e.g. their lethal hypothermia studies) that led to the development of this first modern ethical code, it would transform post-war research in public and private settings.

As a direct result of its members' experiences in World War II, in 1948 the Society for Applied Anthropology articulated the first formalized American anthropological code of ethics. This code stressed that the "anthropologist must take responsibility for the effects of his recommendations, never maintaining that he is merely a technician unconcerned with the ends toward which his applied scientific skills are directed" (Mead et al. 1949:20). It stated that, "the applied anthropologist should recognize a special responsibility to use his skill in such a way as to prevent any occurrence which will set in motion a train of events which involves irreversible losses of health or the loss of life to individuals or

21

groups or irreversible damage to the natural productivity of the physical environment" (Mead et al. 1949:21).

It was no accident that it was the applied anthropologists' professional society, and not the larger, highly academic AAA, that first developed an ethics code. The experiences and traumas of the Second World War forced these anthropologists to take a hard look at what had been and what could be done with their work. The war also left many anthropologists concluding that the military frequently did not listen to their analysis because it went against the institutional assumptions of the agencies which sought their advice. During the war, the academic journal of the AAA continued to publish articles about obscure kinship systems and carry on lofty theoretical debates, but *Applied Anthropology* carried articles detailing the logistics of imprisoning Japanese Americans, wartime labor issues, and forms of social engineering in service of the war, and once the guns of war fell silent those who had been drawn into contributing anthropology so directly to this fight started thinking hard about what it all meant, and what limits should exist.

World War II taught anthropologists to work on directed research projects not of their own design, and the Cold War's showers of previously unimaginable public and private funds for anthropological research shifted anthropological imaginations in ways aligned with geopolitics. The early Cold War brought new lucrative federal funding programs for foreign language study, and Area Study Centers (adopting and spreading the interdisciplinary approach to regional studies developed at the OSS during the war) mixed a new wealth of public and private funds for anthropologists to study the Underdeveloped World at the center of Cold War politics. During the Cold War, the CIA and other intelligence agencies used funding fronts, through either agency controlled dummy foundations or by channeling research monies to "useful" research projects through bona fide research foundations without the recipient's knowledge. These foundations are known as "pass-throughs" or funding fronts. In the mid-1970s, the U.S. Congress' Church Committee determined that during the mid-1960s such maneuvers allowed the CIA to manipulate about half the grants made for international research in the USA. For the most part these were unwitting interactions (Church Committee 1976:182).

Uncounted Cold War anthropologists quietly passed through the revolving door between the academy and intelligence agencies with little notice or concern by their colleagues. Anthropologists covered the Third World, and while most anthropologists were doing the exact academic research they claimed they were, some anthropologists had other agendas. In the early Cold War Frank Hibbin used fieldwork as a cover to secretly plant devices to monitor Chinese atomic bomb tests. During this same period, the AAA Executive Board covertly provided the CIA with a master roster of their membership, including language abilities, foreign contacts, and geographical specialties (Price 2003). Sometimes anthropologists were sponsored by funding fronts and didn't even know that their sponsors were actually the CIA, such as when anthropologists writing about stress in different cultures were funded by the Human Ecology Fund, a CIA front working on the CIA's KUBARK interrogation manual (Price 2007). Through such means anthropologists and other social scientists became unwitting CIA laboratory mules examining questions of mutual interest while earning money and advancing their academic careers. Many anthropologists were oblivious to the political context in which they worked, which Laura Nader characterized the period as "sleepwalking" through the history of anthropology (Nader 1997).

In 1964, the U.S. Army's Project Camelot sought to use anthropologists and sociologists to study patterns of Third World social upheaval and revolution. Project Camelot planned to use anthropologists' and sociologists' research to develop counterinsurgency tactics to quell uprisings (democratic or otherwise) in Latin America. When the Norwegian sociologist Johan Galtung was contacted in a futile effort to recruit him for Camelot's Chilean counterinsurgency program, he publicly exposed the project. A sizable public uproar followed and soon the AAA began scrutinizing programs designed to use social science to inform counterinsurgency.

With anthropologists' outrage, growing suspicions in the international community, public scrutiny and academic criticism, Project Camelot never got off the ground. As Marshall Sahlins wrote at the time, "as a tactic of fomenting Latin American unrest and anti-North American sentiment, Camelot would be the envy of any Communist conspiracy. We have heard of the self-fulfilling prophecy; here was the self-fulfilling research proposal" (Sahlins 1967:73). The American Anthropological Association reacted to Camelot by establishing a committee led by Ralph Beals that wrote a 1967 report on "Background Information on Problems of Anthropological Research and Ethics." The report identified many of the fundamental ethical principles to be articulated in the AAA's first ethics code four years later.

Project Camelot was a flashpoint for academic anger in the mid-1960s, but it was but one of many counterinsurgency programs drawing on anthropologists. Anthropologists worked on Strategic Hamlet Program in Vietnam, and were beginning to work on a number of so-called "Modernization Programs" managed by the U.S. Agency for International Development and other agencies which had rationales similar to those articulated by Thomas Jefferson in his secret congressional briefing. Anthropologists working for RAND in Vietnam supported a number of rural agricultural counterinsurgency programs. In the 1960s, military strategists and intelligence analysts suddenly rediscovered the value of anthropology, and began dreaming that culture might hold answers to their military problems. The Special Operations research Office (SORO) and its cousin-organization CINFAC (Counterinsurgency Information Analysis) published a whole series of crazy sounding (and reading) papers on counterinsurgency related topics like the 1964 classic, "Witchcraft, Sorcery, Magic and Other Psychological Phenomena and Their Implications on Military and Paramilitary Operations in the Congo," or CINFAC's Staff "An Ethnographic Summary of the Ethiopian Provinces of Harar and Sidamo," and a series of counterinsurgency related documents. The military and CIA were in over their head with a mix of overt and covert operations around the world, and they held out hopes that "culture" was the panacea for the forms of social control they envisioned.

For many American anthropologists of the mid-1960s, it was this prospect of using anthropology for counterinsurgency that raised the most fundamental ethical and political questions about applying anthropology to the needs of warfare. Using anthropology to alter and undermine indigenous cultural movements cut against the grain of widely shared anthropological assumptions about the rights of cultures and people to determine their own destiny. In 1968 a full-page ad for a Vietnam War PYSOP Counterinsurgency position appearing in the back of the *American Anthropologist* journal led over eight hundred anthropologists to sign a statement protesting the running of this ad in the *American Anthropologist*. Eric Wolf, Robert Murphy, Marvin Harris, Mort Fried, Dell Hymes, and Harold Conklin later wrote a policy forbidding the Association from accepting advertisements for employment that produced secretive reports. These border incursions by military and intelligence agencies pushed the AAA to undertake steps that led them closer to drafting its first ethics code. And while the Association leadership strove to frame members concerns in terms of ethics, the political issues raised by using anthropology for counterinsurgency drove much of the debate.

In 1967 a self-identified "Radical Caucus" of anthropologists was organized, and using grassroots techniques it seized political power at the AAA's annual meetings, drawing massive crowds to the sessions they organized, flooding the annual business meetings with caucus members who used the meetings to push through political resolutions against anthropological contributions to the war, and supporting a broad platform of progressive issues ranging from anti-discrimination policies and calling for the establishment of an ethics code, to calling on the association to provide childcare at the annual meetings. This movement successfully pressed the AAA's Board to draft an ethics code (known as the Principles of Professional Responsibility) that mandated members "do no harm," disclose funding sources and uses of research, and forbid covert research and the production of secret reports.

In 1970 a graduate student at UCLA stole documents from the files of anthropologist Michael Moerman. These documents established that Moerman and other anthropologists involvement in counterinsurgency operations in Thailand. Copies of these stolen documents were sent to Eric Wolf, the chair of the AAA's Ethics Committee, and to a radical newspaper, *The Student Mobilizer*. After Eric Wolf publicly questioned the propriety of this counterinsurgency work, the AAA Executive Board harshly criticized Wolf, and Eric Wolf resigned as Chair of the Ethics Committee. There were highly charged debates between anthropologists across the country, and the AAA Board appointed an independent committee chaired by Margaret Mead to investigate these matters (Wakin 1993).

But the Mead Committee's report was a disaster. When the committee submitted its report in late 1971, their findings were seen as a cover-up by many of the AAA membership because the report focused most of its criticism not on the anthropologists engaged in counterinsurgency in Southeast Asia, but on Ethics Committee chairman Wolf for making judgments without affording the accused anthropologists due process and for taking actions beyond those procedurally identified in the AAA bylaws and the Ethics Committee's charge. The Radical Caucus packed the 1971 AAA Council meeting and used their numbers to seize control of the agenda, and though the AAA leadership had not wanted the report to be approved or rejected, a motion was made, seconded and adopted which rejected the Mead Report. But more significant than the rejection of the Mead Report was that all the commotion and anger over the weaponization of anthropology in the aborted Camelot Project and Southeast Asia solidified the AAA membership's vote to adopt the Principles of Professional Responsibility, the AAA's first Code of Ethics, in a vote that pushed by the political concerns of warfare.

The AAA's 1971 Principles of Professional Responsibility unambiguously declared that anthropologists should not conduct covert research, should not issue secret reports (to governmental agencies or anyone else) and must work to use pseudonyms to protect the identities and well-being of those they studied. This 1971 code clarified that anthropologists' primary loyalties were to those they studied. In the immediate sense, the establishment of the 1971 AAA Code of Ethics was a disciplinary reaction to CIA and Pentagon counterinsurgency efforts in the Vietnam War; but in the larger sense, it was also the product of a growing awareness of the problems and concerns raised when anthropology is used not only for warfare, but in *any* interactions between anthropology and research participants.

While war brought anthropology ethics, in some sense, military and intelligence agencies' temporary neglect of the discipline contributed to a weakening these ethical proclamations. During the 1980s, as the pressing concerns of abuses in wartime were replaced by market-driven concerns over responsibilities to sponsors; concerns that included loosening prohibitions over secretive reports or reports containing what industry termed "proprietary data." Shifts in anthropology's political economy brought growing desires to produce proprietary reports for industry in the 1980s, which spawned successful efforts to loosen the AAA's Code of Ethics to allow for more secrecy.

This shift troubled many university-based anthropologists because it inverted appropriate relationships between professional ethics and desires to produce or control knowledge. The 1990 relaxation of the AAA's Code of Ethics allowing the production of proprietary, secretive, reports, occurred for reasons of commerce as increasing number of anthropologists worked outside of universities in corporate or governmental settings, but it would be the re-militarized America following the attacks of 9/11 in 2001 that demonstrated how these changes expressed anthropology's commitments and responsibilities during times of war.

President Bush's wars at home, Afghanistan and Iraq brought new uses for anthropology and anthropologists, many of these engagements occurred without ethical complications, while others, especially those involving counterinsurgency went far beyond what the previous generation of anthropologists would considered ethical uses of anthropology. Increasing numbers of anthropologists responded to militarized calls in ways that viewed anthropological ethics as a luxury not to be afforded by those needing anthropology's ethnographic knowledge for warfare. The clearest expression of these views came from anthropologist Montgomery McFate, who openly sought to militarize anthropology with the development of embedded Counterinsurgency teams known as Human Terrain Teams. Doctor McFate led the charge to recruit anthropologists, bluntly admitting that "despite the fact that military applications of cultural knowledge might be distasteful to ethically inclined anthropologists, their assistance is necessary" (McFate 2005:37). Rather than confronting the complexity of ethical relationships, McFate's Human Terrain Teams simply ignored them.

Post 9/11 efforts to militarize anthropology lean on false historical narratives that construct unrealistic interpretations of the possibility of individuals changing entrenched military structures, and an abandonment of normative understandings of professional ethics. The Pentagon, White House, and military contractors painted pictures of Human Terrain Teams as "armed social workers." But using anthropology for counterinsurgency perverts the discipline's potential; and the Human Terrain Program took the research of other ethnographers and applied it for occupations in ways that took the science or art of ethnography and resold it as a sort of social science pornography.

But Ethics can be a Force that Allows Anthropology to Avoid Politics

Somewhere between 1971 and today, American anthropologists lost their collective strong sense of outrage over the discipline being so nakedly used for counterinsurgency. Part of this loss of outrage comes with the degeneration of historical memory as fewer Americans know the history of the CIA's legacy of assassinations, coups and death squads and a history of undermining democratic movements harmful to the interests of American elites. The increasing corporatization of university campuses over the past decades has reduced expectations of academic independence, and has left under-funded departments willing to consider anything that promises to provide funding. Post-9/11 America has become so fervently militarized that many anthropologists privately questioning these developments remain publicly silent because they fear a mob response should Fox News target them as unpatriotic intellectual snobs. Today, news of anthropologists' involvement in counterinsurgency programs still mobilizes a core group of scholars, but the discipline as a whole refrains from stating outright opposition to anthropologically informed counterinsurgency. The growing militarism of American social science since 2001 slowly raised concerns among a large number of anthropologists.

In 2006, these developments pressed the AAA to form a commission, of which I was a member, charged with investigating the issues raised by anthropologists' engagements with military, intelligence and national security agencies; and this commission chose to delineate the ethical issues raised by these engagements (AAA 2007 & 2009). While this examination of professional ethics provided some guidance to the discipline, the Association's inability to critique the *political* issues leaves the primary concerns of many anthropologists unaddressed.

One way that these political issues were addressed was with the formation of the Network of Concerned Anthropologists by a group of colleagues and myself in 2007 helped focus political and ethical opposition to counterinsurgency and the militarization of anthropology. Anthropologist Terry Turner drew upon widespread concerns over the increasing weaponization of anthropology to press the AAA to restore language in the Code of Ethics prohibiting secretive research. Some anthropologists have argued that it is "unfortunate" that revisions of the AAA's Code of Ethics is occurring during a time marked by active warfare—the implication being that political or emotional factors stand to override objective rationality. Such arguments act as if political vacuums existed in nature, laboratories or anywhere. Anthropology's consideration of ethics has *always* been pushed by warfare—and after 9/11, the mercenary nature of counterinsurgency necessarily drives anthropological discussions of ethics.

In 2008, the AAA membership voted to restore general prohibitions against secrecy by adding a section to the Association's ethics code stating that: "anthropologists should not withhold research results from research participants when those results are shared with others" (AAA Code of Ethics VI, 2). Human Terrain Systems, other militarized forms of anthropology, as well as pressures and changes in applied and non-applied forms of anthropology led the AAA Executive Board in late 2008 to appoint an ad hoc committee charged with revising the Association's Code of Ethics (at the time of this writing, I am a member of this committee). Obama's wars and increasing militarization of society casts shadows over this undertaking—but just how these shadows will influence these revisions to the ethics code remains unclear. While the issues addressed by anthropological ethics codes must address routine anthropological activities, war remains the force that pushes the importance of these issues to the fore.

While professional associations like the AAA have historically taken political stances on some issues (most generally dealing with matters of social equality, including statements on race and marriage), and adopted policies linking the discipline to supporting the Second World War, there remains a great resistance to confronting the ways that disciplinary ethics are linked to the political context in which anthropology is practiced. Although the rank and file membership of the AAA have adopted resolutions condemning particular unpopular wars or military actions (the Vietnam War, the Iraq War, etc.), the Association remains skittish in adopting stances on the uses of anthropology in non-defensive wars of aggression, or wars of imperialism. Instead, professional associations like the AAA are pressured to keep the institutional focus on delineating ethical, not political, practices.

On the surface, these distinctions between ethical and political concerns make a certain amount of sense if you follow the logic that professional ethics have legitimate concerns with establishing "best practices." But this reasoning stops short of addressing fundamental issues ranging from the inconsistency of associations supporting some political causes (e.g., racial equality, the Second World War) and not others, and it fails to address just how problematic notions of "best practices" are if they don't include basic political stances like opposing imperialism, neo-colonialism, and supporting the rights of nations to self determination. While professional associations like the AAA, often embrace doctrines of universal human rights (the AAA does), such positions can insolate organizations from adopting positions on specific issues.

These distinctions between ethics and politics limit the critiques that develop within professional associations. Such distinctions mean the difference in organizations, like the AAA, opposing the Human Terrain program's use of anthropologists for ethical reasons (because it does not obtain voluntary informed consent, endangers studied populations etc.), or opposing it for political reasons (because it assists the American military in an unjust project of empire, occupation, and exploitation). As long as professional associations limit these discussions to the realm of ethics, and avoid addressing these political issues embedded in conducting anthropological research in a nation engaging in global military expansion, the critiques of these associations must be limited to critiques of manners and techniques, not of the underlying political program employing anthropology for conquest.

Professional associations focusing on ethics while setting aside politics, ignore the larger political issues of how anthropological engagements with military, intelligence, national security sectors relate to US foreign policy, neo-colonial military campaigns, the Global War on Terror and a growing military reliance on anthropologically informed counterinsurgency. But addressed or not, these political issues remain at the forefront of many anthropologists' concerns over these issues, even while their professional associations generally limit their focus on ethics.

Professional associations like the AAA hope to position themselves as politically neutral, but there is no political neutrality. There is only silence or engagement on these issues—and silence most usually means acquiescence to national policies, which is itself a dangerous political position. The AAA avoids addressing the political meaning of using anthropology in military contexts that include the occupation and conquest of the peoples anthropologists work with and study. It is as if some anthropologists believe that addressing these issues would undermine the scientific (or humanistic) nature of our work—yet the measures of anthropologists' work are generally measured by criteria such as reliability, validity, rigor of method etc., criteria that need not be undermined by directly addressing the political project that seeks anthropologists, our data and methods.

Given the Obama Administration's increased reliance on counterinsurgency's soft power in Afghanistan, the political and ethical issues raised by anthropologists manipulating other cultures in ways aligned with US foreign policy will grow in importance. Anthropologists need to resist limiting their critiques to issues of ethics and bring the political issues of domination to the fore of their critiques.

CHAPTER TWO

THE CIA'S UNIVERSITY SPIES: PRISP, ICSP, NSEP, AND THE BIG PAYBACK

> What is overlooked in the growing, enthusiastic collaboration between the military-industrial complex and academe within the context of developing a powerful post-9/11 national security state is that the increasing militarization of higher education is itself a problem that may be even more insidious, damaging, and dangerous to the fate of democracy than that posed by terrorists who "hate our freedoms.
>
> —Henry Giroux

POST 9/11 CHANGES ON AMERICAN UNIVERSITY CAMPUSES TRANSFORMED university classrooms into covert training grounds for the CIA and other agencies in ways that increasingly threaten fundamental principles of academic openness as well as the integrity of a wide array of academic disciplines. Several programs developed in the past half decade found new ways to secretly place students with undisclosed ties to the CIA, FBI, NSA, the Defense Intelligence Agency and Homeland Security in American university classrooms.

There have long been tensions between the needs of academia and the needs of the National Security State; and even before the events of 9/11 expanded the powers of American intelligence agencies, universities were quietly being modified to serve the needs of intelligence agencies in new and covert ways. The most visible of these reforms was the establishment of the National Security Education Program (NSEP) which siphoned-off students from traditional foreign language funding programs such as Fulbright or Title VI. While traditional funding sources provide students with small stipends of a few thousand dollars to study foreign languages in American universities, the NSEP gives graduate students a wealth of funds (at times exceeding $40,000 a year) to study "in demand" languages, but with troubling pay-back stipulations mandating that recipients later work for unspecified U.S. national security agencies. Upon its debut in the early 1990s, the NSEP was harshly criticized for reaching through an assumed barrier separating the desires of academia and state (Rubin 1996). Numerous academic organizations, including, the Middle East Studies Association and the African Studies Association, Latin American Studies Association, and even the mainstream Boards of the Social Science Research Council and American Council of Learned Societies expressed deep concerns over scholars' participation in the NSEP. And though the NSEP continues funding students despite these protests, there was some solace in knowing so many diverse academic organizations condemned this program.

But while many academics and professional associations openly opposed the NSEP's entrance onto American campuses, there has been little public reaction to an even more troubling post-9/11 funding program which upgrades the existing American intelligence-university-interface. With little notice Congress approved section 318 of the 2004 Intelligence Authorization Act which appropriated four million dollars to fund a pilot program known as the Pat Roberts Intelligence Scholars Program (PRISP). Named after Senator Pat Roberts (R. Kansas, then Chair, Senate Select Committee on Intelligence), PRISP was designed to train intelligence operatives and analysts in American university classrooms for careers in the CIA and other agencies. PRISP now operates on an undisclosed number of American college and university campuses, and after the pilot phase of the program proved to be a useful means of recruiting and training members of intelligence agencies, the program continues to expand to campuses across the country.

PRISP participants must be American citizens who are enrolled full-time in graduate degree programs with a minimum GPA of 3.4, they need to "complete at least one summer internship at CIA or other agencies," and they must pass the same background investigations as other CIA employees. PRISP students receive financial stipends ranging up to $25,000 per year and they are required to participate in closed meetings with other PRISP scholars and individuals from their administering intelligence agency.

In 2003, the *Lawrence Journal World* (11/29/03) describing plans for developing this new program claimed that, "those in the program would be part of the ROTC program specializing in learning how to analyze a variety of conditions and activities based on a thorough understanding and deep knowledge of particular areas of the world" (Simons 2003). Beyond the similar requirements that participants of both programs commit years of service to their sponsoring military or intelligence branches there are few similarities between ROTC and PRISP. ROTC programs mostly operate in the open, as student-ROTC members register for ROTC courses and are proudly and visibly identified as members of the ROTC program, while PRISP students are instructed to keep their PRISP-affiliations hidden from others on campus.

The CIA's website describes PRISP and lists sought academic specialties; these include experts on: China, the Middle East, Asia, Korea, Russia, the Caucasus, Africa and South America, and seeking language training or proficiency in: Chinese, Arabic, Persian, Urdu, Pashto, Dari, Turkish, Korean, or a Central Asian or Caucasian language such as Georgian, Turkmen, Tajik, or Uzbek (https://www.cia.gov/careers/opportunities/analytical/pat-roberts-intelligence-scholars-program-prisp.html, 12/15/10). PRISP also funds Islamic studies scholars and scientists with expertise in bioterrorism, counterterrorism, chemistry, physics, computer science and engineering. When PRISP was first launched in 2005, it was advertised on intelligence recruiting web sights (such as www.intelligencecareers.com or the National Ground Intelligence Center; these links have long since been removed) and was pitched on select university campuses in small, controlled recruiting sessions. In the years since its first funding, PRISP developed a low profile and an individualistic approach to finding candidates for PRISP funding.

When I made initial inquiries about PRISP to Senator Roberts' staff in 2005 concerning the size and scope of PRISP I was given little useful information, but in response to my inquires Senator Roberts' staff referred me to Mr. Tommy Glakas at the CIA. Mr. Glakas was reluctant to discuss many specific details of PRISP, but he did confirm that PRISP then funded about 100 students studying at an undisclosed number of American universities. When I asked Mr. Glakas in 2005 if PRISP was already up and running on college campuses, he first answered that it was, then said it wasn't, then clarified that PRISP wasn't the sort of program that was tied to university campuses-it was decentralized and tied to students, not campuses. When pressed further on what this meant Mr. Glakas gave no further information. He said that he had no way of knowing exactly how many universities currently have students participating in PRISP, claiming he could not know this because PRISP is administered not just by the CIA, but also through a variety of individual intelligence agencies like the NSA, MID, or Naval Intelligence. He stressed that PRISP was a decentralized scholarship program which funds students through various intelligence agencies. Mr. Glakas told me that he didn't know who might know how many campuses had PRISP scholars and he would not identify which campuses are hosting these covert PRISP scholars. PRISP's organizational structure is reminiscent of the sort of limited contact "cells" used by intelligence agencies, where an individual within an intelligence cell has only limited knowledge of other individuals in this same chain of connections—most commonly only knowing their individual "handler," but not knowing the identities of others in the greater chain of connections.

PRISP was largely the brainchild of University of Kansas anthropologist Felix Moos-a longtime advocate of anthropological contacts with military and intelligence agencies. During the Vietnam War Moos worked in Laos and Thailand on World Bank-financed projects and over the years he has worked in various military advisory positions. He worked on the Pentagon's ARPA Project Themis, and has been an instructor at the Naval War College and at the U.S. Staff and Command College at Fort Leavenworth. For years Moos taught courses on "Violence and Terrorism" at the University of Kansas. In the months after the 2001 attacks on the World Trade Center and Pentagon Moos elicited the support of his friend, former CIA DCI, Stansfield Turner to curry support in the senate and CIA to fund his vision of a merger between anthropology, academia, intelligence analysis and espionage training.

Professor Moos initially proposed that all PRISP students be required to master two foreign languages, and to enroll in a battery of university anthropology and history courses to learn the culture history of their selected regions (Kansas University Radio 2003). Moos's vision for PRISP was more comprehensive than the program that eventually developed. Moos proposed having an active CIA campus presence where PRISP students would begin training as freshmen and, "by the time they would be commissioned, they would be ready to go to the branch intelligence units of their choice" (Kansas University Radio 2003).

It is tempting to describe Felix Moos as an anachronistic anthropologist out of sync with his discipline's mainstream, but while many anthropologists express concerns about disciplinary ties to military and intelligence organizations, contemporary anthropology has no core with which to either sync or collide and there are others in the field who openly (and quietly) support such developments. Moos is a bright man, but his writings echo the musty tone and sentiments found in the limited bedside readings of Tom-Clancy-literate-colonials, as he prefers to quote from the wisdom of Sun Tzu and Samuel Huntington over anthropologists like Franz Boas or Laura Nader.

In 2002 I joined Moos (and anthropologists Robert Rubenstein, Anna Simons, Murray Wax and Hugh Gusterson) on one of the first post-9/11 American Anthropological Association panels to examine American anthropologists' contributions to military and intelligence agencies. Moos acted incredulous that all anthropologists would not join his crusade, and he rhetorically asked, "Have anthropologists learned so little since 9/11/2001, as to not recognize the truth-and practicability, in Sun Tzu's reminder that: 'unless someone is subtle and perspicacious, he cannot perceive the substance in intelligence reports. It is subtle, subtle.'" From the dais I could see not so subtle anthropologists in the audience employed by RAND and the Pentagon nodding their heads as if his words had hit a secret chord. Moos was clearly onto something, though at the time it was difficult to imagine just how far reaching these new connections between anthropologists and military and intelligence agencies would become.

Moos became the early post-9/11 leader publicly pushing for more open connections between anthropology and the CIA, but he was rotated out of the public spotlight pretty early on in this discourse. I've heard several different reasons suggested, ranging from the off-putting media effect of his faintly lingering German accent and his penchant for speaking in what has been described as "1940s sound bites." After I published my initial PRISP exposé in *CounterPunch*, other media picked up the story (e.g., Willing 2006) and David Glenn wrote a story on PRISP in *The Chronicle of Higher Education* and later had a live online interview (3/23/05) with Professor Moos answering live questions from readers about PRISP, and his answers showcased his awkward reading from a dated script.

Moos explained to David Glenn how the War on Terror must sweep aside all reticence about bringing the CIA and other intelligence agencies onto our classrooms and into our hearts, arguing that:

> The United States is at war, and thus, simply put, the existing cultural divide between the intelligence community, the U.S. military and academe has become a critical, dangerous, and very real detriment to our national security at home and abroad.
> The former global symmetry of inter-nation conflict has become the asymmetry of terrorism and insurgency. Long gone are the days where academic anthropology might occasionally be applied to tourism and gender studies but not to critical area and language studies with a direct, practical use to national defense.....All of us have to re-examine our perceptions of each other, rather than simply claiming that the CIA in the United States, if not worldwide, now threatens the fundamental principles of academic transparency (Glenn 2005b).

President Bush's declaration that the United States was at war with the concept of "terrorism" was vital to Moos, and something odd happened as he answered almost each of the queries from readers: Moos preferred answering questions with an odd formulaic montra stating, " the United States is at war..." or "we are at war," again and again with repeated answers. The effect was striking like a form of pastiche used by Stephen Colbert, as he would personalize this formula in all sorts of ways, such as when a question from a scholar from Yale was presented, he answered with the phrase, "The United States is at war, and that includes Yale and all American anthropologists…;" and when a scholar from U.C. Santa Barbara challenged him with a question, he began his reply stating "The United States is at war and that includes U.C. Santa Barbara." Finally after nine separate uses of the chanting phrase, "we are at war," one online participant wrote Moos: "You obviously enjoy typing the words, 'we are at war.' Do you think that typing the words, 'we are at war' gives you and the CIA license to ignore the past abuses of intelligence agencies? Who do you think 'we' are at war with anyway?" (Glenn 2005b).

Moos had no answer; all he could muster was a question in reply: "Are you serious?" Moos was certainly serious. In some ways, his was a more honest and forthright presentation of how academia would be expected to become subservient to the needs of state for intelligence gathering and analysis than the claims made by Montgomery McFate and other latter-day national security spokes-anthropologists.

In 1995 Moos testified before a commission modifying the AAA's code on anthropological ethics that anthropologists should be allowed to engage in secretive research, arguing that, "In a world where weapons of mass destruction have become so terrible and terrorist actions so frightful, anthropologists must surrender naïve faith in a communitarian utopia and be prepared to encounter conflict and violence. Indeed they should feel the professional obligation to work in areas of ethnic conflict…moreover, as moral creatures so engaged, anthropologists should recognize the need to classify some of their data, if for no other reason than to protect the lives of their subjects and themselves" (Moos 1995). More recently, when the AAA reinstated ethical prohibitions against secret research in 2008, Moos remained in silence and did not even bother arguing his position with the Association.

It is PRISPs devotion to secrecy that is the root problem of its presence on our campuses as well as with Moos' vision of anthropology harnessed for the needs of state. Moos' fallacy is his belief that the fundamental problem with American intelligence agencies is that they are lacking adequate cultural understanding of those they study, and spy upon-this fallacy is exacerbated by orthodox assumptions that good intelligence operates best in realms of secrecy. America needs good intelligence, but the most useful and important intelligence can largely be gathered openly without the sort of covert invasion of our campuses that PRISP silently brings.

The claim that more open source, non-classified intelligence is what is needed is less far fetched than it might seem. In *Cloak and Gown:*

Scholars in the Secret War, 1939-1961 historian Robin Winks recounts how in 1951, the CIA's Sherwood Kent conducted an experiment in which a handful of Yale historians used nothing but declassified materials in Yale's library to challenge CIA analysts (with access to classified data) to produce competing reports on U.S. military capacities, strengths and weaknesses focusing on a scale of detail down to the level of military divisions (Winks 1996:457-459). The written evaluation of this contest was known as the "Yale Report," which concluded that over 90% of material in the CIA's report was found in the Yale library. Kent further estimated that of the remaining 10% of "secret" materials, only half of this could be expected to remain secret for any length of time. President Truman was so furious with the results of the Yale Report that he suppressed its distribution, arguing that the press needed more restrictions governing the release of such sensitive materials, while Republican pundits joined the furor claiming that Yale liberals were trying to leak state secrets.

Evidence of the power of open intelligence is close at hand, consider only how American scholars' (using publicly available sources) analysis of the dangers for post-invasion Iraq out-performed the CIA's best estimates. As one who has lived in the Middle East and read Arabic news dailies online for years while watching the expansion of American policies that appear to misread the Arab world I suspect that a repeat of the Yale Report experiment focusing on the Middle East would find another 10% intelligence gap, but with the academy now winning due to the deleterious effects of generations of CIA intellectual inbreeding. Perhaps the Agency has become self-aware of these limits brought on by the internal reproduction of its own limited institutional culture, and in its own misshapen view it sees PRISP as a means of supplying itself with new blood to rejuvenate under cover provided by public classrooms. But such secrecy-based reforms are the products of a damaged institutional mind trying to repair itself.

Some might misread criticism of the CIA's secret presence on our campuses as contradicting my critique of the need for more outside and dissenting input in intelligence circles, but such a reading would misunderstand the importance of openness in academic and political processes. The fundamental problems with American intelligence are *exacerbated* by secrecy-when intelligence agencies are allowed to classify and hide their assumptions, reports and analysis from public view they generate self-referential narrow visions that coalesce rather than challenge top-down policies from the administrations they serve. Intelligence agencies do need to understand the complex cultures they study, but to suggest that intelligence agencies like the CIA are simply amassing and interpreting political and cultural information is a dangerous fantasy: The CIA fulfills a tripartite role of gathering intelligence, interpreting intelligence, and working as a supraconstitutional covert arm of the presidency. It is this final role that should give scholars and citizens pause when considering how PRSIP and other university-intelligence-linked programs will use the knowledge they take from our open classrooms.

The CIA has made sure we won't know which classrooms PRSIP scholars attend; this is rationalized as a requirement for protecting the identities of intelligence personnel. But this secrecy shapes PRISP as it takes on the form like a cell-based covert operation in which PRISP students study chemistry, biology, sociology, psychology, anthropology and foreign languages without their fellow classmates, professors, advisors, department chairs or presumably even research subjects (creating serious ethics problems under any post-Nuremberg professional ethics code or Institutional Review Board) knowing that they are working for the CIA, DIA, NSA or other intelligence agencies.

In almost two decades of Freedom of Information Act research I have read too many FBI reports of students detailing the deviant political views of their professors (These range from the hilarious: As anthropologist Norman Humphrey was reported to have called President Eisenhower a "duckbilled nincompoop"; to the Dadaist: wherein former Miss America, Marilyn van Derbur, reported that sociologist Howard Higman mocked J. Edgar Hoover in class; to the chilling: as when the FBI arranged for a graduate student to guide topics of "informal" conversation with anthropologist Gene Weltfish that were later the focus an inquiry by Joseph McCarthy) to not mention the likelihood that these PRSIP students are also secretly compiling dossiers on their professors and fellow students (Higman 1998; Price 2004). I would be remiss to not mention that students are not the only ones sneaking the CIA onto our campuses. There are also unknown thousands of university professors who periodically work with and for the CIA--in 1988 CIA spokeswoman Sharon Foster bragged that the CIA then secretly employed enough university professors "to staff a large university." Most experts estimate that this presence has grown since 2001 (Mills 1991:37).

The quiet rise of programs like PRISP or ICCIE (see Chapter Four) should not surprise anyone given the steady cuts in federal funding for higher education, and the resulting pressures for more mercenary roles for the academy. In the post-World War Two decades, scholars naively self-recruited themselves or followed classmates to the CIA, but increasingly those of us who have studied the languages, culture and histories of peoples around the world have also learned about the role of the CIA in undermining the autonomy of those cultures we study, and the steady construction of this history has hurt the agency's efforts to recruit the best and brightest post-graduates. For decades the students studying Arabic, Urdu, Basque or Farsi were predominantly curious admirers of the cultures and languages they studied, the current shift now finds a visible increase in students whose studies are driven by the market forces of new Wars on Terrorism. If the CIA can use PRISP to indenture students in the early days of their graduate training-supplemented with mandated summer camp internships immersed in the workplace ethos of CIA-the company can mold their ideological inclinations even before their grasp of cultural history is shaped in the relatively open environment of their university. As these PRISP graduates enter the CIA's institutional environment of self-reinforcing Group Think they will present a reduced risk of creating cognitive dissonance by bringing new views that threaten the agency's narrow view of the world. Institutional Group Think can thus safely be protected from external infection.

Healthy academic environments need openness because they, unlike the CIA, are nourished by the self-corrective features of open disagreement, dissent, and synthetic-reformulation. The presence of the PRISP's secret sharers brings hidden agendas that sabotage these fundamental processes of academia. The Pat Roberts Intelligence Scholars Program infects all of academia with a germ of dishonesty and distrust as participant scholars cloak their intentions and their ties to the hidden masters they serve.

INTELLIGENCE SCHOLAR LOAN SHARKS

After I published my initial *CounterPunch* exposé on PRISP in January 2005, secondary stories followed on newspaper wire services, *Democracy Now*, NPR, in the *Chronicle of Higher Ed*. Senator Pat Roberts soon began publicly speaking about the program, assuring the public there were no reasons to worry about PRISP spreading domestic surveillance on campus. Neoconservative anthropologist Stanley Kurtz used his column in the *National Review* to claim that I wouldn't be happy until CIA agents killed themselves, absurdly writing, "So long as CIA recruits openly identify themselves to every Pakistani villager they talk to, Price is happy. Assisted suicide for aspiring CIA analysts may be morally acceptable to Professor Price, but I suspect Roberts Fellows may feel differently" (Kurtz 2005). The *Wichita Eagle* reported, "Roberts noted that legal safeguards against domestic spying are in place that weren't in the 1950s and 1960s, when the anti-Communist fervor of former Sen. Joe McCarthy and FBI chief J. Edgar Hoover created a climate that contributed to agency abuses. Specifically, a 1981 presidential executive order clearly prohibits physical surveillance of American citizens by agencies other than the FBI" (Wichita Eagle 2/13/05). This was a remarkable statement. Pat Roberts, then Chair of the Senate Intelligence Committee, appeared to not even understand that the U.S. Patriot Act dismantled safeguards preventing domestic surveillance by the CIA and other agencies. More revealing is that when pressed by reporters, Roberts and sources at CIA did not dispute the likelihood that having undisclosed CIA operatives amongst the ranks of academics could seriously damage the credibility of American academics conducting domestic and foreign research. This blasé attitude concerning the collateral damage of hapless academic bystanders won Roberts no friends in the academy as most academics realize the damage from such actions can be widespread.

But beyond Roberts' reassuring words on the propriety of secretly sending intelligence agents to our classrooms, there was a quiet enthusiasm for the first cloned offspring of PRISP. And like its progenitor PRISP, this program was birthed in an atmosphere of public silence. In December 2004 when Congress approved the Intelligence Reform and Terrorism Prevention Act (S. 2845), they established a Director of National Intelligence. One of the Director's charges is to oversee a new scholarship program known as the Intelligence Community Scholars Program (ICSP). Though modeled after PRISP, the similarities and differences between these two programs reveal emerging trends not only in intelligence funding, but in the intelligence apparat's new expectations for outcome-based funding in higher education.

The Director of National Intelligence is responsible for determining which specific fields and subjects of study will be funded under ICSP. Like the Pat Roberts Intelligence Scholars Program, the ICSP authorizes directors of various unnamed intelligence agencies to make contractual agreements with students. But unlike the Pat Roberts Intelligence Scholars Program, these ICSP students receive unspecified levels of funding for up to four years of university training. Congress specifies that ICSP participants owe two years of intelligence agency work for every year of funded education, with a ceiling of four years of study allowed unless overridden by the Director of National Intelligence.

Unlike previous intelligence-linked scholarship programs, the ICSP does not specifically limit the expenses incurred by participants. But given that the National Security Education Program's current authorization of over $40,000 of annual "academic" expenses for students, it is reasonable to assume that the ICSP will likewise allow over $160,000 of expenses over a four-year period.

One reason why intelligence agencies are so interested in recruiting social sciences and area studies students in the early stages of their education is because of a desire for early indoctrination of these students. Regardless of such efforts to select and shape these individuals, it seems inevitable that at least some will develop more critical attitudes towards these agencies as a result of their education or experiences with these agencies. But suppose a few ICSP students' studies in a university history class lead them to read works like Philip Agee's *Inside the Company* (Agee 1976) or John Stockwell's *In Search of Enemies* (Stockwell 1979) and they decide they made a mistake in enrolling in the ICSP? If so, they will face serious penalties.

The 2004 Intelligence Reform and Terrorism Prevention Act stated that if ICSP recipients decline to work for their sponsoring intelligence agency upon completing of their education, then the student "shall be liable to the United States for an amount equal to the total amount of the scholarships received[and] the interest on the amounts of such awards which would be payable if at the time the awards were received they were loans bearing interest at the maximum legal prevailing rate, as determined by the Treasurer of the United States, *multiplied by three*" (US Congress 2004, Public Law 108-458:h, 2. b). In other words, spy or have a lousy credit rating for the rest of your life.

Such penalties are routine boilerplate language used in other "payback"-based federal scholarship legislation. But the CIA, NSA, FBI and other intelligence agencies are not like the Department of Education, the NSF, or other mundane federal agencies. After all, CIA lawyers who argue that "water-boarding," intense shaking, *shabah*-posturing, and prolonged-hooding do not constitute illegal torture might just as easily argue that the "maximum legal prevailing" interest rate is that established by the payday loan industry.

Get Ready for the Big Payback

In 2008 I was contacted by a recipient of another pay-back national security related scholarship program who provided me with documentation establishing how the US government was pressuring him to engage in national security related work, of face financial penalties. Over a decade earlier, Nicolas Flattes, then an anthropology student at the University of Hawai'i, was awarded a Boren Scholarship from the National Security Education Program (NSEP), then a relatively new funding source for students in the social sciences studying foreign cultures of strategic interest to U.S. policy makers. Flattes' NSEP scholarship allowed him to travel abroad to study food security issues and sustainable agriculture in southern India, in a gender development studies program focusing on nongovernmental organizations' community initiatives.

Flattes signed a standard NSEP contract stating that after graduation he would work at an approved U.S. governmental agency dealing with national security issues, by posting his resume on NSEP's website or applying to specific federal agencies. All NSEP scholars enter into such payback agreements—though there are conflicting accounts of what participants have been told they must do to meet these demands.

Back in the pre-9/11 days of 1998, Flattes was comfortable with the prospect of fulfilling this national security work after graduation. But the radical shift in militaristic foreign and domestic policy and the ascendancy of unchecked powers for U.S. intelligence agencies quelled Flattes' desire to work in any national security capacity after 9/11.

When Flattes completed his Master's degree in June 2001, he posted his resume as he was required to do under the guideline and he went on to other things. Flattes had no further contact with NSEP until 2008, when he received a letter from the Department of Defense (eventually forwarded from a decade-old address) notifying him that he must either begin work for a U.S. agency involved in national security work, or repay the cost of his scholarship along with penalties. As the parent of a young child, Flattes worked part time and lived on limited income. Upon receiving the letter, he contacted NSEP and tried to work out a five-year payment plan but was told he could either begin work at a national security related position (which would both forgive the debt and provide a salary), or he must repay his loan over a two-year period. After some discussion, he was told he could pay off his loan in three years. Flattes could afford a four-year repayment schedule, but on his budget a three-year schedule was impossible.

NSEP personnel told Flattes that a four-year repayment plan was out of the question, and that if he did not meet NSEP's demands he would have to pay a 28 per cent penalty, could have his wages garnished, and collections would be turned over to a private collection agency. Flattes says he left messages for Boren Scholarship and Fellowship Director Christopher Powers, saying he was sending the first of his four-year payments. Flattes described a bizarre episode that occurred after he sent the first of his four-year payments via Canadian Registered Purolator service, when he received a frightening phone call from someone claiming that FBI and D.C. police were investigating the letter he'd sent as a suspected anthrax scare, and they demanded to know the contents of the envelope. The check Flattes sent to NSEP was never signed for, and he believes this was done to produce a trail of plausible deniability, allowing NSEP to claim he was in default so that they could increase pressure on him to seek national security related work.

After NSEP failed to accept his payment, Flattes received a letter from the Treasury Department demanding repayment of his NSEP scholarship with an added 28 per cent penalty. Flattes' believed that NSEP "had no intention of setting up a payment plan and wanted to turn the matter over to another agency as soon as possible." Flattes told me he felt like he was "being shaken down by a loan shark in a government suit," but instead of being given the choice between paying up now or taking a tire-iron to his kneecap, he was told he could either come up with payments beyond his budget, sell his skills for national security work as part of a terror war he does not support, or he could have his credit rating decimated. Not pleasant choices for a man with a conscience and a child to feed. Flattes acknowledged that he must pay back his scholarship funds. What he objected to is NSEP's harsh tactics and their efforts to pressure him into national security work.

Flattes questioned what events triggered the push for him to fulfill his service requirement at this particular point in time. The NSEP service agreement he signed in 1998 did not specify when this service must be completed (today, the program requires services within three years of graduation). Because Flattes served as a Cryptologic Technician Technical in the U.S. Navy from 1985-1989, he believed the NSEP's actions could be an effort designed to press him back into service involving intelligence work. In the Navy, Flattes specialized in Electronic Intelligence where he obtained "a security clearance that was two levels above Top Secret which is rare for enlisted personnel. This field has definite links and cooperation with U.S. intelligence agencies. Basically you work for one, you work for all in a sense." Flattes says he had specialized training in areas that would now be of direct interest to intelligence agencies

47

regardless of specific changes over the last two decades, and he can't help but wonder if his NSEP debt was being used to try and leverage him into intelligence work that he is unwilling to undertake in the political setting of post 9/11 America.

The significance of the NSEP's pressure on Flattes is not that he has to pay back his scholarship funds: he contractually agreed to do this when he signed his NSEP contract. The significance of Flattes' account is threefold: first, Flattes raises the possibility that NSEP may be using his debt to pressure him to get him to do classified national security work; second, it documents the forms of coercion awaiting participants in intelligence and national security payback scholarship programs, who come to think better of working in national security settings once they finish their education; finally, his treatment counters claims that scholars participating in NSEP will not later be forced to either complete their national security requirements or pay back funds with penalties.

Perhaps the most unusual element of Flattes' case is that we, the public, have some knowledge of it. Flattes' willingness to speak out helps establish how the coercive potential of NSEP and other national security linked payback programs leverage scholars into governmental service supporting policies that they personally oppose. Because of the private nature of the repayment demands, it is unknowable how routine such high-pressure demands are.

Institutional privacy policies prevented Boren Scholarship Director, Christopher Powers, from commenting on the specifics of Flattes' case, but he did tell me that the "vast majority of [NSEP funded scholars] to date have fulfilled the program's service requirement through a variety of jobs throughout the federal sector and in higher education." But the public does not know how many former NSEP recipients have caved to the program's demands and quietly slunk off to work for the CIA, NSA, FBI, Homeland Security or other agencies designated to meet contractual obligations of servitude. We don't know how many NSEP scholarship recipients later work in intelligence or national security settings. That some meet their payback requirements in ways that have little or nothing directly to do with national security does not diminish the significance of those who do, and such connections between scholars and national security are the stated reason for NSEP's existence.

Because NSEP's "payback" is always distant, fluid and ill-defined at the time that students join the program, participants cannot know what they are agreeing to do when they receive these funds. Faculty advisors at students' institutions often play a key role in students' NSEP decisions.

Over the past decade, numerous NSEP recipients have told me that they were informally told by academic advisers and others that student wouldn't really have to undertake national security work at a later date and that the program's obligations were routinely downplayed when they applied to the program. Some NSEP scholars have been told that if they later find work teaching in universities, their national security service requirement may be considered met, though the wording of contracts has varied on this point over the years. For example, Flattes' 1998 NSEP service agreement states his agreement to be "employed in a national security position in the Federal Government or work in the field of higher education in [his] study-related area," while current Boren Scholarships information states that fulfilling NSEP national security requirements by working in education "is available only after exhausting all opportunities to fulfill the requirement in the Federal Government in accordance with conditions established by NSEP." Current NSEP scholars banking on a career in academia as a hedge against required national security work underestimate the odds of securing such work and risk facing the same sort of coercion as Flattes is experiencing.

Misinformation on NSEP's payback requirements is widespread. Back in 2000, after I criticized NSEP's payback obligations in an article published in *The Nation* (Price 2000), Adam Frank, then an anthropology graduate student doing NSEP sponsored research in Shanghai, wrote a letter to *The Nation* complaining that I had misrepresented NSEP's payback requirements. Frank claimed that he and other NSEP scholars had been told they really didn't have to fulfill their NSEP contracts' payback clause. Frank's claims that NSEP funding was really just like Fulbright funding or any other research funding were point by point exactly the same talking points I heard a few weeks earlier when a disgruntled NSEP administrator unhappy with my critique had tried to intimidate me on the telephone. Frank's view of NSEP as being fundamentally like the Fulbright program appeared to hinge on his misunderstanding that he could never be pressured to work for a branch of the government concerned with national security (views that nine months later would be more difficult to maintain in post-9/11 America). Frank claimed that NSEP's goals were rooted in "peace" not war, writing:

> One of the post-cold war "peace dividend" programs of the senior Bush Administration, NSEP was created in the early 1990s by an act of Congress. Administered by the Defense Department, the program is similar to the older (and less conspicuously named) Fulbright program: NSEP provides money for research abroad in a wide variety of academic fields. What distinguishes NSEP from Fulbright is that it comes with a service obligation that requires recipients to make a "good faith effort" to find employment in a "security related" government agency within five years of graduation. If they cannot find such employment, they may complete their service agreement through teaching at the college level.
>
> ...NSEP scholars fulfill the requirement to work for the government simply by posting their resume to the NSEP website (beyond that, they are neither assisted in finding government work nor compelled to do so); only a tiny percentage of the research funded by NSEP in the past five years has explicit links to security issues; and "security-related agencies" include more than twenty Congressional subcommittees, the International Trade Office and the Treasury Department among others (Frank 2001).

Arguing that the National Security Education Program is similar to the "less conspicuously named" Fulbright program is like saying borrowing money from a loan shark is similar to borrowing money from a bank. It is true that the loan shark and the bank both loan money, and they will both reinvest loan payments in what they hope are profitable ventures, but the stark differences between forms of customer service and collection services render these comparisons incongruous. I would not argue that Fulbright's agenda has been completely separate from the state's agenda, but comparing NSEP to Fulbright ignores how, despite the truth that both programs fund scholars doing research both related and unrelated to the needs of state, NSEP directly ties scholars' future to unspecified national security needs. In replying to Frank, I wrote that:

My concern with NSEP derives from the inherent conflict it presents to practitioners in a field whose commitment and loyalty must be to those we study—not to those who pay our way through graduate school.

I do not know who told Frank that his only mandated payback to NSEP was "posting [his] resume to the NSEP website." This is clearly not true. The Defense Department states that all grantees must post resumes and seek federal employment at an NSEP-approved national security oriented agency. Participants are allowed to request that their resumes not be circulated among the CIA, DIA and NSA—though the [FBI], the State Department and many other agencies that are the soft-core interface of our national security state's apparatus do not appear on this list of off-limits agencies....

Incidentally, just in case Frank was planning not to follow through with the required "good faith effort" to seek national security-related employment upon graduation, he should be forewarned that NSEP policy states that "recipients are required to reimburse the U.S. Government for the full amount of assistance provided by the NSEP Fellowship, plus interest, should they fail to fulfill the service requirement." True, NSEP fellows can fulfill their payback requirement at US institutions of higher education after their good-faith effort to find employment at NSEP-approved government agencies, but given the job market for anthropologists, anyone counting on repaying NSEP through such an anticipated maneuver is living in denial.

...Under the most basic concept of informed consent, anthropologists receiving NSEP funding must inform those they study that upon their graduation they are required to seek employment from a limited list of national security-related government agencies. But I am sure that Adam Frank has done this in Shanghai and that the University of Texas has required him to do so in compliance with its Human Subject Review Board's policies (Price 2001).

But of course, while U.S. scholars are required to present research proposals to Institutional Review Boards or Human Subject Review Boards, these panels do not universally require NSEP research applicants to disclose to research populations that they have future commitments to work for the government in undetermined national security employment—though such disclosures are mandated by ethical codes of professional organizations such as the American Anthropological Association or the American Sociological Association. Pressing university Institutional Review Boards to require all NSEP recipients to disclose that they are required to pursue future national security employment to all research participants might be a good campaign for campus activists or professional organizations concerned about the damage being inflicted by NSEP. University Institutional Review Boards know that their failure to abide by basic ethical requirements to disclose funding sources and obligations could jeopardize their ability to receive federal grants.

Even within the ranks of those participating in various national security linked payback programs, there exists an informal hierarchy of disdain. The secrecy, front-end linkage with intelligence agencies, and the extreme levels of servitude of the PRISP and ICSP programs give the willies to some NSEP loyalists. When PRISP first appeared on the scene, one scholar who had received NSEP funds in graduate school and later worked with NSEP in another capacity wrote to me that "NSEP is very upset about the PRISP fellowship because they feel they'll be tainted by it, because they don't like the secrecy aspects, and because they fear some enterprising young PRISP-er could end up being killed and/or could threaten NSEP-ers in the field. As you probably know, NSEP recipients are not allowed to be working for the government in any capacity during the period of their award." Like these other payback programs, NSEP holds the potential of becoming a revolving door between the worlds of academia and national security. Nicolas Flattes wondered if NSEP and other national security payback programs were providing a way for U.S. intelligence agencies to get around the ban limiting intelligence personnel from traveling to foreign countries or maintaining contact with individuals in countries listed as hostile.

Flattes told me that "there are two reasons given for this ban. One is that an intelligence operative may accidentally reveal security secrets to an agent from a hostile country. The other reason is that an operative may be influenced or bribed by an agent from a hostile country and intentionally compromise national security. I think this has a great bearing on the NSEP, PRISP, and other similar government programs. Since an intelligence agent is usually unable to travel in or to a hostile or unfriendly, country this makes academics good surrogates and even undergraduate students could be a useful intelligence tool. They can travel freely, and have no obvious association with an intelligence agency.

They can provide invaluable information about countries and places that U.S. intelligence agents are unable to visit."

Flattes sees these payback programs as providing unique opportunities for those who will face travel and contact restrictions when they later work for intelligence agencies. All former students facing hard choices on how to pay for their education have my sympathy. The education industry's means and relations of production provide increasingly narrow choices for students not of independent means, and as American foreign policy becomes ever more tied to invasion, occupation and counterinsurgency, the state's needs for social science swell. Programs like Robert Gates' Minerva Consortium (see chapter three) provide funds for scholars located outside the government's walls in ways that simultaneously subdue what might have been independent academic critiques of national policy while producing knowledge for the state and empire; while indentured payback programs like NSEP, ICSP, and PRSIP can help produce those who can harness and use knowledge within the walls of government. Through such financial means academics are increasingly becoming if not comfortable, then compliant appendages of the state.

But the most troubling elements of ICSP and PRISP are those indicating how academia is increasingly tethered to hidden patrons and clients. If you connect the dots from "non-payback" programs like Fulbright and Title VI to "payback" programs like the National Security Education Program (NSEP), PRISP and then ICSP, the changes in these funding programs suggest directional changes and likely reiterations to come.

While the shift from non-ideological programs like Title VI, or some would argue even NSEP to some degree, to intelligence-agency-linked programs indicates an obvious change, the subtle variations between PRISP and ICSP may indicate future funding developments. From this vantage point, the National Security Education Program appears to be an unstable transitional evolutionary form. The transient independence of NSEP students during their studies is not to the liking of intelligence agencies, and PRISP and ICSP take direct steps to tie students to specific agencies increasingly early, also irrevocably. Changes in the evolution of specific "payback" requirements from NSEP to PRISP to ICSP also indicate an escalation in mandatory employment periods. In a budgetary world of zero sum gains, both PRISP and ICSP bring a growth of intelligence-linked scholarships in a time when traditional independent academic funding programs face cutbacks, and these conditions of scarcity will draw students to these "payback" programs.

While PRISP and ICSP are transforming aspects of higher education without the consent of the universities, many institutions are cultivating closer relations with intelligence agencies. New campus intelligence consortia are forming. Most of these are organizations like the National Academic Consortium for Homeland Security (did they really think we wouldn't call it: NACHoS?) which aligns research and teaching at member institutions with the requirements of the war on terror. But NACHoS is more of a programmatic loyalty marker than it is a key to inner sanctum funding. Member institutions range from Clackamas Community College to MIT. Interestingly, some of the universities that one might suspect would be NACHoS apex institutions (Harvard, Yale, Chicago etc.) are missing from the rolls.

The 251 universities in the consortium (www.homelandsecurity.osu. edu) declare their vague commitment to studying national security issues, antiterrorism, developing new Homeland Security technologies and to "educate and train the people required by governmental and nongovernmental organizations, to effectively accomplish international and homeland security roles and responsibilities". While such proclamations may sound like advertisements for a left-handed monkey wrench, they can function as welcome mats or hobo signs for students secretly holding PRISP or ICSP funding as they shop around for spook-friendly campuses.

There's an unexamined world in which second and third tier universities are being used to train future intelligence personnel; whether it is backdoor connections between the CIA and FBI with fundamentalist Christian homeschoolers at places like Patrick Henry College, or the ICCAE pilot program at Trinity Washington University (see Chapter Four), or no-bid contracts for Homeland Security training at Mercyhurst College, in Tom Ridge's hometown, Erie, Pennsylvania (see Field 2005). There are fortunes to be made by universities interested in cashing in on the national security craze, according to Steven R. David, director of Johns Hopkins University's security certificate program, "Homeland security is probably going to be the government's biggest employer in the next decade" (Kinzie & Horwitz 2005). As Dana Priest and William Arkin's *Washington Post* investigative series on "National Security Inc." (7/20/10) and "Monitoring America" (12/20/10) documents, the spread of public and private sector "national security" employment has been one of the fastest growing parts of the American economy (Priest & Arkin 2010).

From one perspective, the changes brought by PRISP, ICSP or NACHoS to university campuses are changes of degree, not of kind. There is little new in the purpose of such funding programs other than their sheer nakedness and impatience of intent. Throughout the Cold War federal funding produced hordes of scholars and highly educated functionaries happy, willing and capable of carrying out the desires of state. The number of dissident scholars is easily exaggerated, but the impacts have mattered.

Obama Ramps Up PRISP

While news of the Pat Roberts Intelligence Scholars Program generated concern within progressive elements of the U.S. academic community, the coming of the Obama Administration did not bring a reduction in PRISP funding. Instead, the Obama Administration's 2010 budget ended PRISP and ICSP's status as pilot programs and designated these programs as ongoing budget items.

As the continuities and disjunctures between the Bush and Obama administrations first came into focus in 2009, it became increasingly clear that while Obama's domestic agenda had some identifiable breaks with Bush's, at its core, the new administration remained committed to staying the course of American militarization. The United States now had an articulate, nuanced president who supported elements of progressive domestic policies, could even comfortably say the phrase LGBT in public speeches, while funding military programs at alarming levels and continuing the Bush administration's military and intelligence invasion of what used to be civilian life.

One clear manifestation of this continuity came in the spring of 2009 when Dennis C. Blair, Director of National Intelligence, announced plans to transform PRISP from a pilot project into a permanent budget item. Blair also announced plans to establish a "Reserve Officers' Training Corps" to train unidentified future intelligence officers in US college classrooms. Like students receiving PRISP funds, the identities of students participating in these programs would not be known to professors, university administrators or fellow students—in effect, these future intelligence analysts and agents would conduct their first covert missions in our university classrooms.

None of the affected academic disciplines will offer resistance and some may quickly warm to announcements of any new funding stream. Traditionally, the disciplines of political science, history or area specialists coming from the humanities have seldom resisted such developments; but for disciplines like anthropology, these undisclosed intelligence-linked programs present devastating ethical and practical problems, as the non-discloser of funding and links to intelligence agencies flies in the face of the basic ethical principles of the discipline. But even without the problems for individual disciplinary ethics codes, the presence of these undisclosed secret sharers in our classrooms betrays fundamental trusts that lie at the core of honest academic endeavors.

While the National Intelligence Director's move to make PRISP a permanent budget item damaged the academic freedom and integrity of American universities, it was not questioned by university administrators facing crashed university endowments and dwindling budgets. That some administrators would so easily accommodate themselves and their institutional integrity for the promise of funds should be of little surprise, but we should be concerned that the combined forces of the current economic collapse conjoined with President Obama's ability to bring a new liberal credibility to the this warmed-over Bush era project will induce more faculty and students to seriously consider participating in these programs. Times are hard and as funds get scarce it will be increasingly difficult for many to say no.

Establishing PRISP as a permanent budgetary item sped through congress in part because supporters claimed they were both supporting education funding, and military and intelligence sectors, with a bonus feel-good work-ethic mandate thrown-in by requiring students to payback their funds through required future governmental service. This push was accomplished without an outside assessment of PRISP as a pilot program. Because of the lack of transparency surrounding PRISP, we have little idea what is really going on with the program. In 2008 I identified one social science recipient of PRISP funds who explained to me that PRISP had been such a failure in finding social scientists to fund that PRISP had sought them out and provided them with funds for work that was already underway just to spend-down the PRISP budget. Given these difficulties with the program, I wonder if the current expansion of PRISP is a supply-side effort to troll the pool of increasingly underfunded and debt-carrying desperate young scholars with few other funding options.

Professional associations like the American Association of University Professors, the American Psychological Association and the American Anthropological Association need to establish professional policies establishing their opposition to members receiving PRSIP or ICSP funds. PRISP risks further blurring already hazy borders marking proper independent academic roles, and it stands to confuse academic identities in ways that many will not even realize. Some of these processes are reminiscent of a recurrent motif in Philip K. Dick's stories where protagonists becomes unclear of their own agency and identity; becoming unsure of their own histories and memories, or true political alliances—in effect becoming undercover agents with identities unknown even to themselves. As this new generation of programs covertly brings undeclared and unidentifiable students into our universities they disrupt university identities and transforms the roles of all who teach, research, study and work there in ways that they will not necessarily understand—as institutions of higher learning further lose their independence and become unwitting agents of state intelligence functions.

CHAPTER THREE

SOCIAL SCIENCE IN HARNESS: THE GRAVITATIONAL DISTORTIONS OF THE MINERVA INITIATIVE

In Paracelsus's time the energy of universities resided in the conflict between humanism and theology; the energy of the modern university lives in the love-affair between government and science, and sometimes the two are so close it makes you shudder.

—Robertson Davies, *The Rebel Angels*

FROM THE 1930S INTO THE 1960S, TROFIM LYSENKO'S CRACKPOT biological theories provided the Soviet Union's leadership with scientific justifications for the forced collectivization of farms and other centralized policy dreams. Lysenko rejected Mendelian genetics and Darwinian models of natural selection in favor of Lamarkian notions of inheritability of acquired characteristics, and for decades all Soviet biologists needed to work in ways that did not challenge Lysenko's doctrine. Lysenko's claim that changes occurring in an individual during their lifetime could be passed on to their offspring seemed to offer scientific proof supporting the Soviet dream that rapid revolutionary formations could transform not just society, but nature itself. So powerful was Lysenko's impact that the bogus experimental data he produced to justify his work stood unchallenged for decades as valid empirical work. Soviet biologists learned to align their work with the state's conception of the world, and the careers of those dissidents who would not so align their views fell by the wayside.

The demands of conforming scientific knowledge with the ideological positions of a powerful state stunted the development of Soviet biology for decades. But today, American social science faces new forms of ideologically controlled funding that stand to transform our universities' production of knowledge in ways reminiscent of the Soviet Union's ideological control over scientific interpretations. As non-directed independent funding for American social scientists decreases, there are steady increases in new directed funding programs such as the Pat Roberts Intelligence Scholars Program, the National Security Education Program, and the Intelligence Community Scholars Program. These programs leave our universities increasingly ready to produce knowledge and scholars aligned with the ideological assumptions of the Defense Department.

A further step along this trajectory came with Secretary of Defense Gate's announcement on April 14, 2008, of the formation of the Minerva Consortium, a Defense Department program designed to further link universities to Defense's prescribed views and analysis. Gates announced Minerva in a speech to presidents of research universities assembled at a meeting of the Association of American Universities (Gates 2008). The comments of these university presidents reported in the press described them as pleased beyond measure by the relatively paltry funds that Gates promised.

Gates' initial proposal only offered his audience funds "in the millions, not tens of millions," sums that once dispersed across several universities would only be table scraps in most university budgets. But these university presidents realize the great potential for future feasts of funds if they can corral their faculty to think in ways in sync with Minerva. Gates' announcement came three weeks before California's Governor Schwarzenegger announced that the University of California's flagship East Asian Studies program would be cutting its offerings due to $40 million in budget cuts. Gates' silence on these larger systemic issues while pulling the academy in towards a program designed to produce limited, directed knowledge speaks volumes. And these hard times for university budgets will likewise make universities less able to pass on whatever crumbs the Pentagon gives from its lavishly stocked table.

Gates envisioned that the Minerva initiative would consist of "a consortia of universities that will promote research in specific areas. These consortia could also be repositories of open-source documentary archives. The Department of Defense, perhaps in conjunction with other government agencies, could provide the funding for these projects" (Gates 2008).

Minerva issued requests for proposals, their initial interests consist of projects working on: "Chinese Military and Technology Research and Archive Programs," "Studies of the strategic impact of religious and cultural changes within the Islamic World," an "Iraqi Perspectives Project," "Studies of Terrorist Organization and Ideologies," and "New approaches to understanding dimensions of national security, conflict and cooperation." All of these are important topics of critical study, but the ideological narrowness of the Defense Department's approach to and presuppositions of these topics will necessarily warp project outcomes in much the same ways that Lysenko warped the development of Soviet biology. Broken institutions can't repair themselves, and agencies bound to neo-imperial desires of occupation and subjugation will not be receptive to scholarly work seeking to correct this national blunder.

Because of the narrowness of scope and assumptions about the causes of problems facing America, Gates' Minerva plan harms America's strategic capabilities as it will inevitably fund scholars willing to think in the narrow ways already acceptable to the Defense Department. If Gates really wants to better inform American policy, intelligence and military decisions, he should focus his power and energies on increasing the dwindling generalized social science, area study centers (though these have since their WWII inception have always had a Lysenkoian glow of state directed purpose), and language training programs. But Gates is instead supportive of the world that brought us secretive "pay-back" programs locking students into national security servitude in their most formative years. With Minerva he extended his reach into universities' more general social science community.

Even as the budgetary funds for Minerva were rapidly increasing, anthropologist Catherine Lutz observed the funds available for social scientists are (relative) chickenfeed:

> The Minerva money is a tiny fraction of the US military's huge annual research and development budget ($85 billion in 2009): by way of comparison, the total NSF budget is $5 billion and the federal budget for the National Institute of Health is $29 billion for the same period). But the money remains significant for several reasons: it is a large amount relative to other grant money in anthropology (the largest

> funder of anthropological research worldwide, Wenner-Gren, dis-
> perses $5 million a year); it represents an important attempt to garner
> ideological acceptance among anthropologists for doing military
> research (Lutz 2008).

It's not that the U.S. government has historically funded all social sciences approaches equally. It hasn't, and this has historically created its
own problems. To pick one obvious example, the funding of American
social science during the 1940s and 50s finds a lack of funding for scholars openly engaging in Marxist or even explicitly materialist much less
class-based analysis. During the fruitful years of the 1960s and 70s, the
US government shifted to a model of funding that cast financial seeds
broadly, with expectations that general funding would produce knowledge and scholars of use to the needs of state. And that it did, even
though it funded critics of American policies openly studying critical
theory, dependency theory, the culture of poverty, and stratification of
race, class and gender just as it funded modernization theory, development, and other theories linked with sustaining the status quo. This open
model of funding was productive for all, and it produced plenty of scholars who thought in ways aligned with the needs of state. The U.S. government got a good return for its investment whether they realized it or not.

In anthropology there is an overwhelming disciplinary amnesia concerning the extent to which research has been directed by the Pentagon
and intelligence agencies in the past. There has been a broad spectrum
of overt and covert control over this funding, with the full range running
from secret directing of funding of unwitting scholars doing research
of interest to the CIA and others, to the open, massive funding of a full
spectrum of social science and language projects through agencies like
the NSF or Fulbright Programs.

In efforts to find middle ground, in 2008 the leadership of the
American Anthropological Association (AAA) suggested that rather
than running the selection and management of Minerva through the
Department of Defense, the program could be run through "external"
agencies such as the National Science Foundation (NSF). In a letter from
AAA President Setha Low to Jim Nussle of the US Congressional Office
of Management and Budget, President Low argued that,

The Association wholeheartedly believes that social science research can contribute to reduction of armed conflict but we believe that as *Project Minerva* moves towards implementation, its findings will be considered more authoritative if its funding is routed through the well-established peer-reviewed selection process of organizations like the National Science Foundation, the National Institutes of Health, and the national Endowment for the Humanities.

Secretary Gates identified four areas of work that Project Minerva might fund: an archive of sources on Chinese military and technology developments; work on documents captures in Iraq; research on relationship between terrorism and religion, especially Islam; and the "New Disciplines Project," which seeks to leverage anthropology and other disciplines historically under-utilized by the U.S. military (Gates specifically mentioned history, anthropology, sociology and evolutionary psychology, voicing the hope that support for these disciplines might produce new areas of study analogous to efforts undertaken during the Cold War).

We believe that it is of paramount importance for anthropologists to study the roots of terrorism and other forms of violence, and to seek answers to the urgent questions voiced by many in the United States and other countries since the attacks of September 11. However we are deeply concerned that funding such research through the Pentagon may pose a potential conflict of interest and undermine the practices of peer review that play such a vital role in maintaining the integrity of research in social science disciplines. From a practical standpoint, we believe it would be more efficient and more likely to produce authoritative results if Pentagon support for such research was managed through such agencies as the National Science Foundation (NSF), the National Institute of Health (NIH), and the National Endowment for the Humanities (NEH). (S. Low to J. Nussle 5/28/08).

Minerva eventually decided to split its grant review process into two camps, with an open unclassified and a separate closed peer review process. But even the openly reviewed Minerva grants show signs of being tainted with the narrow assumptions of the Pentagon funders. Anthropologist Hugh Gusterson wrote in the *Bulletin of Atomic Scientists:*

When research that could be funded by neutral civilian agencies is instead funded by the military, knowledge is subtly militarized and bent in the way a tree is bent by a prevailing wind. The public comes to accept that basic academic research on religion and violence "belongs" to the military; scholars who never saw themselves as doing military

> research now do; maybe they wonder if their access to future funding
> is best secured by not criticizing U.S. foreign policy; a discipline whose
> independence from military and corporate funding fueled the kind
> of critical thinking a democracy needs is now compromised; and the
> priorities of the military further define the basic terms of public and
> academic debate (Gusterson 2008).

Minerva seeks to increase the military's understanding of other cultures. This is a different project than the Cold War funding programs that openly sought to increase policy makers' understanding of other cultures. The Bush Doctrine's proximity to Minerva suggests a program designed to give the tools of culture to those in the military who will be told where to invade and occupy, not to those who might be asked of the wisdom of such actions. As legions of troop supporting SUV drivers with affixed magnetic yellow ribbons insist on reminding us: the troops don't pick the wars they fight, they follow orders.

Beyond existential questions of desertion, this is certainly true; and anthropologists adding to the military's cultural repertoire in ways that Minerva will pay anthropologists and others to do, will likewise follow orders to produce specific knowledge. What's next? Will academics be driving gas guzzling SUVs with Harris Tweed magnetic ribbons proclaiming: "support the anthropologists (they don't decide when we go to war and who we fight)"? Social scientists cannot ignore the political context in which their knowledge will be used in limited ways by those who fund it, and Minerva's mission does not seek to alter the basic uses to which this knowledge will be put. Minerva seeks to increase the efficiency of implementing the Bush Doctrine, not the questioning of it.

The projects funded by Minerva all study subjects of interest to the Pentagon in particular, limited, ways that in turn influence the questions asked and answers found. For example, from the 2009 funding cycle, Minerva funded: Susan Shirk's (UCSD) study of how Chinese technology relates to their national security; Mark Woodward's (Arizona State University) research mapped "the diffusion and influence of counter-radical Muslim discourse;" David Matsumoto (SFSU) studied cross cultural facial expressions of emotion (with obvious uses for doomed efforts to identify and recognize terrorists). The 2010 joint NSF/DoD Minerva grants include: Martha Crenshaw (Stanford) "mapping terrorist organizations;" Eli Berman (UCSD) presenting a workshop on "The Political Economy of Terrorism and Insurgency." The 2010 DoD funded Minerva Grants had even more direct military applications, with Suzanne Logan's (USMC) research on "Iraqi and Terrorist Perspectives;" William Spain's (Naval War College) on "Iraqi and Terrorist Perspectives/Culture and Strategy;" and Judith Yaphe and Kamal Beyoghlow's researching "Religious and Cultural Change in the Muslim World" (http://minerva. dtic.mil/funded.html). Many of the Minerva projects funded efforts to make social forces legible in particular ways are designed to produce new forms of if not control, then predictive understanding.

Minerva doesn't appear to be funding projects designed to tell Defense why the US shouldn't invade and occupy other countries. Its programs are more concerned with the nuts and bolts of counterinsurgency, and answering specific questions related to the occupation and streamlining the problems of empire. Minerva instead generates select views that conceptualize enemies and problems in ways that are already familiar and understood by those who fund this research. There is no Minerva funded research of dissent and warning, Minerva funds only those who already are aligned with Defense's basic vision of the world. This sort of Soviet model of directed social science funding will make America's critical perspective more narrow precisely at an historical moment when we need a new breadth of knowledge and perspective.

Gates and others at Defense need to hear from independent, unindentured critical scholars who will tell them that counterinsurgency won't work the way that the current social science salesmen are pitching it to the Pentagon and the think tanks of Dupont Circle's hegemony row would have them believe, and the Minerva Consortium will not take social science in this needed critical direction.

The problem with Gate's Minerva vision is the problem with Soviet science: ideologically dependent science's purse strings cannot lead to good results. If Gates really wanted good social science, not social science that tastes good (and familiar to the Pentagon's limited palate), he would be lobbying Congress to increase the funding of generalized social science—including dissident social science—not pushing to Sovietize the social sciences.

CHAPTER FOUR

SILENT COUP: HOW THE CIA WELCOMED ITSELF BACK ONTO AMERICAN UNIVERSITY CAMPUSES WITHOUT PUBLIC PROTEST

> Worship of the state has become a secular religion
> for which the intellectuals serve as priesthood.
>
> —Noam Chomsky

THROUGHOUT THE 1970S, 80S AND 90S, INDEPENDENT GRASSROOTS movements to keep the Central Intelligence Agency off American university campuses were broadly supported by students, professors and community members. The ethos of this movement was captured in Ami Chen Mill's 1990 book, *C.I.A. Off Campus: Building the Movement against Agency Recruitment and Research* (Mills 1991). Mills' book presented tactics for campus activists to resist CIA campus incursions, but it also gave voice to the multiple reasons why so many academics during this period opposed the presence of the CIA on university campuses; reasons that ranged from the recognitions of secrecy's antithetical relationship to academic freedom and the production of critical knowledge, to political objections to the CIA's unbridled use of torture and assassination, to efforts on campuses to recruit professors and students, and the CIA's longstanding role in undermining democratic movements around the world. For those who lived through the dramatic and shocking revelations of the Church Committee Hearings and other congressional inquiries in the 1970s documenting the CIA's routine institutional involvement in global and domestic atrocities, it made sense to many in our universities to construct and maintain institutional firewalls between an agency so deeply linked with these actions and educational institutions dedicated to at least promises of free enquiry and truth. But the last dozen years has seen the retirements and deaths of generations of academics who had lived through this history and had been vigilant about keeping the CIA off campus; and with the terror attacks of 9/11 came new campaigns to bring the CIA back onto American campuses.

In post-9/11 America, the Bush administration spun a narrative that was accepted by Congress and the media claiming that one of the reasons that the 9/11 attacks occurred was because the US did not have well trained analysts who understood the Middle East. Rather than acknowledging that shortcomings in US policy and intelligence were related to the extreme narrowness of political perspectives allowed to exist within agencies like CIA, State, and Defense Department, governmental agencies moved to spread their own narrowness of institutional knowledge by exporting the CIA's dysfunctional institutional culture and groupthink externally to universities.

Henry Giroux's book, *The University in Chains: Confronting the Military-Industrial Academic Complex*, details how shifts in university funding over the past two decades brought increased intrusions by corporate and military forces onto university campuses in ways that transformed the production of knowledge (Giroux 2007). Over the past twenty years, U.S. universities shifted from a reliance on traditional funding sources for research and classroom instruction as both private and public universities welcomed private corporations' money and external research agendas. This shift in corporatization increased most universities reliance on outside corporate funds and an acquiescence towards external agendas positioned university administrators to see post-9/11 advances by intelligence agencies as just another revenue stream.

After 9/11, intelligence agencies pushed campuses to see the CIA and campus secrecy in a new light, and as traditional funding sources for university research did not keep up with perceived funding needs, military and intelligence agencies launched a well-financed bureaucratic push to gain footholds on university campuses in a soft campaign that largely escaped public notice, though privately on each campus where these intelligence programs nest and reproduce, shock waves of concern, outrage and disapproval quietly internally emerged among faculty and students.

Post-9/11 scholarship programs like the Pat Roberts Intelligence Scholars Program (PRISP) and the Intelligence Community Scholarship Programs (ICSP) now sneak unidentified scholars as secret sharers with undisclosed links to intelligence agencies into university classrooms. A new generation of so called "flagship" programs have taken root on campuses, and with each new flagship our universities are transformed into vessels of the militarized state as academics learn to sublimate their unease about these relationships. The programs most significantly linking the CIA with university campuses are the: "Intelligence Community Centers of Academic Excellence" (ICCAE, pronounced "Icky") and the "Intelligence Advance Research Projects Activity" (IARPA); both programs share a vision of quietly using existing universities to train present and future intelligence operatives by establishing at least partially non-transparent programs on these campuses that can piggyback onto existing educational programs. Campuses that can learn to see these outsourced programs as nonthreatening to their open educational and research missions are rewarded with a wealth of funds, useful contacts within intelligence agencies for professors and students, and other less tangible benefits.

These new programs are different from the Cold War's language and area study center funding programs that provided funds for students and faculty to somewhat independently study languages, regions and topics of interest to the American national security state. Cold War language programs like those funded by the 1958 National Defense Education Act, funded things like the study of Russian Language and Soviet culture and history (or later, Latin American language and culture) in ways beneficial to the needs of state without linking scholars to agencies in ways that so obviously limited scholarship. While there were troubling instances where these programs covertly interfered with academic freedom, the extent that these programs funded critical scholarship demonstrates a break with present trends. These past programs created critical scholarship without front loading academics with the intelligence communities institutional world view.

On January 25th, 2010, James O'Keefe and three other individuals were arrested in connection with efforts to wiretap Democratic Sen. Mary Landrieu's office in the Hale Boggs Federal Building in downtown New Orleans. One of the individuals arrested was Mr. Stan Dai, who was arrested a few blocks away from Landrieu's office in a car with a small radio listening device. Independent journalist Lindsay Beyerstein soon identified Stan Dai as a former Assistant Director of Trinity Washington University's ICCAE program. The extent of Mr. Dai's ongoing connections with intelligence agencies remains unclear, but in the summer of 2009 he gave a public talk on the topics of terrorism and torture at a multi-campus "CIA Day" student program in the Junior Statesmen of America's summer school. Dai's arrest makes him ICCAE's reluctant poster child, a status that belies ICCAE supporters routine claims the program is simply another federally funded academic program, essentially no different from funding programs like Fulbright, the National Science Foundation or the Department of Agriculture. This is ludicrous; none of these other federally funded programs openly link scholars with military or intelligence agencies.

After Beyerstein blogged of Dai's connections to ICCAE, *Newsweek* interviewed Ann Pauley, Vice President of Trinity Washington University, who confirmed Dai's work in the ICCAE campus program. Pauley described Trinity's program as seeking "to expose female and minority students to the kind of work spy agencies do and potentially interest them in becoming intelligence officers." The publicity surrounding Dai's arrest was certainly one way of "exposing students to the kind of work spy agencies do." Pauley assured *Newsweek* that Dai's work with ICCAE was only on an administrative level, but *Newsweek* determined that "online records indicate Dai did interact with high-ranking intelligence personnel" (Newsweek 2010). Dai pled guilty to charges of "entering real property belonging to the United States under false pretenses," was fined $1,500, and sentenced to two years probation.

It should be no surprise that ICCAE personnel would be arrested in a bungled blackbag operation. The history of American intelligence agencies is full of characters mixed up in harebrained misadventures, and when universities succumb to the economic pressures to bring ICCAE on campus they need to know they are embracing ignoble institutional histories packed with a motley cast of characters like E. Howard Hunt, G. Gordon Libby and Edwin Wilson. Given the CIA's well documented history and university administrators' refusals to acknowledge that there are fundamental differences between intelligence agencies and universities, this state of denial guarantees we can expect to see more connections between ICCAE-linked personnel and all sorts of nefarious activities.

Today's shift to bringing programs like ICCAE onto American campuses is but one part of the growing acceptance of what anthropologist Catherine Lutz calls "the military normal," as the American military and intelligence state continues to grow in uninhibited ways that increasingly take over all facets of our culture. It isn't enough that U.S. military spending makes up 49% of the planet's military budget: this core militarism reaches into all elements of cultural life until its presence is seen as proper, normal and good. This is how culture works; pastoralist cultures tend to idealize the virtues and imagined personality traits of cattle into countless facets of daily life and religion (it's no coincidence that the Lord is my shepherd came from semi-nomadic shepherds), insect eaters normalize what to us is grotesque, hunters and collectors value egalitarianism and sharing, collective cultures shun the private, capitalists come to see selfishness, bragging, and greed as virtues, and private gain is valued over public good. That economic cultural values are internalized, viewed as natural virtues is not surprising to anthropologists; so in this anthropological sense we should expect a military economy the likes of which the world has never seen before should spread an acceptance of militarization into all forms of social life. We should expect citizens in such a society to be encouraged to accept as normal conditions where basic medical care, food and education are seen as secondary importance to financing the uncontrolled growth of military spending.

ICCAE is part of larger efforts to coax Americans into seeing intelligence agencies as a normal part of life; as a way to get us to internalize surveillance as a new element of American freedom. None of us are immune from such subtle internalizations. When editing a first draft of an article on ICCAE, Alexander Cockburn pointed out to me how many times I had used the word "community," in various ways, including seamlessly switching between references to academic and citizen "community" resistance efforts to CIA campus programs and non-ironically referring to the spy agencies as "the intelligence community"—this being the self-christened innocuous phrase of desensitized preference used by a broad range of intelligence agencies ranging from the CIA to the Defense Intelligence Agency. The soft inviting glow of using "community" to refer to spy agencies devoted to anti-democratic means, imperialism, torture, and any-means-necessary is but one small example of how we are all being socialized to accept intelligence agencies intrusions as part of the normal fabric of American life. In the movie, *Three Days of the Condor*, Mr. Higgins (Cliff Robertson), tells Joe Turner (Robert Redford) that someone within "the community" must be behind the killings that have Turner on the run. Turner repeats Higgins' phrase back to him, saying "community" with disdain. Higgins clarifies, saying "intelligence field," and Turner says, "Community! Jesus, you guys are kind to yourselves. Community!" The CIA's colonialization of America's consciousness has progressed so well that the words "intelligence community" has taken on a normal soft and natural feel.

But even in the extreme militarization found in America today, it is the public silence surrounding this quiet installation and spread of programs like ICCAE and IARPA on campuses that is extraordinary. Since 2005 ICCAE has more rapidly progressed along a trajectory of bringing the CIA and other intelligence agencies openly to multiple American university campuses than any previous intelligence agency's intrusion onto American campuses since the Second World War. Yet the program has spread with little public notice or organized multi-campus resistance. In 2004 a $250,000 grant was awarded to Trinity Washington University by the Intelligence Community for the establishment of a pilot "Intelligence Community Center of Academic Excellence" program. Trinity was in many ways an ideal campus for a pilot program, as a vulnerable, tuition driven struggling financial institution in the D.C. area, the promise of desperately needed funds and a regionally assured potential student base linked-with or seeking connections to DC-based intelligence agencies made the program financially attractive.

In 2005, the first wave of ICCAE centers were installed at ten university campuses: California State University San Bernardino, Clark Atlanta University, Florida International University, Norfolk State University, Tennessee State University, Trinity University, University of Texas El Paso, University of Texas Pan American, University of Washington, and Wayne State University. Between 2008-2010 another wave of expansion brought ICCAE programs to another eleven campuses: Carnegie Mellon, Clemson, North Carolina A&T State, University of North Carolina-Wilmington, Florida A&M, Miles College, University of Maryland, College Park, University of Nebraska, University of New Mexico, Pennsylvania State University, and Virginia Polytechnic Institute. But the CIA and FBI aren't the only intelligence agencies that ICCAE brings to American university campuses. ICCAE quietly brings a smorgasbord of intelligence agencies to campuses with fifteen agencies, such as the National Security Agency, Defense Intelligence Agency, and Homeland Security on our campuses.

Roberto González's research explores how ICCAE's university programs are but part of a larger project that also seeks to connect intelligence agencies with American students in high school and even younger. In *Militarizing Culture*, González notes that the Office of the Director of National Intelligence's program plan encourages grantees to "consider coordinating summer camps for junior high students…[they] should be at least one week in duration with high energy programs that excite the participants" (González 2010:39). He also describes programs tailored especially for high school students, such as Norfolk State's "simulation exercise in which faculty asked Nashville-area high schoolers to locate ten simulated 'weapons of mass destruction' hidden in the city" and the University of Texas Pan American's high school summer camp which featured talks "from speakers from intelligence community agencies, such as the CIA and FBI." González poses the question: "Couldn't these young people play a more constructive role in our society if they were aggressively recruited into careers in medicine, engineering, or education" rather than spy work (González 2010:49)?

ICCAE's stated goals are to develop a "systematic long-term program at universities and colleges to recruit and hire eligible talent for IC agencies and components," and to "increase the [intelligence recruiting] pipeline of students...with emphasis on women and ethnic minorities in critical skill areas." Specifically, ICCAE seeks to "Provide internships, co-ops, graduate fellowships and other related opportunities across IC [Intelligence Community] agencies to eligible students and faculty for intelligence studies immersion," and to "support selective international study and regional and overseas travel opportunities to enhance cultural and language immersion" (http://www.dni.gov/cae/). In other words, ICCAE seeks to shower fellowships, internships, scholarships and grants on universities willing to adapt their curriculum and campuses to align with the political agenda of American intelligence agencies, and installing corridors connecting ICCAE campuses with intelligence agencies through which students, faculty, students studying abroad and unknown others will pass. These ICCAE sponsored centers have different names at different universities, for example, at the University of Washington, ICCAE funds established the new Institute for National Security Education and Research (INSER), Wayne State University's center is called the Center for Academic Excellence in National Security Intelligence Studies (CAE-NSIS) and Clark Atlantic University's program is the Center for Academic Excellence in National Security Studies (CAENS).

Even before 2008's economic downturn, there were decreased traditional funding sources for students and faculty conducting research in university environments—but further reductions in funds exacerbated a funding environment characterized by extremely scarce financial resources. Layoffs of university staff became a common occurrence at many universities. Such scarcity of funds leads scholars to shift the academic questions they are willing to pursue and suspend previous ethical and political concerns about funding sources; and many scholars who are unwilling to set aside ethical and political concerns are keenly aware of institutional pressures to keep their outrage and protests in-house and remain publicly silent.

In 2010, Alumni and professors at historically black colleges and universities wrote me with accounts of the ways that ICCAE and other programs linked to the FBI and CIA are increasingly embedding themselves on these campuses to increase minority recruitment for intelligence agencies. This correspondence shared concerns that Howard University and Miles College figured prominently on the list of new ICCAE institutions. One Howard alumnus wrote me that various efforts to connect the campus with CIA personnel have made Howard "CIA central;" while a Howard professor wrote me about the university's consortium relationship with Virginia Polytechnic Institute and State University connecting the FBI, Homeland Security and the CIA with Howard faculty and students; writing, "these agencies would love to make connections with our students, and the amount of funds they can offer to students without financial means makes it difficult for many to say no." American intelligence agencies need transformational overhauls, but moving the FBI and CIA onto historically black colleges and universities won't transform the FBI, it will transform these institutions in ways they aren't critically considering. With the generational loss of memory of the roles these agencies played in the domestic and international suppression of minority power movements, one wonders if the FBI will try and sponsor a Fred Hampton Intelligence Scholarship designed to recruit students from historically black colleges and universities.

The targeting of minority populations on campuses clarifies systemic problems with intelligence agencies trying to reform themselves. The United States never had anything like a truth and reconciliation commission to sort out past accountabilities for these agencies; instead, it has named the headquarters of our secret police after J. Edgar Hoover himself, embracing the agency's links to Hoover's shameful practices. If the FBI and CIA want to use ICCAE as a front to set up shop on our campuses, they must be held publicly accountable for their own institutional history, but they have yet to produce a public history clarifying exactly where they break with past atrocities, and the lack of critical public discourse on ICCAE further reduces the possibility that these campus intelligence centers will bring about needed reforms.

The *Washington Post* published two articles mentioning ICCAE after the program had quietly been running for a few years, but there has been no critical coverage of these programs in the national press; there certainly has been no mention of the faculty and student dissent that these programs create. Despite the lack of media coverage of student and faculty misgivings over ICCAE programs coming to campuses, some traces of dissent can be found in internet records of faculty senate minutes from various campuses. These records show things like, when Dean Van Reidhead at the University of Texas PA, brought a proposal for ICCAE to establish a center on campus, some faculty and graduate students spoke out against the damages to academic freedom that the program would likely bring. At the senate meeting where this was raised, the minutes record that faculty "representatives spoke against and for UTPA submitting a proposal to compete for federal money to establish an Intelligence Community Center for Academic Excellence (ICCAE)." At this meeting, graduate students "listed the following demands: 1) inform the community via press release about the possible ICCAE proposal, 2) release the proposal draft for public review, 3) establish a community forum on ICCAE, and 4) abolish the process of applying for ICCAE funds" (UTPA Senate 4-26-06). And at UTPA, as at other ICCAE campuses, administrators noted these concerns and continued with plans to bring intelligence agencies to campus.

The online minutes of the University of Washington Faculty Senate and Faculty Council on Research, record shadows of dissent that are so vaguely referenced they are easily missed. For example, while points raised in debates and discussions in the UW's senate are generally item-ized and characterized in the minutes on other topics, the minutes for the December 4, 2008 meeting publicly gloss over even the nature of the issues raised when Christoph Giebel, acting as a member of the University of Washington's AAUP Executive Board, submitted a request to the Faculty Senate for information concerning INSER's contacts with intelligence agencies. These minutes simply read: "…both Giebel and Jeffry Kim [INSER director] answered a series of good questions that resulted in a fair, tough and serious conversation," but what these "good questions" were and the nature of this "tough and serious con-versation" were not mentioned in the minutes, as if "good questions" were not important enough to enter into a public record (UW Faculty Senate Minutes, 12/4/08, pp 5). Likewise, the nature of faculty objec-tions to INSER are glossed over in the January 29, 2009 University of

Washington Senate minutes which simply reported that: "a number of email communications have come through the faculty senate that reflect a range in attitude towards the INSER program" (UW Faculty Senate Minutes 1/29/09, pp 3).

A significant portion of this faculty "range in attitudes towards the INSER program" could best be characterized as outraged. I have heard from faculty at a dozen of the ICCAE flagship campuses that some form of internal dissent has occurred on each of their campuses, and professors at the University of Washington have sent me documents clarifying the extent of the campus' anguish over intelligence agencies' insertion onto their campus; an insertion whose success can best described as a silent coup for the CIA.

The faculty and students' public silence at ICCAE universities in the face of these developments needs some comment. While some public attitudes towards the CIA changed after 9/11, the post-9/11 political climate casts a pall of orthodoxy over critical discussions of militarization and national security, and the rise of anti-intellectual rightwing media pundits attacking those who question increasing American militarization adds pressure to muzzle vocal dissent on anything framed as a national security matter—faculty at public universities often feel these pressures more than their colleagues at private institutions. There are also natural inclinations to try and keep elements of workplace dissent internal, but two factors argue against such a public silence. First, most of the ICCAE institutions are publicly funded universities drawing state taxes; the state citizens funding these universities deserve to be alerted to concerns over the ways these programs can damage public institutions. Second, university administrators have been free to ignore faculty's harsh, publicly silent, internal dissent. Keeping dissent internal has not been a very effective tactic; institutions like the CIA don't want to operate in the sort of sunlight that public scrutiny brings, and these ICCAE programs deserve lots of public scrutiny.

In a healthy step towards moving beyond internal private critiques of ICCAE programs, multiple professors at the University of Washington provided me internal memos sent from professors to administrators. These memos document the form and breadth of internal faculty dissent on this campus over administrators' October 2006 decisions to bring the CIA and other intelligence agencies on campus. University of Washington professors are not alone in these internal critiques, my contacts with professors at other ICCAE universities finds that similar internally expressed concerns are happening on the other ICCAE campuses.

In 2008, AAUP campus executive board member and history professor, Christoph Giebel led efforts in the University of Washington Faculty Senate to pressure the administration to publicly answer faculty questions about university contacts with ICCAE. The campus attention that Giebel generated triggered a wave of memos from departments to the administration questioning the appropriateness of establishing an ICCAE center on campus. Giebel took his concerns public and he worked hard to try and raise public awareness of these developments. He worked to get local newspaper reporters interested in covering plans to bring the CIA onto campus, but beyond a small piece in a local alternative paper, the local media completely ignored these developments (Spancenthal-Lee 2008)

Initially, the University of Washington's administration appeared to appreciate the concerns raised by faculty. In October 2005, David Hodge, University of Washington's Dean of Arts and Sciences met with School of International Studies faculty to discuss proposals to establish affiliations with US intelligence agencies after International Studies faculty wrote the administration expressing opposition to any affiliation linking them with the CIA and other intelligence agencies (though one faculty member reported Hodge was less diplomatic in private). This group of faculty wrote that such developments would, "jeopardize the abilities of faculty and students to gain and maintain foreign research and study permits, visas, and open access to and unfettered interaction with international research hosts, partners, and counterpart institutions;" and they worried that any such relationships would "endanger the safety and security of faculty and students studying and conducting research abroad as well as their foreign hosts." One participant in these meetings told me that the administration initially acknowledged that there were real risks that students and faculty working abroad could lose research opportunities because of negative views of having a CIA-linked program on campus, and that these concerns led the administration initially to not pursue an affiliation with these intelligence agency-linked programs.

But these privately raised concerns did not derail the administration's interest in bringing intelligence agencies on campus, and the following year the administration decided to establish the new ICCAE funded Institute for National Security Education and Research (INSER) on campus. But even after INSER's opening, concerned memos continued to come from faculty across the campus. Letters voicing strong protest from at least five academic units were sent by groups of concerned faculty to Deans.

In October 2008 Professors Bettina Shell-Duncan and Janelle Taylor, composed a challenging memo that was approved by the anthropology faculty as a whole, and sent to Dean Howard, Dean Cauce, and Provost Wise, raising concerns about INSER's presence on campus, and the damage INSER could bring to the University and its students, writing,

> As anthropologists, we also have more specific concerns relating to the nature of our research, which involves long-term in-depth studies of communities, the majority of which are located outside the United States. Some of these communities are very poor, some face repressive governments, and some are on the receiving end of U.S. projections of military power. Recognizing that anthropologists often "study down steep gradients of power" ([Paul] Farmer 2003), our profession's Code of Ethics requires first and foremost that we cause no harm to the people among whom we conduct research (Shell-Duncan to Howard, Cauce & Wise, 10/31/08).

Shell-Duncan & Taylor tied disciplinary concerns to anthropology's core ethical issues and also raised apprehensions that INSER funding could convert the university into a hosting facility for "military intelligence-gathering efforts." This memo voiced concerns over reports that INSER personnel would debrief some students completing studies abroad. Specifically, concerns were raised about,

> 1) the reports that students are required to submit to INSER at the end of their studies, and 2) the "debriefing" that they are required to undergo upon their return. Although our faculty have already been asked [to be] academic advisors for students with INSER funding, we have never been given any information on the guidelines for the

> reports, or the nature, scope or purpose of the debriefing process.
> This is of particular concern given that National Security is not an
> academic field of study, but a military and government effort. Unless
> and until we are provided with clear and compelling information that
> proves otherwise, we must infer that these reports and debriefings
> are in fact military intelligence-gathering efforts (Shell-Duncan to
> Howard, Cauce & Wise, 10/31/08).

This memo cited a 2007 report written by a commission (of which I was a member, and was a report co-author) charged by then American Anthropological Association President Alan Goodman to critically evaluate a wide variety of engagements between anthropologists and the military and intelligence agencies, referencing this report, the memo argued that this AAA report found that while:

> some forms of engagement with these agencies might be laudable,
> the Commission also issued cautions about situations likely to entail
> violations of the ethical principles of our profession. In particular,
> the members of the Commission expressed serious concern about "a
> situation in which anthropologists would be performing fieldwork on
> behalf of a military or intelligence program, among a local popula-
> tion, for the purpose of supporting operations on the ground. This
> raised profound questions about whether or not such activities could
> be conducted under the AAA's Code of Ethics, not to mention the
> requirements of most human studies review boards." Among the
> recommendations reached by the Commission was that "anthropolo-
> gists must ... remain cognizant of the risks engagement entails to
> populations studied (through information-sharing about fieldwork,
> applications of knowledge gained from fieldwork, tactical support and
> operations), to the discipline and their colleagues, and to the broader
> academic community. The AAA's Code of Ethics should remain the
> focal point for discussions of professional ethics" (Shell-Duncan to
> Howard, Cauce & Wise, 10/31/08).

Professors Shell-Duncan & Taylor concluded by asking the administration for,

> a clear and detailed account of the process by which the Institute for
> National Security Education and Research was formed, and request
> assurances that this was done in accord with our shared governance
> procedures. We would like clarification of the role that students are
> playing in military intelligence gathering, and whether and how that
> information is made clear to the student or to their academic advi-

sors. We would like clear and detailed information on the nature and requirements of the reports that students are asked to prepare, and information about the dissemination of these reports. And finally, we would like information about the scope, nature and parties involved in the debriefing process. Without disclosure of such information, it is impossible for us to know if we are acting within the scope of the Code of Ethics of the American Anthropological Association (Shell-Duncan to Howard, Cauce & Wise, 10/31/08).

This record finds the Anthropology Department doing all they could to express concerns and to press for answers. A public accounting of the processes leading to the establishment of INSER has yet to occur; the silence of administrators over the details of how these ICCAE programs come to campuses is not unique to the University of Washington. Sober questions about the roles that students will play in military intelligence gathering also remain unanswered, as do questions of what information about links or agreements for future employment between students and intelligence agencies is being disclosed to academic advisors.

Other academic departments wrote the administration expressing concerns; in November 2008, members of the Latin American Studies division in the Henry M. Jackson School of International Studies complained to the administration in a memo that:

in light of the US Intelligence Community's extensive track-record of undermining democracies and involvement in human rights violations in Latin America and elsewhere, we find it unconscionable that the UW would have formal ties with the newly created Office of the Director of National Intelligence (ODNI), let alone involve our students in an exercise of gathering intelligence information and assist it with its public relations campaign among children in our local schools. The most recent examples of the US Intelligence Community's inexcusable behavior in Latin America are torture at Guantanamo detention centers, collaboration with the infamous School of the Americas, the backing of paramilitary forces as part of the "drug war," the shooting down of a civilian aircraft in Peru, and support for the failed coup in Venezuela…

…Some would argue that UW should engage the Intelligence Community as a method of constructively influencing or reforming it. To our mind this argument is naïve and misguided at best. The training we provide is unlikely to change the deeply entrenched institutional cultures among the various entities, such as the CIA, which form a part of ODNI. In effect, then, we would be enabling the Intelligence Community to be more effective at carrying out their indefensible activities. It is our position that until the ODNI and the various sectors of the Intelligence Community which it oversees demonstrate a clear break from their anti-democratic practices, then the UW, as a global leader, should not be partnered with it. We realize that the UW faces a number of financial constraints, perhaps now more than ever, but the needs for monies can never justify collaboration with an Intelligence Community which is responsible for hundreds of thousands of deaths and immeasurable human suffering throughout the world (Jonathan Warren, Chair of Latin American Studies, to Secretary Killian, Vice Provost Hason, Dean Cauce and Dean Howard 11/25/08).

This argument voiced historical concerns that the CIA's unapologetic role in human rights violations, torture, assassination, and thuggish policies supporting brutal dictators throughout the third world, but it is the reference in the closing paragraph acknowledging that the University of Washington "faces a number of financial constraints" that touches on university administrator's motivation for embracing the CIA in the face of faculty unease in ways that undermines principles of shared governance.

A letter from a broad group of faculty from the Southeast Asian Studies Center anchored its concerns in the CIA's dark history. They wrote that their,

particular concerns are related to the history of US relations with Southeast Asia [(SEA)], and fall into two inter-related categories:

Firstly, the particular history of intelligence operations in SEA and the ongoing legacies of these interventions in the countries, and among the communities that we interact with, in our study aboard and our research activities, makes us particularly aware of how any apparent connection with the US intelligence apparatus could be perceived. We have study aboard programs in 5 countries: Indonesia, Viet Nam, Thailand, Cambodia and Philippines. All of these countries have witnessed political manipulations and instances of violence directly related to US intelligence agency activities: the beginnings were in Indonesia in the 1950s and 1960s, and in the Philippines from the mid 1950s through the 1970s, under Cold War doctrines. Covert activities in Thailand, Vietnam and Cambodia are well known, due to the public scrutiny that resulted from the very overt nature of much of the American war in Indochina. While these may seem to be episodes of the past, memories and legacies are still powerful forces in those countries, and our partners remain particularly sensitive to associations with intelligence activities.

These histories make us particularly concerned that professional standards of disclosure and transparency are maintained in our relationships with our partner institutions. Such transparency is not possible when we may be unwittingly including IC [e.g. Intelligence Community] Scholars in our programs. As we try to work through these histories, we do so in the expectation that the ethics of our profession guide us in our international activities in relation to our counterparts. As we consider our study abroad programs, some of which now require home-stays, we are most concerned about not only the safety and security of our students, but of our hosts and host institutions, who may be seriously damaged by any association with students funded under this program.

In short, having INSER money directly tied to UW programs and students, will taint our reputation, and will endanger the viability of our research, and will endanger us and our counterparts. Like our Jackson School colleagues, we request that the University address our concerns in a public forum (Judith Henchy & Christoph Giebel, to UW Administration, Dec. 2008).

But the administration's actions appeared less concerned with the damage to the university's reputation, the viability of research and endangerments of researchers and subjects than it was with the funding and opportunities that ICCAE provided.

Members of the History Department questioned whether the administration had considered how the presence of INSER on campus would taint professors and students, because, "the professional bodies of many disciplines and professional programs have barred members from participating in programs funded by groups like the CIA due to the ethical conflicts such a relationship would involve. Did the administration take this into account in the process of creating INSER? Are there steps taken in the administration of funds from INSER to prevent faculty from unknowingly compromising their professional and ethical obligations?" (Purnima Dhavan & Adam Warren to Chair Lovell undated letter). Given the lack of transparency surrounding decisions to establish INSER on campus and that ICCAE programs attract secondary secretive funding through programs like PRISP or ICSP, the odds of compromising these professional obligations increase. Given this lack of transparency, many of these transgressions will be unwitting and unknown to many involved.

Among the problems facing the University of Washington's administration in creating INSER was to find an existing academic structure where they could park such a stigmatized program; because the social sciences represented hostile territory, administrators looked to the Information School (I-School). But librarian and Information School faculty weren't happy about having to house INSER.

International Studies Fund Group Librarians privately raised multiple concerns; concerns about transparency, about developing a program outside the normal standards of peer review, and the damage they would receive from having INSER housed within their administrative structure, concerns that this relationship would naturally generate suspicions that the I-School was facilitating intelligence "data mining and exploitation." A letter signed by a dozen faculty from the International Studies Fund Group Librarians expressed deep concerns that that housing "a CIA Officer in Residence" would pollute perceptions of them in ways that could "damage our ability to serve the [other campus constituencies]," arguing that their long standing "strategy of impartial professionalism" across the campus,

> has enabled us to create collections of such depth over the years. It is also this professional independence that has in the past protected us from undue scrutiny by the governments of the countries that we visit and from which we solicit information sources—sometimes of the most sensitive nature—for our scholarly collections. We feel that the presence of the INSER program, not just on campus, but in the very professional school that purports to train librarians in the ethics of their mission, is damaging to our credibility as independent professionals serving the scholarly endeavor. Indeed, in some instances, it could endanger our personal safety and liberty as we travel on behalf of the Libraries to certain areas of the world where the US foreign policy apparatus that INSER represents is not perceived as a benign force (Judith Henchy, Michael Beggins et al. to Bill Jordan & Tim Jewel, undated memo).

Many I-School faculty were unhappy with having to manage such a problematic program and the prospect of being left holding the bag when something goes wrong with one of INSER's intelligence agency partners was not something anyone in the I-School wanted to contemplate.

* * *

Taken as a whole, this correspondence of professorial dissent produces a broad critique of the damaging impacts that INSER brings to the University of Washington. While some critics of the CIA's presence on campus will be encouraged to find faculty privately pushing administrators to avoid such pitfalls for ethical, historical, political and very practical reasons; but it's not clear that these private critiques really mattered precisely because they remained so private. It is striking that activists at the University of Washington have organized protests over their Provost Phyllis Wise's, membership on Nike's board, yet public campaigns against the administration's invitation to the CIA remain publicly dormant.

Today, INSER hosts at least one CIA funded post-doc on the UW campus. It is unknown how many CIA linked employees or CIA linked students are now on the University of Washington's campus. We don't know what all members of the so called "intelligence community" on campus are doing, but those scholars who study the history of the agency know that in the past CIA campus operatives have performed a range of activities, activities that included using funding fronts to get unwitting social scientists to conduct pieces of research that were used to construct an interrogation and torture manual, these contacts have been used to recruit foreign students to collect intelligence for the CIA, they've debriefed graduate students upon return from foreign travel, we know the CIA has cultivated relationships with professors in order to recruit students (Mills 1991; Price 2007). When universities bring IACCE programs to their campus, they are bringing this history with them, and as students from IACCE universities travel abroad, suspicions of CIA activity will travel with them and undermine the safety and opportunities to work and study abroad for all.

ICCAE campus administrators are quick to mouth smooth assurances that these are simply government funded academic programs, akin to National Science Foundation, or Fulbright, or other governmental programs, they are telling half-truths; half-truths that do not confront the history of the very agencies they seek to embed in our classrooms and that ignore how ICCAE transforms the universities that host it.

Taking Stock and Breaking the Silence

University of Washington faculty unease about ICCAE programs is not an anomaly; it isn't the only institution with apprehensions about intelligence agencies' rapid move into education; professors and staff at other ICCAE schools have privately voiced these same concerns. These concerns move beyond universities. I've spoken with staff and administrators at international education NGO's who are so troubled by the rapid advances of intelligence agencies into new flagship programs, that they are considering switching careers.

Conservative ideologues like to argue that academics do not want the CIA on campus because of claimed un-American tendencies; such claims make good scarecrows to frighten away the uninformed, but these claims are even sillier than claims that ICCAE is just like any other governmental funded academic program. While the American public is expected to have little historical memory of the specifics of the CIA's history, academics in disciplines like anthropology, sociology, political science and history know this history too well to be easily distracted by hasty jingoistic arguments that will not confront this history.

There are lots of good reasons to keep the CIA off of our campuses, the most obvious ones stress the reprehensible deeds of the agency's past (and present), and while not denying these powerful arguments, for me the best reason is that this move further diminishes America's intelligence capacity while damaging academia. ICCAE, like the Pat Roberts Intelligence Scholars Program, the Intelligence Community Scholars Program or the Minerva Consortium strives to expand the knowledge of military and intelligence agencies by moving operations onto university campuses, but this will not be their primary impact. The primary impact will be to transform segments of universities so that they learn to limit themselves and to adapt to the cultures of the intelligence agencies, and as these processes occur, our intelligence capacity, and scholarship, will diminish and narrow. ICCAE mimics the Soviet model of central-ized, state directed scholarship, and this tactic will stifle the indepen-dent development of the braches of scholarship it touches as scholars follow those who can learn to think in the ways desired by the CIA and ICCAE. The memo from the Latin American Studies got half of this point in observing that, "the training we provide is unlikely to change the deeply entrenched institutional cultures among the various entities, such as the CIA," if one adds to this a dose of institutional back-flow we can see how this "entrenched institutional culture" overflows into the universities that house ICCAE programs and learn to chase their funds. These dynamics will weaken American universities and our intelligence capacities, as scholars learn to think in increasingly narrow ways.

If the United States wants intelligence reform, it needs to fund inde-pendent scholarship: not narrow down the range of discourse on our campuses by paying cash-strapped universities to house revolving doors between the academy and the CIA. If the CIA, FBI, Homeland Security and the Pentagon want to change the way they approach problems they should encourage Congress to fund research and education on American university campuses without restrictions (as they did with significant self-interested returns throughout the Cold War); and they should resist the urge to spread their tendrils—spreading the institutional limits and problems that they are trying to eliminate—onto American campuses.

But there are other damages that will follow intelligence agencies' presence on campus. Bringing intelligence agencies onto campuses damages academic inquiry and threatens academic freedom. In my book on McCarthyism's impact on anthropology (*Threatening Anthropology*) I used tens of thousands of FOIA documents to show how increased presence of intelligence operatives and informers on American cam-puses wounded the development of anthropology as endless dossiers were compiled on academics disagreeing with US policies on war, race, class, gender etc. This is one of the things that intelligence agencies do: they collect intelligence on those they come in contact with, and especially those they see as different. Paul Lazarsfeld and Wagner Thielens' classic book, *The Academic Mind: Social Scientists in a Time of Crisis*, is full of examples of how intelligence agencies on campuses deadened academic freedom in the 1950s. In one example, a professor tried to caution a student that his comments in class were close to following "the Communist *Pravda* line," and the professor tried to warn the student to be more careful. But the student's response was:

> "In the university anything goes, any idea—just so it's within the bounds of propriety and decency." At the end of the session [the student] announced that he knew the incident would be reported since there were unknown intelligence men in the class. I felt that I ought to report this incident, but I felt like a rat. A friend who is also teaching in the military told me to cover myself. I phoned the next day to the civilian security man, and explained the situation to him. I later learned that the F.B.I. had already heard most of the conversation. I didn't have to repeat the story to them. They had already received reports of the incident (Lazarsfeld & Thielens 1958:210).

Universities need to be places where people can freely explore ideas, but ICCAE inevitably brings chills to open classrooms. How long will it take until students at ICCAE universities start to wonder about who's reporting on free-flowing discussions in classes; with cadres of future FBI and CIA employees on campus, those who question such things as the wisdom of American drug policies, immigration policies and spending on military and intelligence programs will find themselves choosing between silence, softening what might have been harsh honest critiques, or speaking their mind. Academic enquiry suffers in such environments. As ICCAE students graduate and begin careers at the CIA, NSA, FBI and other agencies requiring security clearances, accounts of all sorts of academic discussions stand to make their way into intelligence files as clearance background checks comb through records on any known "subversive" acquaintances these individuals encountered during their university years.

These problems are not intended outcomes of ICCAE bringing the CIA, FBI, Homeland Security etc. on campus; but as unintended consequences, these problems will emerge. The history of how this worked in the past is pretty clear, and these problems are why legislation prohibiting forms of domestic political surveillance (later undone with the Patriot Act) were written. It's easy to see this past as prologue, and now that the Patriot Act removed vital legal firewalls prohibiting these forms of domestic political surveillance, the stage has been set for a dark renaissance to begin.

Because ICCAE's successful embedment on campuses depends on institutional memory-loss, silence and a lack of student and faculty resistance, academics opposed to these developments can draw on their professional strengths to break the silence and fill the sizable gaps in the public's memory of the CIA's institutional history. Historians and political scientists can develop curriculum drawing on scholarly materials and primary sources to teach students the unsanitized details of the CIA's history. If faculty remain in control of the curriculum, then documenting this past may be one of the best ways to defend the present.

The CIA and other intelligence agencies have always relied on secrecy for their operations, and with the public silence over ICCAE's intelligence-gateway onto our campus communities; this silence has been a real boon for the CIA's quiet entrance onto our campuses. If students, faculty and citizens are concerned about ICCAE's impact on our universities, then breaking the silence is the simplest and most effective tactic available.

Anyone who wants specific information on contacts between university administrators and ICCAE officials or other members of intelligence agencies can use state public records laws and the federal Freedom of Information Act to request these records. Given university administrators' claims that everything is above board, these records should not be blocked by national security exemptions, and if they are, this would be important information. In most states, public records laws can be used to access the correspondence of public employees. Concerned members of individual campuses can use these tools to access correspondence and verify claims by university administrators about the nature of their contact with ICCAE.

Faculty, staff, students, alumni and community members concerned about ICCAE's presence on university campuses should form consortiums online to share information from various campuses and make common cause. ICCAE has made significant and rapid headway because of the internal and campus-specific, isolated nature of resistance to ICCAE. Something like an "ICCAE Watch" or "CIA Campus Watch" website could be started by a faculty member or grad student on an ICCAE campus, providing forums to collect documents, stories and resistance tactics from across the country. Philip Zwerling has written about how a group of undergraduate and graduate students at the University of Texas Pan American organized themselves to protest the CIA's campus presence, and to raise awareness (Zwerling 2009:256-257). Other campuses resisting the CIA's campus expansion need to open channels of communication with each other.

Finally, tenured professors on campuses with ICCAE programs, or on campuses contemplating ICCAE programs, *need to use their tenure* and speak out, on the record, in public: the threats presented by these sorts of developments are exactly why tenure exists. If professors like the idea of bringing the CIA on campus (they need to read more about the history of the agency…), fine, they have the right to publicly express these views, but the split between the strongly voiced internal dissent while remaining publicly silent has helped usher the CIA silently back onto American university campuses, and if this move is to be countered, it must be done publicly with academic voices demanding that the CIA and other members of intelligence agencies explain them self and their history in public.

The intelligence community thrives on silence; and the only way for academicians to challenge the threats to academic independence and integrity that ICCAE presents is for tenured professors to speak out and raise their concerns in public.

PART II MANUALS:
DECONSTRUCTING
THE TEXTS OF
CULTURAL WARFARE

CHAPTER FIVE

THE LEAKY SHIP OF HUMAN TERRAIN SYSTEMS

> The fact that some social scientists have received [Human Terrain Systems] so warmly reveals historical amnesia and a profound lack of imagination.
>
> —Roberto González

IN THE FALL OF 2007, A NEW FORM OF ANTHROPOLOGICALLY INFORMED counterinsurgency was publicly announced as the Bush administration and U.S. military placed great hopes on a new program known as Human Terrain Systems (HTS). The Human Terrain program embeds social scientists, such as anthropologists, with troops operating in battle theatre settings as members of Human Terrain Teams (HTT). These teams are part of counterinsurgency operations designed to provide military personnel with cultural information that will help inform troop activities in areas of occupation. Since the first public acknowledgement of HTS in 2007, it has been criticized by anthropologists for betraying fundamental principles of anthropological ethics, as being politically aligned with neo-colonialism, and as being ineffective in meeting its claimed outcomes. For the most part, the mainstream media has acted as cheerleaders for the program by producing a seemingly endless series of uncritical features highlighting what they frame as kind hearted individuals trying to use their knowledge of culture to save lives; while misrepresenting the reasons and extent of criticism of the Human Terrain program.

Supporters of Human Terrain claim the program uses embedded social scientists to help reduce "kinetic engagements," or unnecessary violent contacts with the populations they encounter. The idea is to use these social scientists to interact with members of the community, creating relationships to reduce misunderstandings that can lead to unnecessarily violent interactions (Kamps 2008; Stannard 2007).

Human Terrain Systems is not some neutral humanitarian project, it is an arm of the U.S. military and is part of the military's mission to occupy and destroy opposition to U.S. goals and objectives. HTS cannot claim the sort of neutrality claimed by groups like Doctors Without Borders, or the International Committee of the Red Cross. HTS's goal is a gentler form of military domination. Pretending that the military is a humanitarian organization does not make it so, and pretending that HTS is anything other than an agent of the military engaging in a specific form of conquest is sheer dishonesty.

One of the most remarkable things about the Human Terrain program has been the ongoing uncritical, fawning coverage of the program uniformly presented by the American media. From the first coverage of the program by David Rohde in the *New York Times* in 2007, to a dozen glossy magazine profiles and dozens of national newspaper stories, a consistent hopeful news narrative has prevailed portraying Human Terrain "social scientists" not as the violators of minimal professional ethics standards that they have been chastised by the Executive Board of the American Anthropological Association, but instead as sensitive humanitarians.

David Rohde's 2007 front page *New York Times* article framed the functional, political and ethical issues surrounding HTS in distorted ways that set the stage for much of the debates and discussions that followed (Rohde 2007). I spoke with Rohde as background for the story, patiently explaining details and historical background, and like other reporters who would follow, Rohde trimmed off elements of the story that overly complicated a simple narrative. Most importantly he uncritically included an incredible claim by Army Col. Martin Schweitzer (82nd Airborne Division), who claimed that after HTS anthropologists embedded with units, their "combat operations had been reduced by 60 percent" (Rohde 2007). After reading this unbelievable claim in Rohde's article, I filed a Freedom of Information Act (FOIA) request with the Army, requesting any records that would substantiate or support Schweitzer's outrageous claim. In reply to my FOIA request I received a series of emails from Col. Schweitzer, who conceded that he had no actual data on this and had simply given figures that expressed what seemed to be occurring (see Price 2010). Yet, these exaggerated figures took on a life of their own and would not die and were recycled in dozens of news stories, with Col. Schweitzer himself later repeating them, unchallenged, in congressional testimony. Years later, Spencer Ackerman politely questioned the veracity of Col. Schweitzer's claims, writing that,

> The first test of the HTS went almost too well to be believed, with a local commander in Afghanistan crediting his Human Terrain Team with an astonishing 60 to 70 percent drop in the number of bombs-and-bullets strikes he had to make. The program grew exponentially, to 27 teams in Iraq and Afghanistan. But no commander ever made a similar boast about HTS' influence. And complaints about the program's recruits metastasized, making the program look like an unworthy enterprise (Ackerman 2010).

A few early boosters of Human Terrain Systems eventually called for its closure (most notable, the British journal *Nature*), and some journalistic coverage shifted from uncritical praise to more reserved critical writing (e.g. Noah Shachtman's writings on *Wired's* military *Danger Room* blog)(Nature 2008a & 2008b; Shachtman 2009). Even while there were plenty of obvious clues that the program was not working as HTS claimed, most media coverage remained uncritical in its thinly veiled support for a program that still has not had to answer the fundamental critiques of its critics, and Human Terrain continues on its trajectory of counterinsurgency domination.

As the Human Terrain Systems story developed in the years following Rohde's *New York Times* story in late 2007, the press moved beyond its initial scandal-instincts feeding off the human interest generated by the controversy and disciplinary outrage over anthropologists assisting military occupations and it refused to hold Human Terrain Systems answerable for the questions and critiques launched by its critics. With time, the media became the key supportive enabler of HTS. Since September 2007, I have probably spent at least forty hours speaking with journalists from *Elle, More, USA Today, Newsweek, Time, AP, New Yorker, New York Times, Wired, Harper's, Washington Post*, etc. patiently explaining what the critical issues for anthropologists are when a program like Human Terrain Systems embeds anthropologists with troops engaged in counterinsurgency operations in occupied battle settings in Iraq and Afghanistan (see: Burleigh 2007; Ephron & Spring 2008; Featherstone 2008; Gezari 2009; Kamps 2008; Packer 2006; Rohde 2007; Shachtman 2007; Stier 2007; Vergano & Weise 2008). Sometimes portions of these critiques show up along the way in the final stories, but in most cases, the arguments and critiques against the efficacy, ethical, neocolonial politics as well as the practical impossibility of HTS working as advertised are ignored, or worse yet, they are presented as absurd caricatures. In October 2007 I was contacted by the Diane Rehm Show and was scheduled to have a one-on-one face-off with Montgomery McFate, moments before going on the air I was told that the military had insisted on not sending McFate alone, so with the two additional military spokespersons, the standard Pentagon to citizen ratio of arguments and airwave domination were then three-to-one (Rehm 2007). In a number of cases I heard from reporters (who sometimes send along portions of their original draft to have me check sections to see if their quotes of me in the draft are correct) telling me, without apparent irony, that my words and the words of other critics were removed from final versions of stories in order to not overly complicate the narrative. That's one way to keep the story presented to the public in simple terms: remove critics' views from the story.

Alternative press journalists like Amy Goodman at *Democracy Now* or Lindsay Beyerstein at *In These Times,* the great writer Dahr Jamail at *Truthout,* or foreign journalists in Holland, Finland, Germany, Spain or the UK have had no problems describing the fundamental problems for their readers, but the mainstream American press seems committed to keeping the story one-sidedly simple and manifestly jingoistic (Democracy Now 2007; Jamail 2010). Between 2008-2010, American journalist John Stanton wrote a remarkable series of damaging exposés detailing the failures of Human Terrain management and the program's overall inefficiency in the field (see Stanton 2009). Stanton's work drew largely on unidentified disgruntled Human Terrain personnel and paints a picture of fiscal mismanagement, poor field supervision, lack of training before sending social scientists into life-threatening situations, and a non-working "reach-back system" that was supposed to connect deployed field Human Terrain personnel with personnel located at HTS headquarters at Ft. Leavenworth. While most of the mainstream media reprinted the talking points provided by Human Terrain Systems' personnel, Stanton, Roberto González, and a few independent journalists like Laurie Beyerstein wrote critical pieces examining the controversies and problems of the Human Terrain program (Beyerstein 2007; González 2008, González & Price 2007, NCA 2009; Stanton 2009).

Beyerstein's piece in *In These Times* was one of the first pieces to push back against the uniform narrative uncritically echoing the program's narrative that HTS reduces harm among occupied populations. Beyerstein wrote in 2007 that,

> Unlike other publicly funded researchers, HTT anthropologists do not have to clear their research methods with any kind of internal review board. They are tasked with collecting whatever operationally relevant cultural information the brigade commander needs. It's not a free-for-all, as the HTT are bound by the same rules that apply to any U.S. contractor on the battlefield. They operate in what the military calls a "non-permissive environment," under the supervision of military commanders. Nevertheless, it's a far cry from the strict standards that govern human subjects research in peacetime.
>
> HTS is reluctant to set specific ground rules for research in advance because the program is still in an exploratory phase. "We don't know what we don't know," says Fondacaro, "There's no internal review board because this is all uncharted territory."
>
> It's easy to envision circumstances in which HTTs might compromise the anthropological injunction to do no harm. While HTTs don't participate in combat, they do offer direct support to combat brigades. The participating anthropologists also have no control over how their work might be used by the brigade commander. If anthropologists figure out who the local power brokers are, commanders can use that information to make a peaceful proposition, or to call in an air strike. Human terrain is analogous to geographical terrain. The same maps can be used to build a bridge or blow one up.
>
> "Targeting and kinentic operations are something that must be done, part of the military," says Fondacaro. He stresses that the goal of HTT is to move towards less violence, and less harm to innocent people when force is used (Beyerstein 2007).

Over the years, Human Terrain's saleswoman, anthropologist Montgomery McFate, adopted a policy of not answering the academic critiques of her many critics regardless of the documentation of her critics. This policy allowed Dr. McFate to avoid answering some pretty serious questions; questions about her reported involvement in the surveillance of an American gun control group (Ridgeway et al., 2008); questions about the unattributed writings of other anthropologists appearing in the new Counterinsurgency Field Manual (Price 2007); Questions about why, rather than acknowledging that Human Terrain Teams raise complex ethical issues to be negotiated, she has instead moved forward without even trying to publicly address these issues (AAA 2007 & 2009). And while this approach works well in the political environment of Washington, D.C., where accountability and memories are short, this is the most non-academic approach imaginable—academics engage with each other when disputes arise, they answer critiques with data and arguments rather than rely on silence and professionals to spin stories in the press.

Dr. McFate's position of leaving critiques unanswered appears to have become that of HTS, and a compliant corporate media has followed this lead as it increasingly refused to report on the problems, corruptions, and complexities of HTS, instead only providing the public with narratives that would have them believe that HTS anthropologists are good caring people trying to lessen harm, while critics are either invisible or portrayed as ivory tower America-hating kooks.

WIKILEAKS AND THE *HUMAN TERRAIN SYSTEMS HANDBOOK*

In December 2008, Julian Assange emailed me word that Wikileaks had just received a leaked copy of the (Unclassified) *Human Terrain Systems Handbook*, asking me to write an analysis of the *Handbook* for *CounterPunch* and the Wikileaks site. Someone inside Human Terrain was so dissatisfied that they were attacking the program from within.

The leaked *Handbook* illuminated how Human Terrain Teams envisioned their role, and how these teams were conceived of as supplanting the roles that Civil Affairs units traditionally played in assessing the needs and conditions of occupied populations. The leaked *Handbook* described Human Terrain Teams as bringing "another aspect of the population: the average persons' perspective. When the HTT incorporates the 'grass-roots' perspective with government and tribal perspectives gathered by the CA and PRT Teams, a more robust clear picture on the needs of the entire population emerges. This in-depth picture can then be infused into planning and military decision making processes to increase positive outcomes" (Finney 2008a:34). The *Handbook* explained how Human Terrain Teams incorporate military-embedded anthropologists and other social sciences who interview members of local populations in war zones, often with armed Team members, sometimes wearing uniforms. The descriptions and details in the *Handbook* revealed how the program imagined anthropological techniques and research could inform military engagements with occupied and enemy populations.

Because of the complex ethical issues involved in conducting ethnographic fieldwork for occupying military forces in war zones, the Human Terrain Program is viewed by most anthropologists as being extremely problematic. In 2007 and again in 2009, the American Anthropological Association's Executive Board produced statements condemning the Human Terrain program for its inattention to basic anthropological ethical concerns for voluntary informed consent and the well-being of studied populations (AAA 2007 & 2009).

It was clear even back before this HTS Manual was leaked in 2008, that little seemed to be working right at Human Terrain. Two Human Terrain social scientists had already been killed and numerous HTS social scientists had come under physical attack. Murder charges were filed against Human Terrain Team member Don Ayala. Ayala was accused of executing a detained and cuffed man believed to have attacked and burnt his Human Terrain Team colleague.

INSIDE THE LEAKED *HANDBOOK*

The *Human Terrain Team Handbook's* author is listed as Army Captain (Retired) Nathan Finney. Finney's qualifications as an "anthropologist" consist of the Bachelors Degree he earned in anthropology at the University of Arizona in 2002; after earning his Bachelors degree,

Finney served in the Army for four years, he writes that when, "later while serving in the Army Reserves, I can across an opportunity to use my bachelor's degree in service of the Army" (Finney 2008b:7). Finney's understanding of anthropological ethics is as cursory and confused as his understanding of culture.

The leaked *Human Terrain Team Handbook* informs us of the goals for Human Terrain Teams. These teams are to support the military units in which they embed by providing,

> the unit the reasons why the population is doing what it is doing
> and thereby providing non-lethal options to the commander and
> his staff. Military units have incorporated systems to identify and
> address threats for the entirety of its history, and more recently created
> systems for the inclusion of subject-matter experts in law enforcement,
> economics, etc. All of these elements gather information and include
> their recommendations on courses of actions for the commander. The
> knowledge gap that HTTs counter is population-focused and designed
> to assist the unit in preventing friction with members of the local
> population by identifying local dynamics, grievances and motivations,
> assessing governmental effectiveness and making recommendations
> on how to address them (Finney 2008a:26).

This statement demonstrates the *Handbook's* deeper underlying logic that anthropologically based non-lethal subjugation is good, while lethal subjugation is bad. The *Handbook* intentionally ignores basic ethical and political questions about whether anthropologists should contribute to the subjugation of the people they study. The *Handbook* ignores more traditional political and ethical considerations of anthropologists' responsibilities to not work against the interests of research participants. Such traditional anthropological considerations lie outside the concerns of the *Handbook*, which takes anthropologically aided subjugation as an acceptable goal from the outset.

The *Handbook* claims that Human Terrain personnel produce "expert human terrain & social science advice based on a constantly updated, user-friendly ethnographic and socio-cultural database of the area of operations that leverages both the existing body of knowledge from the social sciences and humanities as well as on the ground research conducted by the team" (Finney 2008a:28). But as reports by John Stanton and disgruntled HTS employees clarifies, the needed software and the "tactical overwatch reach-back links" at the Ft. Leavenworth Reachback Research Center have never worked as planned, with failed software systems and personnel reportedly unable to use the system (Stanton 2009).

The *Handbook* describes how a Human Terrain "toolkit" can be used to make subjects living in military occupied areas understandable to the U.S. military forces occupying them. This toolkit is used in ways designed to make populations (to borrow from James Scott's *Seeing Like a State*) "legible" and thus controllable (Scott 1999). The *Handbook* states that:

> HTTs will use the Map-HT Toolkit of developmental hardware and software to capture, consolidate, tag, and ingest human terrain data. HTTs use this human terrain information gathered to assist commanders in understanding the operational relevance of the information as it applies to the unit's planning processes. The expectation is that the resulting courses of actions developed by the staff and selected by the commander will consistently be more culturally harmonized with the local population, which in Counter-Insurgency Operations should lead to greater success. It is the trust of the indigenous population that is at the heart of the struggle between coalition forces and the insurgents (Finney 2008a:34).

Human Terrain social scientists' mission is thus expressed in terms of engineering the "trust of the indigenous population." The *Handbook* clarifies how Human Terrain Systems envision its role as a tool by occupying military forces. In this role, "the HTT will research, interpret, archive, and provide cultural data, information, and knowledge to optimize operational effectiveness by harmonizing courses of action within the cultural context of the environment, and provide the commander with operationally relevant, socio-cultural data, information, knowledge and understanding, and the embedded expertise to integrate that understanding into the commander's planning and decision-making processes" (Finney 2008a:35). Like many other contemporary articulations of anthropologists' working with the military, the *Handbook* compartmentalizes the project as something separate from larger neo-imperial missions of invasion and occupation.

Consistent with claims by Montgomery McFate and others supporting Human Terrain Systems, the *Handbook* insists that Human Terrain Teams should not engage in "Lethal Effects Targeting." But the *Handbook* remains silent on how the supposedly non-classified collected Human Terrain data will be protected from the "unintended" uses by others. It does state that "The commander has an intelligence section for lethal targeting, what they require is a section that can explain and delineate the non-lethal environment (e.g. tribal relationships and local power structures), as well as the second and third order effects of planned lethal and non-lethal operations" (Finney 2008a:82).

Human Terrain Systems naively believes that it can control the uses to which its data is put by others. In a similar state of denial, the *Handbook* includes the admonition that personnel should: "avoid direct involvement in tactical questioning. Tactical questioning is a function of the intelligence world and designed to elicit primarily lethal-targeting information. It would also endanger relationships with the local population if HTTs are seen being involved with the "interrogating" of friends/family" (Finney 2008a:83). This statement shows how HTT falsely envisions that the world of intelligence gathering and processing is neatly compartmentalized and that intelligence officers could not possibly have access to HTT reports. It is as if HTT personnel's avoidance of "direct involvement" with the intelligence community means that whatever passive involvement they have with the intelligence community is acceptable. The *Handbook* does not address the possibility that when Human Terrain Personnel collect information reporting identities of cooperative and compliant individuals or groups as "not" Taliban or "not" sympathetic to al-Quaida, that those other individuals or groups occupying the negative space of these composite pictures risk becoming targets.

Roberto Gonzalez observed that the Human Terrain Handbook shares a,

> striking resemblance between some suggested HTT methods—for example, the appropriately named 'SPIIEOP'—and methods employed during the infamous Vietnam War-era CORDS/Phoenix Program. Specifically, CORDS/Phoenix 'census grievance' teams collected census and ethnographic data and interviewed people about their

needs, complaints and sentiments towards the Viet Cong—in much the same way that HTT members are instructed to do. 'Census grievance' data was submitted to databases that Phoenix operatives used to detain, torture and kill 26,000 suspected Viet Cong supporters (Gonzalez 2009:28).

Pointing out these clear historical connections of method and purpose rankle Human Terrain supporters, who insist they operate outside of any form of structural or historical forces that would limit or necessarily link their efforts to any such outcome. Some HTS supporters imagine themselves to be reworking large bureaucracies from within with declared good intentions and visions of reduced harm, as if the larger social forces governing human history are only for lesser beings who do not share their wisdom and nobility of purpose.

The academic lineages exposed in the leaked *Handbook* are enlightening. The *Handbook* cites and draws heavily from the work of American anthropologist Russell Bernard and anthropologist James Spradley—both highly regarded research methodologists. The *Handbook* recommends several specific ethnographic tools, some of which are standard software packages used by many anthropologists. The *Handbook* describes how the "core software components (Analyst Notebook, ArcGIS, Anthropac, UCINet and NetDraw) allow the team to conduct network analysis, Modeling and Pattern analysis and geo-spatial analysis that place those people and events in place and time" (Finney 2008a:47). The *Handbook* includes sample interview forms that can be used to catalog members of occupied populations in remote databases. There are discussions of qualitative and quantitative data collection and analysis written at a high school or middle school level of sophistication, describing such techniques as producing ethnographic field notes or conducting structured and unstructured interviews.

James Spradley's 1979 "Taxonomy of Ethnographic Questions" and his "Elements in the Ethnographic Interview" are cited and reproduced in full. The *Handbook* includes a list of an interesting knowledge-tree of local concerns that military occupiers should be aware of—this list includes such items as knowledge of local archaeological resources, hand gestures, shortages of water, electricity and other resources. The list provides a matrix to be used by anyone wishing to inventory items needed when attempting to establish full spectrum dominance over a given occupied people.

The *Handbook* envisions HTT social scientists gathering and coding ethnographic data in the field, and using these technological tools to analyze this data in the field, but there is something odd in the *Handbook's* brief presentations of information on the collection and analysis of this data. The *Handbook's* references to these ethnographic tools places blind trust in technological aids as if these tools can take the place of human theoretical understanding of what the data means.

The inclusion of these specific methodologies, toolsets, interview and inventory sets is an artifact of Human Terrain Systems' focus on neo-positivist notions that social control of the human landscape can be achieved by the recording of, and then manipulation of key variables in these environments. At a theoretical level, the Human Terrain project is reliant on a form of social engineering where the anthropologists working inside the program seem to believe they are reducing harm for the studied occupied populations, but the program itself is designed to manipulate these populations as studied objects—objects to be controlled for what has been determined as "their own good." The revelations of Human Terrain training insider John Allison (see chapter nine) clarify that the quick and dirty approach to methods in the HTS training classes used simplistic, atheoretical notions of culture and a mixture of marketing research techniques loosely bundled as anthropological field methods.

The most startling methodological revelation in the *Handbook* comes when the current Human Terrain project connects itself to past anthropological efforts to catalog disparate cultural traits in the Human Relations Area File, a project with financial roots firmly planted in George Peter Murdock and other anthropologists' efforts to catalog cultures during the Second World War. The *Handbook* states that,

> As part of the research, we will eventually use the Organization of
> Cultural Materials schema in order to contribute our research results
> to an existing database of cultural practices and social systems known
> as the Human Relations Area Files (HRAF) housed at Yale University.

> This practice allows us to provide significant, abundant, and contemporary socio-cultural information that others around the world may use in their own research. This practice will also allow us to tie into the HRAF database and compare the existence of one social practice, symbolic system, or historical process in our area of operations with others elsewhere in the world. Such cross-cultural analysis enables us to get closer to explaining causation and make weak assertions of what will likely happen in the population in the near future (Finney 2008a:56).

With this statement Human Terrain comes full circle and connects to World War II projects using anthropological data to inform military interactions with occupied peoples, yet there is no expressed awareness of the many failures of the HRAF project, or of the problems faced by World War Two users of Murdock's data (Price 2008). Instead, the *Handbook* blindly marches towards a high-modern world of imagined social engineering where handheld data units provide occupiers with the sort of specific data readings that Captain Kirk, Science Officer Spock and their red shirted human terrain ensigns had in the original *Star Trek* series. But this project isn't exploring where no [hu]man has gone before, it is only a broken high tech version of colonial projects that many anthropologists hoped had become part of a shameful disciplinary past.

Plans to link HTS data to the Human Relations Area Files also links Human Terrain's counterinsurgency operations with HRAF's poorly understood Cold War counterinsurgency research projects. The most absurd of the HRAF-linked counterinsurgency programs from the 1960s involved the military's Special Operations Research Office's interest in expanding HRAF's cross cultural indexing system to include categories that could be used to code data for U.S. counterinsurgency operations. As the U.S. military today increasingly prepares for rapid deployment counterinsurgency operations around the globe (with AFRICOM operations taking on an increasing importance), we can expect that these old broken efforts to prepare readily available geographically-specific counterinsurgency information databases will be revived and made available as handheld iPhone like devices to be used by culturally confused personnel embedded with troops. Such high tech efforts to fill in cultural gaps will remain attractive to military contractors and military personnel entrapped in engineering problem solving mindsets, and there are fortunes to be made for military contractors generating poor quality data (pirated from the published ethnographic literature) to be used in ridiculous mobile-global counterinsurgency databases. The *Handbook's* vision of providing HRAF ready data reporting thus fulfills the dual purposes of creating the self-serving pretense that HTT is engaged in scholarly activity, while also collecting data organized in ways that can be retrieved as part of what may become a larger counterinsurgency database.

In a few places the *Handbook* makes fleeting suggestions that issues of research ethics are being dealt with by someone or something else. Without explanation, the *Handbook* states that "an accompanying document is written outlining how the research will comply with the protection of human research subjects according to 45 CFR 46 to ensure the research falls within accepted ethical guidelines" (Finney 2008a:55). My correspondence with HTT defector John Allison (see Chapter Nine) clarified that HTT training includes little meaningful discussions of ethnographic ethics, and while ethics were briefly mentioned in Allison's training sessions, the larger focus was on training HTT social scientists to comply with the needs of the military units with whom they embed. The *Handbook* claims that, "the results of our research provide non-target data that suggests Courses of Action to the commander and his staff. Our research is performed in the same manner in which academic social scientists conduct their research and is similarly rooted in theory and complete with ethical review boards" (Finney 2008a:56). It is difficult to evaluate the claims of non-targeting. In his book *American Counterinsurgency: Human Science and the Human Terrain*, anthropologist Roberto González quotes U.S. Army, Lt. Colonel Gian Gentile, scoffing at suggestions that such cultural data would not be used for targeting in active war situations, responding to similar claims by Human Terrain anthropologist Marcus Griffin, Gentile wrote:

> Dear Dr. Griffin: *"Don't fool yourself. These Human Terrain Teams whether they want to acknowledge it or not, in a generalized and subtle way, do at some point contribute to the collective knowledge of a commander which allows him to target and kill the enemy in the Civil War*

in Iraq. I commanded an Armored Reconnaissance Squadron in West Baghdad in 2006. Although I did not have one of these HTTs assigned to me (and I certainly would have liked to) I did have a Civil Affairs Team that was led by a major who in his civilian life was an investment banker in New York City and had been in the area I operated for about 6 months prior. He knew the area well and understood the people and the culture in it; just like a HTT adviser would. I often used his knowledge to help me sort through who was the enemy and who was not and from that understanding that he contributed to I was able to target and sometimes kill the enemy. So stop sugarcoating what these teams do and end up being a part of; to deny this fact is to deny the reality of the wars in Iraq and Afghanistan. I am in favor of this program of HTTs and see great utility in it for combat commanders. I understand the debate too between these field anthropologists who are part of the HTTs and academia. I think academia is wrong to chastise these people for being a part of the HTTs. But I also think that people like you should call a spade a spade and accept the reality of the effects that these HTTs produce. (Lieutenant Colonel Gian P. Gentile in Gonzalez 2008:70-71, emphasis added).

The *Handbook's* claim HTT's research is "complete with ethical review boards" contradicts the information I have garnered in my interviews with former HTT social scientists, or HTT social scientists in training. I am skeptical that HTT has in fact implemented any meaningful ethical training, or used "ethical review boards" in any ongoing meaningful way.

Human Terrain Systems is a failed attempt to approach problems of subjugation or occupation with tools and understanding of cultural nuance and culturally appropriate manipulation. Many anthropologists like myself oppose these methods on ethical and political grounds. The ethical problems of voluntary informed consent, and protection of research participants in such battle settings are ignored by Human Terrain, as is the political reality that anthropology is being used to aid and abet the forced occupation and subjugation of others.

Human Terrain supporters like Montgomery McFate argue that it represents a nonviolent alternative to the use of force, but these supporters fail to address the larger political context of supporting conquest and subjugation, instead choosing poses in which they present themselves as if it is they who are actually "insurgents" working within and against the military as they try and teach the military to use less-lethal means of achieving conquest. The leaked *Handbook* shows that this is not insurgency against the military; it is a betrayal of what might have been anthropology's promise to represent those we study in ways that reflect not only who they are, but their own self interests.

In the summer of 2010, years of Human Terrain Systems disfunctionality finally took their toll as Steve Fondacaro and Montgomery McFate left their leadership of the Human Terrain Systems program; Fondacaro was reportedly forced out, McFate left with him. A half a year later, in an interview with Spencer Ackerman, Fondacaro admitted that "thirty to 40 percent of the [Human Terrain System's social scientists] were not qualified" to do their jobs (Ackerman 2010). Fondacaro shirked all personal responsibility for this disaster, instead blaming BAE Systems, the private contractors running and profiting from the HTS sham. Fondacaro claimed that BAE's hiring practices saddled him with a herd of hires lacking sufficient regional cultural experience, the requisite social science skills, or the physical stamina required to successfully embed with the military. McFate joined Fondacro's efforts to blame BAE for HTS's multiple failures, complaining that BAE's vetting of HTS hires was so poor that they hadn't even caught that one of their employees had an outstanding homicide arrest warrant (Ackerman 2010).

But even as Fondacaro finally contradicted his years of lies about the high quality of their HTT social scientists and blamed BAE for the program's disasters, McFate and Fondacro both continued to deny their own roles in the program's many failures. McFate and Fondacaro were complicit in these hires, in the public cover-up of how poorly things were going, in conning the taxpayers with upbeat evaluations of the program; and they were handsomely paid for their central roles in building the program that they would later criticize after cashing in on the boondoggle.

Despite a steady drumming by the corporate media's coverage pitching Human Terrain Systems as a miraculous cure-all for America's counterinsurgency woes, in December 2010, after a report by the House Armed Services Committee (highly critical of HTS), the U.S. House's defense funding bill stated that it would only provide 85% of HTS's budget funds until, "the Army submits to the congressional defense committees each of the following: (1) A validation of all HTS requirements including any prior joint urgent operational needs statements. (2) A certification that policies, procedures, and guidance are in place to protect the integrity of social science researchers participating in HTS including ethical guidelines and human studies research procedures" (111th Congress, 2nd Session, H.R. 6523).

In other words, despite HTS's steady media barrage of pro-HTS propaganda, the House Armed Services Committee finally put Human Terrain Systems on notice that it needs to produce evidence supporting its remarkable claims of reducing "kinetic engagements," and the program must demonstrate that it is in compliance with normal ethical research guidelines used for human subjects. Over three years of criticism coming from numerous anthropologists, the Network of Concerned Anthropologists, a critical American Anthropological Association commission report (AAA 2009), and critical articles by progressive journalists pushed the House Armed Services Committee to conduct its own investigation leading to this (minor) hold on program funding.

The methodological and political difficulties of designing a fair and honest means of evaluating a battlefield program like HTS are significant enough that it would be possible to concoct a scientific-looking study with low-validity that won't negatively evaluate the program's effectiveness. Evaluating HTS social scientists' compliance with normal standards of research ethics will present very serious problems for the program, and it seems impossible that the program can legitimately pass this second requirement.

But lying beyond the technicalities of evaluating outcomes and ethics remains the immovable politics of using anthropology for occupation. No clean bill of health from independent social science contractors evaluating the efficiency or ethical propriety of Human Terrain Teams can overcome the core political problems of using anthropology for neo-colonial occupations and subjugations.

CHAPTER SIX

COMMANDEERING SCHOLARSHIP: THE NEW COUNTERINSURGENCY MANUAL, ANTHROPOLOGY, AND ACADEMIC PILLAGING

> If I could sum up the book in just a few words, it would be: "Be polite, be professional, be prepared to kill.
>
> —John Nagl, pitching the new *Counterinsurgency Field Manual* on *The Daily Show*

Soon after the U.S. Army and Marine Corps published their new *Counterinsurgency Field Manual* (No. 3-24), in December 2006, the American public was subjected to a well orchestrated publicity campaign designed to convince them that a smart new plan was underway to salvage the lost war in Iraq. In policy circles, the *Manual* became an artifact of hope, signifying the move away from the crude logic of "shock and awe" toward calculations that rifle-toting soldiers can win the hearts and minds of occupied Iraq through a new scholarly appreciation of cultural nuance.

At the time of this media blitz, things were going poorly in Iraq, and the American public was assured that the *Manual* contained plans for a new intellectually fueled "smart bomb" for an Iraqi victory. This contrivance was bolstered in July 2007, when the University of Chicago Press republished the *Manual* in a stylish, olive drab, *faux*-field ready edition, designed to slip into flack jackets or Urban Outfitter accessory bags (US Army & USMC 2007). The Chicago edition included the original forward by General David Petraeus and Lt. General James Amos, with a new forward by counterinsurgency expert Lt. Col. John Nagl and introduction by Harvard's Sarah Sewell. Chicago's republication of the *Field Manual* spawned a media frenzy, and Nagl became the *Manual*'s poster boy, appearing on NPR, ABC News, NBC, and the pages of the *NYT*, *Newsweek*, and other publications, pitching the *Manual* as the philosophical expression of Petraeus' intellectual strategy for victory in Iraq (see Ephron 2006; Kaplan 2007; Kerley 2006; NPR 2007; Sutherland 2008).

The Pentagon's media pitch claimed the *Manual* was a rare work of applied scholarship, and old Pentagon hands were shuffled forth to sell this new dream of cultural engineering to America. Robert Bateman wrote in the *Chicago Tribune* that it is "probably the most important piece of doctrine written in the past 20 years," crediting this success to the high academic standards and integrity that the Army War College historian, Conrad Crane, brought to the project. Bateman touted Crane's devotion to using an "honest and open peer review" process, and his reliance on a team of top scholars to draft the *Manual*. This team included "current or former members of one of the combat branches of the Army or Marine Corps." As well as being combat veterans, "the more interesting aspect of this group was that almost all of them had at least a master's degree, and quite a few could add 'doctor' to their military rank and title as well. At the top of that list is the officer who saw the need for a new doctrine, then-Lt. Gen. David Petraeus, Ph.D" (Bateman 2007).

The *Manual*'s PR campaign was extraordinary. In an August 23, 2007, *Daily Show* interview, John Nagl hammed it up in uniform with Jon Stewart, but amidst the banter Nagl stayed on mission and described how Gen. Petraeus collected a "team of writers [who] produced the [*Manual*] strategy that General Petraeus is implementing in Iraq now." When Jon Stewart commented on the speed at which the *Manual* was produced, Nagl remarked that this was "very fast for an Army field manual; the process usually takes a couple of years"; but for Nagl this still was "not fast enough". The first draft of each chapter was produced in two months before being reworked at an Army conference at Ft. Leavenworth. The speed at which the *Manual* was produced should have warned involved academics that corners were being cut, but none of those involved seemed to worry about such problems. The *Counterinsurgency Field Manual*'s insertion into mainstream American popular culture was part of the military's larger scheme to use willing glossy outlets to convince the

American public that new military uses of culture would lead to success in Iraq. While one conservative magazine criticized these efforts (e.g. *The Weekly Standard*), the liberal press (*New Yorker, Elle, More, Wired, Harper's etc.*) climbed on board, running glossy uncritical profiles of the cultural counterinsurgency's pitchmen in glamorous write-ups portraying this new generation of anthropologists as a brilliant new breed of scholars who could build culture traps for foreign foes and capture the hearts and minds of those we'd occupy (see: Burleigh 2007; Featherstone 2008; Kamps 2008; Marlowe 2007; Packer 2006; Shachtman 2007). The willing press pitched the Pentagon's message that top scholars were now using scholarship to prepare America for victory in Iraq.

The American public was assured that in Iraq and Afghanistan, the military was implementing the *Manual*'s approach to the use of culture as a battlefield weapon. Human Terrain Teams embed anthropologists with troops operating in Iraq and Afghanistan, and the *Counterinsurgency Field Manual* was hailed as the intellectual tool guiding their coming success.

THE SECRETS OF CHAPTER THREE

The heart of the *Manual* is Chapter Three's discussion of "Intelligence in Counterinsurgency." Chapter three introduces basic social science views of elements of culture that underlie the *Manual*'s approach to teaching counterinsurgents how to weaponize the specific indigenous cultural information they encounter in specific theaters of battle. General Petraeus bet that troops working alongside Human Terrain System teams could apply the *Manual*'s principles to stabilize and pacify war-torn Iraq.

When I read an online copy of the *Manual* in early 2007, I was unimpressed by its watered-down anthropological explanations, but having researched anthropological contributions to the Second World War, I was familiar with such oversimplifications. Like any manual, it is written in the dry, detached voice of basic instruction. But when I re-read Chapter Three a few months later, I found my eyes struggling through a crudely constructed sentence and then suddenly being graced with a flowing line of precise prose, "A ritual is a stereotyped sequence of activities involving gestures, words, and objects performed to influence supernatural entities or forces on behalf of the actors' goals and interest" (FM 3-24, 3-51).

The phrase "stereotyped sequence" leapt off the page. Not only was it out of place, but it sparked a memory. I knew that I'd read these words years ago. With a little searching, I discovered that this unacknowledged line had been taken from a 1977 article written by the anthropologist Victor Turner, who brilliantly wrote that religious ritual is, "a stereotyped sequence of activities involving gestures, words, and objects, performed in a sequestered place, and designed to influence preternatural entities or forces on behalf of the actors' goals and interests" (Turner 1977:183).

The *Manual* simplified Turner's poetic voice, trimming a few big words and substituting "supernatural" for "preternatural". The *Manual* used no quotation marks, attribution, or citations to signify Turner's authorship of this barely altered line. Having encountered students passing off the work of other scholars as their own, I know that such acts are seldom isolated occurrences; this single kidnapped line of Turner got me wondering if the *Manual* had taken other unattributed passages. With a little searching in chapter three alone I found about twenty passages showing either direct use of others' passages without quotes, or heavy reliance on unacknowledged source materials.

The numerous instances I found shared a consistent pattern of unacknowledged use. While any author can accidentally drop a quotation mark from a work during the production process, the extent and consistent pattern of this practice in this *Manual* is more than common editorial carelessness. The cumulative effect of such non-attributions is devastating to the *Manual's* academic integrity, and claims of such integrity are the heart and soul of the Pentagon's claims for the *Manual*.

The use of unquoted and uncited passages is pervasive throughout this chapter. For example, when the *Manual's* authors wanted to define "society" they simply "borrowed" every word of the definition used by David Newman in his *Sociology* textbook (cf. FM 3-24 3-20, Newman 2006:16), they lifted their definition of "race" from a 1974 edition of Encyclopedia Britannica (cf. FM 3-24 3-25, Encyclopedia Britannica.

"Race." 1974, vol. 15.), and their definition of "culture" was swiped from Fred Plog and Daniel Bates' *Cultural Anthropology* textbook (cf., FM 3-24 3-37; Plog & Bates 1988:7). The *Manual's* definition of "tribe" was purloined from an obscure chapter by Kenneth Brown (cf., FM 3-24 3-27; Brown 2001:206), and not only is Victor Turner's definition of "ritual" hijacked without attribution but the *Manual's* definition of "symbols" was a truncated lifting of Turner (cf., FM 3-24 3-51 ; Turner 1967:19). Several sections of the *Manual* are identical to entries in online encyclopedia sources. The *Manual's* authors used an unacknowledged truncated version of Anthony Giddens' definition of "ethic groups" (cf., FM 3-24 3-26; Giddens 2006:487). Max Weber's definition of "power" is taken from *Economy and Society* and used without attribution (cf., FM 3-24 3-55; Weber 1922:53). And so on. Each of these passages was taken without the use of either quotation marks or any acknowledgement that real scholars had originally written these words.

Other sections of the *Manual* have unacknowledged borrowings from other sources. Roberto González discovered that the *Manual's* Appendix A was "inspired by T.E. Lawrence, who in 1917 published the piece 'Twenty-seven articles' for *Arab Bulletin*, the intelligence journal of Great Britain's Cairo-based Arab Bureau" (González 2010:79). González compared several passages of Lawrence with David Kilcullen's Appendix A, and found parallel constructions where paragraphs were reworded but followed set formations between the two texts. González observed that while these parallel constructions can be seen, "Lawrence is never mentioned in the appendix." González shows that "Kilcullen's other written work makes a passing reference, but does not acknowledge the degree to which Lawrence's ideas and style have been influential" (González 2010:81).

A complicating element of the *Manual's* reliance on unattributed sources is that the *Manual* includes a bibliography listing of over 100 sources, yet not a single source I have identified is included. My experience with students trying to pass off the previously published work of others as their own is that they invariably omit citation of the bibliographic sources they copy, so as not to draw attention to them. Even without using bibliographic citations, the *Manual* could have just used quotes and named sources in a standard journalistic format, but no such attributions were used in these instances.

Examples of Lifted Text

In some sentences, the *Manual* directly follows the vocabulary and structure of identifiable sentences in other works. For example, the *Manual's* entry for "ethnic groups" says:

> "An *ethnic group* is a human community whose learned **cultural practices, language, history, ancestry**, or **religion** distinguish them from others. **Members of ethnic groups see themselves as** different **from other groups in a society and are** recognized as such **by others**" (US Army & USMC 2006: 3-26).

Elements of this definition follow the model sentence patterns of a passage in Anthony Giddens' 2006 *Sociology* text discussing ethnicity:

> "Different characteristics may serve to distinguish ethnic groups from one another, but the most usual are **language, history**, or **ancestry** (real or imagined), **religions** and ...**Members of ethnic groups see themselves as** culturally distinct from **other groups in a society, and are seen by those other** groups to be so in return" (Giddens 2006:487)

Comparisons of Unacknowledged Sources for Passages in *The Counterinsurgency Field Manual*

Here are specific examples of portions of the *Counterinsurgency Field Manual*, derived from other unacknowledged sources. The hyphenated numbers preceding passages indicate the citation used in the *Counterinsurgency Manual*. **Bold writing** indicates the portion of the passage that has been used without attribution from another source; indented passages present the original unacknowledged source passage (references for source passages appear in parenthesis).

Counterinsurgency Manual, section 3-20: Society

"...**sociologists define society as a population living in the same geographic area that shares a culture and a common identity and whose members are subject to the same political authority**" (US Army & USMC 2006:3-20).

UNACKNOWLEDGED SOURCE:

"Formally, **sociologists define society as a population living in the same geographic area that shares a culture and a common identity and whose members are subject to the same political authority.**" (Newman 2006:19)

Counterinsurgency Manual, section 3-24: Groups

"**A group is two or more people regularly interacting on the basis of shared expectations of others' behavior** and who have **interrelated status and roles**" (US Army & USMC 2006: 3-24).

UNACKNOWLEDGED SOURCE:

"**Group: two or more people regularly interacting on the basis of shared expectations of others' behavior; interrelated statuses and roles.**" (Silbey 2002)

Counterinsurgency Manual, section 3-25: Race

"A *race* is a **human group that defines itself or is defined by other** groups **as different by virtue of innate physical characteristics.** Biologically, there is no such thing as race among human beings; race is a social category" (US Army & USMC 2006: 3-25).

UNACKNOWLEDGED SOURCE:

[Race] "refers to **a human group that defines itself or is defined by others as different by virtue of innate** and immutable **physical characteristics**" (Encyclopedia Britannica 1974).

Counterinsurgency Manual, section 3-26: Ethnic groups

"**Members of ethnic groups see themselves as different from other groups in a society and are** recognized as such **by others**" (US Army & USMC 2006: 3-26).

UNACKNOWLEDGED SOURCE:

Members of ethnic groups see themselves as culturally distinct from **other groups in a society, and are seen by those other** groups to be so in return" (Giddens 2006: 487).

Counterinsurgency Manual, section 3-27: Tribes

"Tribes are generally defined as *autonomous, genealogically structured groups* in which the rights of individuals are largely determined by their ancestry and membership in a particular lineage" (US Army & USMC 2006: 3-27).

UNACKNOWLEDGED SOURCE:

"[A Tribe is an] autonomous, genealogically structured group in which the rights of individuals are largely determined by their membership in corporate descent groups such as lineages" (Brown 2001:206).

Counterinsurgency Manual, section 3-37: Culture

"Culture is a system of shared beliefs, values, customs, behaviors, and artifacts that members of a society use to cope with their world and with one another" (US Army & USMC 2006: 3-37).

UNACKNOWLEDGED SOURCE:

"The system of shared beliefs, values, customs, behaviors, and artifacts that the members of society use to cope with this world and with one another." (Plog & Bates 1988:7).

Counterinsurgency Manual, section 3-44: Values

"A value is an enduring belief that a specific mode of conduct or end state of existence is preferable to an opposite or converse mode of conduct or end state of existence" (US Army & USMC 2006: 3-44).

UNACKNOWLEDGED SOURCE:

"A value is an enduring belief that a specific mode of conduct or end state of existence is personally or socially preferable to an opposite or converse mode of conduct or end state of existence" (Rokeach 1973:5).

Counterinsurgency Manual, section 3-51: Cultural Forms

"A ritual is a stereotyped sequence of activities involving gestures, words, and objects performed to influence supernatural entities or forces on behalf of the actors' goals and interest" (US Army & USMC 2006: 3-51).

UNACKNOWLEDGED SOURCE:

Religious ritual is "**a stereotyped sequence of activities involving gestures, words, and objects, performed** in a sequestered place, and designed **to influence** preternatural **entities or forces on behalf of the actors' goals and interests**" (Turner 1977:183).

Counterinsurgency Manual, section 3-51: Cultural Forms

"**Symbols** can be **objects, activities,** *words,* **relationships, events,** or **gestures**" (US Army & USMC 2006: 3-51).

UNACKNOWLEDGED SOURCE:

"The **symbols** I observed in the field were, empirically, **objects, activities, relationships**, **events, gestures,** and spatial units in a ritual situation" (Turner, 1967:19).

Counterinsurgency Manual, section 3-55: Power and Authority

"**Power is the probability that one actor within a social relationship will be in a position to carry out his or her own will despite resistance.**"

UNACKNOWLEDGED SOURCE:

"**Power** [Macht] **is the probability that one actor within a social relationship will be in a position to carry out his or her own will despite resistance**" (Weber 1922:53).

Several sections of the manual are identical to entries in online encyclopedia sources like www.answers.com. For example, the *Handbook's* definition of "language" is the same as that on http://www.answers.com/topic/duration-poem-4), portions of other entries appear on wikipedia. Because such online entries are not dated, it cannot be demonstrably shown which text is the original, but the overall pattern of unacknowledged use suggests that the *Handbook* relied on these sources.

The inability of this chapter's authors to come up with their own basic definitions of such simple sociocultural concepts as "race," "culture," "ritual," or "social structure" not only raises questions about the ethics of the authors but also furnishes a useful measure of the *Manual* and its authors' weak intellectual foundation. In all, I quickly found over a dozen examples of lifted passages from uncredited source.

When I published an exposé in October 2007 documenting the extent of the *Manual's* unacknowledged "borrowed" passages in *CounterPunch*, the military had a variety of responses (Price 2007). U.S. Army Spokesman Major Tom McCuin issued a doublespeak statement declaring a mistakes-were-made-but-the-message-remains-true admission that passages were indeed used in an inappropriate manner. Major McCuin officially proclaimed Army's official position to be that:

> the messages contained in the manual are valid, regardless of any discussion of academic standards. Any argument over missing citations should in no way diminish the manual's utility in the current counter-insurgency fight.…The Human Terrain System is recognition of the fact that academic study and applied social science has practical uses, and those who have chosen to devote their time and efforts to exploring non-lethal alternatives to combat are making a vital contribution to the nation's efforts to secure a peaceful, stable and secure future for the people of Iraq and Afghanistan. The long term by-product of their heroic efforts will be better informed military decisions that minimize casualties and suffering, and ultimately, optimized policy decision making within government that is harmonized with the ethical principles social science values the most (McCuin 2007).

Less-officially, a mob of blood-boiling COIN believers furiously blogged on the *Small Wars* website and sent emails attacking me, my credentials, and my reputation and discussed plots designed to get me fired from my job or cause me trouble in the workplace. The comments were a pretty good example of the state of anti-intellectual currents prevailing in American. These were blog rants of angry warriors carrying on in ways that demonstrated they did not understand academia or even basic principles of academic freedom, the discourse failed to address how the *Manual* was being used to sell the American public on the war, much less that the use of these unsourced passages ran counter to *Manual's* own claims that the work of others was properly cited and acknowledged.

Montgomery McFate issued no statement concerning the sourcing problems in the manual, and to the best of my knowledge, to this day she has never explained what happened. John Nagl issued a statement claiming that the *Manual*, as military doctrine, did not need footnotes or attributions of any type—this was of course counter to the *Manual's* own claims (Nagl 2007). Nagl's response skirted the issue of the *Manual's* lifting exact sentences (and of slightly modifying others) and reproducing them in the manual without quotation marks as if the problem was simply one of missing footnotes and citations and not of quotations. Nagl wrote that it was his "understanding that this longstanding practice in doctrine writing is well within the provisions of "fair use" copyright law." A few military scholars, like historian Lt. Col. Gian Gentile of West Point publicly criticized Lt. Col. Nagl's excuses and argued that the academic credibility of the *Manual* has been undermined.

Lt. Col. Gentile posted a public letter on the Small Wars Journal website to Nagl, stating that scholarship matters, and asking Nagl to publicly respond to how this stealing of the work of others had happened. He wrote that he agreed with Nagl that my piece had an angry strident tone and was using a critique of Human Terrain Teams because a deeper disapproval of anthropologists contributing to warfare, but then he wrote:

> However, in all of the responses to the Price piece to include yours not one has offered a satisfying explanation of the passages that are used in the Coin manual that Price shows to be directly lifted from other sources. Now the garden variety explanation for this has been oh yes, oh well what should we realistically expect since it is a doctrinal manual and it can not be cluttered with footnotes and quotation marks.
>
> But I look at it this way, like you I have an advanced degree (a PhD in history from Stanford University). I was not an author of the Coin manual. You were along with others like Dr Conrad Crane. Con was in fact a senior mentor of mine at Stanford and read and critiqued my dissertation. So I have to tell you that if I was involved with the writing of this manual and even understanding the limits of using footnotes, if I would have pulled so many direct quotes from other sources and placed them in quotations and then found out that the publisher had removed the quotations then I would have taken that to be a "fall on my sword issue" for me. Is that the way it was with you, Con, and the other scholars who were involved with the writing of this manual?

> Again and to sum up, I am looking for an explanation for the reason so many passages from the manual were pulled directly from other sources (as the Price piece demonstrates) but were not set off in quotations in the manual. I mean heck on page 1-4 of the manual the publishers did find it in their means to use quotation marks to quote directly from TE Lawrence; So why not these other passages? (Gian P. Gentile to Nagl 11/2/07 http://smallwarsjournal.com/blog/2007/11/desperate-people-with-limited/)

Gentile's questions are fundamental questions that still demand answers. Nagl chose silence to these direct questions about how and why the passages of others appeared in the *Manual*. Montgomery McFate and others involved in the production of these chapters have joined Nagl in the silence over how this occurred; a silence assisted by a national media uninterested in holding the military accountable.

In one sense, the particular details of how the *Manual* came to reprint the unacknowledged writings of scholars do not matter. If quotation marks and attributions were removed by someone other than the chapter's authors, the end result is the same as if the authors intentionally took this material. The silence on the reproduction of these passages, the lack of any authorial *erratum*, and the failure to add quotation marks even when Chicago Press republished the *Manual* seems to argue against the likelihood of a simple editorial mix-up, but who knows. The ways that the processes producing the *Manual* so easily abused the work of others inform us of larger dynamics in play, when scholars and academic presses lend their reputations, and surrender control, to projects mixing academic with military goals.

Criticizing the *Manual's* rejection of the most basic of scholarly practices is not (as Nagl later tried to argue) holding it to external standards, it is to hold the manual to its own standards (Nagl 2007). Lt. Col Nagl later argued that using the un-attributed passages of others is acceptable when writing military doctrine. But the preface of the University of Chicago Press's edition of the *Manual* clearly says: "This publication contains copyrighted material. Copyrighted material is identified with footnotes. Other sources are identified in the source notes" (US Army & USMC 2007:xlviii). According to doctrine's preface: doctrine *should* have footnotes; and Nagl remains silent on the glaring contradiction.

The instances in which the *Manual* does use quotes and attributions provides one measure of its status as an extrusion of political ideology rather than scholarly labor, as these instances most frequently occur in the context of quoting the apparently sacred words of generals and other military figures—thereby, denoting not only differential levels of respect but different treatment of who may and may not be quoted without attribution.

After my critique was published in *CounterPunch*, the Small War's website posted a document full of citations and quoted passages that purported to be an original draft of one the problematic section of the *Manual's* third chapter (COIN Draft n.d.). Even as a draft this document has a *lot* of problems. While it has an impressive use of footnotes, there remain sentences (often marked with footnotes) that have no quotation marks yet are the words of others. I don't know the provenance of this document, but even if it were the original draft of a chapter that was later altered by unknown citation-and-quote-removing editors, it does not answer basic questions of why McFate, Nagl or others remained silent when the University of Chicago Press republished a work they would have then known to have contained the unacknowledged work of others. If this is what happened, why was no errata forthcoming? The mysterious production of this claimed early draft without any explanation solves nothing, and raises more questions than it answers.

The numerous footnotes in this supposed "draft" document do shed more light on the extent of anthropologists whose work was consulted in the production of this chapter; these anthropologists include: Clifford Geertz, E.E. Evans-Pritchard, Napoleon Chagnon, Raymond Firth, A.R. Radcliffe-Brown, Ralph Linton, Bronislaw Malinowski, and Sherry Ortner. I assume that many of the "draft's" cited non-anthropologist radicals such as C. Wright Mills, Antonio Gramsci or Pierre Bourdieu, would have been disgusted to have his work used for such manipulative needs of military occupation (See Chapter Eleven for a critique of the worthless form of theory this haphazard mixing of social theory produces).

The few published critical examinations of the *Manual* focus on the text's provenience and philosophical roots. In *The Nation,* Tom Hayden links the *Manual* to the philosophical roots of U.S. Indian Wars, reservation policies, and the Vietnam War's Phoenix Program (Hayden 2007). Roberto González observed that the *Manual*

> reads like a manual for indirect colonial rule—though 'empire' and 'imperial' are taboo words, never used in reference to US power. The authors draw historical examples from British, French and Japanese colonial counterinsurgency campaigns in Malaya, Vietnam, Algeria and China. They euphemistically refer to local leaders collaborating with occupying forces as the 'host nation' (rather than indirect rulers) and uniformly describe opponents as 'insurgents'. Yet they never mention *empire*—hardly surprising, since *FM 3-24* is a document written for the US Army and Marine Corps, and from a perspective ensconced within US military culture. Indeed, is it possible to imagine that any US Army field manual would ever use such terms?
>
> Instead, *FM 3-24*'s authors imply that a culturally informed occupation—with native power brokers safely co-opted by coalition forces, community policing duties carried out by a culturally sensitive occupying army, development funds doled out to local women, etc.—will result in a lighter colonial touch, with less 'collateral damage' and a lower price tag (González 2010:83).

That a press as drenched in "reflexive" critiques of colonialism as Chicago would publish such a manual is an ironic testament to just how depoliticized many of postmodernism's salon bound critiques have become; and a *New York Times* op-ed by University of Chicago anthropologist, Richard Shweder, voiced a stance of soft postmodern inaction from which the travesties of Human Terrain could be lightly critiqued while anthropologists are urged not to declare themselves as being "counter-counterinsurgency" (cf., Shweder 2007, Gusterson & Lutz 2007).

THE POLITICS OF REPUBLICATION

The role of University of Chicago Press in bringing the *Manual* to a broader audience is a crucial element of understanding my critique of how the manual was publicly praised, while *fake* scholarship was a critical element of the *Manual*'s domestic propaganda function. That such shoddy scholarship passed so briskly through the press' editorial processes raises questions concerning Chicago's interest in rushing out this *faux* academic work—though some authors writing about the flap following revelations of these problems misunderstood the importance of the University of Chicago Press's role in transforming the *Manual* into a work of domestic propaganda (e.g. Wasinki 2007). Rushing a book through the production process at an academic press in about half a year's time is a blitzkrieg requiring a serious focus of will. There was more than a casual interest in getting this book to market—whether it was simply a shrewd recognition of market forces, or reflected political concerns or commitments. The Press enjoyed robust sales of a hot title (it was one of Amazon's top 100 in September 2007); but it did not adequately consider the damage to the Press' reputation that could follow its association with this deeply tarnished service manual for Empire.

To highlight the *Manual*'s scholarly failures is not to hold it to some over-demanding, external standard of academic integrity. It is important to recognize that claims of academic integrity are the very foundation of the *Manual*'s promotional strategy. Somewhere along the line, Petraeus' doctorate became more important than his general's stars, touted by Petraeus' claque in the media as tokening a shift from Bush's "bring 'em on" cowboy shoot-out to a nuanced thinking-man's war.

In a September 2007 phone call, University of Chicago Press acquisitions editor, John Tryneski, told me the *Manual* went through the standard peer review process, but there are unusual dynamics in reviewing an already published work whose authors are not just unknown (common in the peer review process), but essentially unknowable. Tryneski acknowledged that peer reviewers came from policy and think tank circles. When I asked Tryneski if there had been any internal debate over the decision by the Press to disseminate military doctrine, he said there were some discussions and then, without elaboration, changed the subject, arguing that the Press viewed this publication more along the lines of the republication of a key historic document. This might make sense if this was an historic document, not a component of a campaign being waged against the American people by a Pentagon, surging to convince a skeptical American public that Bush hasn't already lost the war in Iraq.

Chicago's republication of the *Manual* was a transformative event for the document. This transformed the *Manual* from an internal document of military doctrine into a public document designed to convince a weary public that the war of occupation could be won. But the act of republication also forced arguments of academic legitimacy. It is remarkable that the scholars who worked on the *Manual* remained silent about attribution problems when they learned of Chicago's plans to republish the *Manual*. If, as some later claimed, quotation marks and citations had been removed by others after the initial draft was submitted, these authors should have alerted the University of Chicago Press of this. In at least one case, one of the authors of *Manual* chapter three was notified that Chicago would be republishing the manual, but no such warning was forthcoming.

That militaries commandeer food, wealth, and resources to serve the needs of war is a basic rule of warfare—as old as war itself. Thucydides, Herodotus and other ancient historians record standard practices of seizing slaves and food to feed armies on the move; and the history of warfare finds similar confiscations to keep armies on their feet. But the requirements of modern warfare go far beyond the needs of funds and sustenance; military and intelligence agencies also require *knowledge*, and these agencies commandeer ideas for use to their own purposes in ways not intended by their authors.

COMMANDEERING SCHOLARSHIP FOR DIRTY WARS

The requisitioning of anthropological knowledge for military applications has occurred in colonial contexts, world wars and proxy wars. After World War II, Carleton Coon recounted how he produced a 40-page text on Moroccan propaganda for the OSS by taking pages of text straight from his textbook, *Principles of Anthropology*. "[He] padded it with enough technical terms to make it ponderous and mysterious, since [he] had found out in the academic world that people will express much more awe and admiration for something complicated which they do not quite understand than for something simple and clear" (see Price 2008: 251).

The most egregious known instance of the military's recycling of an anthropological text occurred in 1962, when the U.S. Department of Commerce secretly, and without authorization or permission from the author, translated into English from French the anthropologist Georges Condominas' ethnographic account of Montagnard village life in the central highlands of Vietnam, *Nous Avons Mangé la Forêt*. The Green Berets weaponized the document in the field. The military's uses for this ethnographic knowledge were obvious, as assassination campaigns tried to hone their skills and learn to target village leaders. For years, neither publisher nor author knew this work had been stolen, translated, and reprinted for militarized ends. In 1971, Condominas described his anger in learning of this abuse, saying:

> I must admit having been shocked, but not by the disdain for international copyright laws which such an act indicates—on the part of a bureaucracy which is at the origin of these laws, and shows such indignation when others bypass them—or by the lack of courtesy shown the author, because I well know that technocrats have little respect for those who indulge in unprofitable occupations. Not! That which irritated me above all was the translation, very bad by the way, had been distributed to the all too famous 'green berets.' How can one accept, without trembling with rage, that this work, in which I wanted to describe in their human plenitude these men who have so much to teach us about life, should be offered to the technicians of death—of *their* death! I know very well that these mercenaries, these well-oiled machines with human faces, are too proud of their lack of culture to be interested in that of others, especially if it is filled with poetry and without the sense of money or technology. But you will understand my indignation when I tell you that I learned about the 'pirating' [of my book] only a few years after having the proof that Srae, whose marriage I described in *Nous Avons Mangé la Forêt*, had been tortured by a sergeant of the Special Forces in the camp of Phii Ko' (Condominas 1973:4).

Today, anthropologists serving on militarily "embedded" Human Terrain Teams study Iraqis and Afghans with claims that they are teaching troops how to recognize and protect noncombatants. But as Bryan Bender reports in the *Boston Globe*, "one Pentagon official likened [Human Terrain anthropologists] to the Civil Operations and Revolutionary Development Support project during the Vietnam War. That effort helped identify Vietnamese suspected as communists and Viet Cong collaborators; some were later assassinated by the United

States" (Bender 2007). This chilling revelation clarifies the role that Pentagon officials envision for anthropologists in today's counterinsurgency campaigns.

MILITARIZED ANTHROPOLOGY

There is a real demand within the military and intelligence agencies for the type of disarticulated and simplistic view of culture found in the *Manual* not because it is innovative—but because, beyond information on specific manners and customs of lands they are occupying, this simplistic view of culture tells them what they already know. This has long been a problem faced by anthropologists working in such confined military settings. My research examining the frustrations and contributions of World War II era anthropologists identifies a recurrent pattern in which anthropologists with knowledge flowing against the bureaucratic precepts of military and intelligence agencies faced often impossible institutional barriers. They faced the choice of either coalescing with ingrained institutional views and advancing within these bureaucracies, or enduring increasing frustrations and marginalized status. Such wartime frustrations led Alexander Leighton to conclude in despair that "the administrator uses social science the way a drunk uses a lamppost, for support rather than illumination" (see Price 2008:197). In this sense, the *Manual's* selective abuse of anthropology—which ignores anthropological critiques of colonialism, power, militarization, hegemony, warfare, cultural domination and globalization—provides the military with just the sort of support, rather than illumination, that they seek. In large part, what the military wants from anthropology is to offer basic courses in local manners so that they can get on with the job of conquest. The fact that so many military anthropologists appear disengaged from questioning conquest exposes the fundamental problem with military anthropology.

As the occupations of Iraq and Afghanistan present increasing concrete problems for the *Manual's* lofty claims of counterinsurgency, the *Manual's* "authors" and defenders take on an increasingly cult-like devotion to thier guiding text, a devotion that even finds some betraying the lost cause of Iraq in an effort to save the *Manual's* sacred doctrine. In a December 24, 2007 interview, Charlie Rose gently questioned Sarah Sewell about ongoing disasters in Iraq; Sewell quickly disserted the war she had been recruited to rationalize in order to save the *Manual*, insisting: "the surge isn't the field manual; Iraq is not the field manual. And I think many Americans tend to conflate these things at their peril. And I think they risk of throwing out the baby with the bathwater. If and when we look back on Iraq, it will not mean that the manual was wrong, it will mean that Iraq had very different problems, starting with the legitimacy of the invasion to begin with" (Rose 2007). With this twisted logic, the *Counterinsurgency Field Manual's* use as an instrument of domestic propaganda comes full-Orwellian-circle, as the public is asked to forget that just months prior to these revelations of poor scholarly practices in the *Manual*, a barrage of media appearances by Lt. Co. Nagl and others had pitched the *Manual* as the intellectual foundation for victory in Iraq.

But those selling the American public the *Counterinsurgency Field Manual* know full well that counterinsurgencies, just like "insurgencies[,] are not constrained by truth and create propaganda that serves their purposes," (FM 3-24: 5-23) and the *Manual's* tactics are embraced by intellectual counterinsurgents battling the American public's wish to abandon the disastrous occupations of Iraq and Afghanistan.

CHAPTER SEVEN

THE MILITARY LEVERAGING OF CULTURAL KNOWLEDGE: THE 2004 STRYKER REPORT EVALUATING IRAQ FAILURES

We can no longer pretend to be the anthropologist as hero,
as Lévi-Strauss once called the anthropologist embarking on
adventures into the unknown. We are on the other side of the
looking glass, where the dark side of the image we cast is
reflected in the eyes of those who observe us.

—June Nash

In December 2004, Wikileaks released the, "Army Stryker
Brigade Initial Impressions Report on Operations in Mosul, Iraq." This
document was produced by the Center for Army Lessons Learned at
Ft. Leavenworth, and provides an internal view on the Army's late-2004
self-perception of how the occupation was going and outlines perceived
military shortcomings in Mosul (CFALL 2004). Given David Petraeus'
role in the occupation and management of Mosul, some elements of the
document prefigured Petraeus' push for increased reliance on cultural
knowledge for counterinsurgency.

The report's six chapters cover the topics of: Command and Control,
Digital Systems, Non-Lethal Operations, Stryker Vehicle Performance
and Survivability, Intelligence, and Operations. Much of the report eval-
uates how specific hardware was performing in Iraq; other discussions
focus on the lack of theatre specific training, or evaluate the merits of
building new interrogation centers instead of using preexisting structures. While the shortcomings of specific military gear could be dealt
with by replacements, retrofits and redesigns, the cultural shortcomings
of the occupation presented more serious obstacles. The report's residual
image is of a pelagic military only beginning to become aware of the
depths of their own ignorance of the complex environment they are

attempting to occupy and dominate. Even at this early stage the Army had reasons to know it was in over its head.

The report remarks on the military's weak understanding of the culture they were occupying, but it also documents that the military understood how to use members of the media, and it praises the compliance of embedded media for not reporting on the failures of American occupiers. The report recounts that,

> An embedded media representative was staying with elements of the brigade and had been granted access to an event where school supplies were to be handed out to needy students. The unit took the reporter to a school which they had recently built. When they arrived they were surprised to find that no children were present and that an Iraqi family was homesteading in the building. The Iraqi police were unwilling to remove the family and no school supplies to be issued. Fortunately the reporter elected not to cover the event, which could have made us look bad, since we didn't know what was going on with the school after we funded its construction. The reporter understood what had happened and had other good coverage to use [rather] than airing any of this event (CFALL 2004).

The section's "Lessons Learned" summary concludes that "assisting the media in getting the type of coverage they want will ultimately enhance the opportunity for more favorable coverage."

The most anthropologically interesting section of the report is chapter five's Topic M: Cultural Differences' discussion of the management of tactical information. This section's chief observation is that "cultural differences have created a challenging environment for the Stryker brigade." It was this sort of "cultural differences" and "challenging environments" that would later provide the impetus for establishing Human Terrain Teams now deploying anthropologists and other social scientists to assist in the military's occupation of Iraq.

The "Cultural Differences" section discussion states that:

> Real-world experience for intelligence analysts and collectors is irreplaceable. Cultural differences have created a challenging environment for the Stryker brigade. The tribal multi-ethnic and historical alliances and allegiances have made it difficult for HUMINT [Human Intelligence] and SIGINT [Signal Intelligence] collection. Communications channels, linguistic dialects and slang terms and

cultural customs and courtesies make collection even more challenging. These barriers also affect the analysis of intelligence. Use of theater and national level assets has helped the brigade overcome many challenges. Attached and reach-back capabilities aided analysis and collectors overcome a steep learning curve. Many analysts and collectors argue no training could fully prepare an intelligence professional for the challenges. Real-world experience for intelligence analysts and collectors is irreplaceable. Training of this caliber cannot be replicated at national training centers. Hired interpreters have enhanced the capability of intelligence professionals in both collection and analysis. Databases developed in country and via production from theater and national level assts in CONUS [the Continental United States] on topics such as tribes, the spelling of names and regional affiliations were used as resources to assist the brigade with intelligence production.

INSIGHTS/LESSONS LEARNED

* Cultural understanding is an endless endeavor that must overcome leveraging whatever assets are available.
* Cultural training prior to deployment, reach-back capabilities, and a resourceful and knowledgeable use of assets available in country is the key to overcoming challenges (CFALL 2004).

This section observes that the military's occupation was weakened by the sort of lack of cultural knowledge that Gen. Petraeus would later focus upon. It recognizes that the Stryker brigade's cultural ignorance weakened their day-to-day effectiveness and interfered with the collection and interpretation of intelligence. The recommended solution for these shortcomings is increased training with "real-world experience" and the development of "reach-back capabilities aided analysis." This "reach-back" analysis refers to the development of remote high-tech databases located off the battlefield (on a stateside base such as Ft. Leavenworth) that can be consulted and supplemented from the battlefield. This call for a U.S. based cultural database with information on tribes and regional information describes the sort of reach-back databases now being compiled and used by Human Terrain Teams in Iraq.

The "lessons learned" component of this section provides a clear view of the military's expectations of how anthropological or cultural knowledge is to be used to meet military needs. In observing that "cultural understanding is an endless endeavor that must be overcome *leveraging whatever assets are available*," the military's choice of "leveraging," beautifully clarifies how the military conceptualizes anthropologists and others providing occupying troops in Iraq with cultural information: they are seen as priers of knowledge; tools to be used for the extraction and use of knowledge ("assets") in ways that military commanders see fit.

It was concerns over this sort of "leveraging" (the functional use of anthropologists as pry-bars deployed to act upon human and cultural "assets" used by the military) that led the American Anthropological Association's Executive Board to declare its disapproval of the military's Human Terrain Systems as "an unacceptable application of anthropological expertise (AAA 2007)."

Obviously, the limited scope of this 2004 Center for Army Lessons Learned report precluded addressing fundamental issues raised by the Bush administration's reliance on false pretenses to illegally invade Iraq. Such issues are not among those included with the designated "Lessons Learned" because at this level, the army follows rather than sets policy. But the same cannot be said for the free-agent social scientists who are not part of the military and are now working as contractors on Human Terrain Teams "leveraging" culture in service of the military occupation of Iraq. These individuals willfully choose to ignore the ethical alarms being sounded by their peers as they voluntarily surrender their disciplinary skills to better "leverage" cultural "assets" for whatever ends the military dictates.

Given the problems identified in this 2004 report, it makes sense that the army would strive for a more culturally nuanced occupation; after all, it is the nature of occupying armies to seek to subjugate and occupy nations (legally, or illegally) with as little trouble as can be arranged. But anthropology's abetment of this cause slides it askew from any central ethical principles of the field, and it reveals something of the lesser demons of the field's nature. Granted, anthropology's past has plenty of shameful instances of anthropologists applying their skills to leverage occupied peoples in colonial and neocolonial settings, but the common contemporary understanding that such manipulative leverages are part of a *shameful* past does not influence those seeking their fortune outside the ethical standards of their discipline's mainstream.

I like the notion of a "Center for Army Lessons Learned," but the existence of such a center controlled by the army dooms any prospect that the learned lessons might ever be anything beyond minor tactical or technological adjustments. There is no hope of learning more important lessons about not becoming mired in imperial quagmires or unjust wars. I suppose if one were to conjure a Center for Anthropological Lessons Learned, its central findings might include admonitions to not betray or "leverage" the people one studies and lives amongst.

Although those directing the war appear to have discovered ways to use anthropology to more efficiently achieve their goals, they don't care that anthropology becomes what it is used for. But anthropologists need to worry about these uses. As a member of my anthropological moiety, Kurt Vonnegut, once noted, "Shrapnel was invented by an Englishman of the same name. Don't you wish you could have something named after you?" (Vonnegut 2005:88).

CHAPTER EIGHT

RENDERING CULTURAL COMPLEXITIES AS STEREOTYPE: ANTHROPOLOGICAL REFLECTIONS ON THE SPECIAL FORCES ADVISOR GUIDE

> Men are more apt to be mistaken in their generalizations
> than in their particular observations.
> —Niccolo Machiavelli

IN THE YEARS SINCE SEPTEMBER 2001, UNITED STATES MILITARY AND intelligence agencies have acknowledged institutional short comings concerning their knowledge of other cultures. Agencies ranging from the Army to CIA have sought to address these deficiencies with a range of initiatives; initiatives that are doomed to fail because these same agencies are selectively funding programs designed in ways that reinforce rather than expand the institutional views of these agencies.

These new programs will likely expand knowledge for consumption by the military; but the types of knowledge are intentionally limited by these programs' designs so that only certain elements of academic knowledge are sought, while other branches of knowledge are ignored. Anthropology's concerns with ethical principles of voluntary informed consent and taking measures to not harm studied populations, anthropological inquiries into structures of power, or the nature of neo-imperialism are routinely ignored, as if these were epiphenomenal baggage unrelated to the ways, means and meaning of the discipline. It is as if some in the military want to "part-out" the discipline of anthropology. The sort of anthropology these new military linked programs seek to generate are limited, as anthropology's historical examinations of power relations, para-colonialism and imperialism and other critical forms of

139

anthropology are bypassed for elements of anthropology thought to be easily adaptable for military goals.

That individuals embedded in resilient social structures would seek new information, yet resist fundamental structural change is a cultural dynamic familiar to anthropologists. Social structures are resilient formations that can resist change in all sorts of ways and when left to their own devices organizations and other social formations often select narratives that reinforce things they already know. As Marshall Sahlins observed, "you would have to be pretty naive to think anthropologists as individuals could have significant influence in the private counsels of the Department of Defense or State Department, except as their expert advice were in line with existing policies" (MS to DP 10/31/07).

One example of the way these processes work is shown in the writing of U.S. military manuals designed to help individuals and institutions interface with other cultures. Such examples show how these agencies select specific limited views of culture (views that reaffirm rather than challenge) to self-conceptualize these relationships. A leaked *Special Forces Advisor Guide* handbook provides one example of the ways that branches of the U.S. military selectively seek and use specific anthropological theories and data. In 2008 Wikileaks provided me with an embargoed copy of the 2008, *Special Forces Advisor Guide* (TC-31-73), a 130 page manual instructing Special Forces personnel on the doctrinal approach to successful operations in foreign environments (U.S. Army 2008). The *Guide* discusses a wide range of issues ranging from conducting cross-cultural negotiations to counterinsurgency, but the *Guide* primarily instructs Special Forces personnel in how to best approach interactions with their counterparts while working in other cultures as advisors, occupiers, or visitors.

Given the push in the U.S. for more anthropologists to work for military agencies, the *Guide* provides an important opportunity for anthropologists and others to critically consider not only the ends to which this desired anthropology will be put, but also the types of anthropology that the military seeks.

The *Guide's* information is presented to help Special Forces personnel overcome intercultural issues so that they may more easily achieve mission objectives. Most of the Special Forces *Guide* contains the sort of common sense advice often presented to people planning on working in another culture: readers are warned that the whole world isn't just like United States, and if they don't alter their approach to other cultures, they will have problems. The sections of the *Guide* of greatest relevance for anthropologists summarize Special Forces' specific views of culture—views that are long-abandoned anthropological conceptions of culture areas, but which continue to hold clear attractions for Special Forces.

As I read the *Special Forces Advisor Guide* the response it produced was similar to that of reading a contemporary physics text relying on theories of æther to explain radio broadcasts, a chemistry text basing its analysis on the inherent qualities of earth, wind and fire, or a geology manual with a chapter on Adam and Eve. The *Guide* conceptualizes culture as nothing more than a measurable set of values that can be understood, compensated for, and therefore not only navigated but engineered to one's advantage; in the context of the Special Forces interests in these matters, this includes tasks of empire. While the status of culture remains contested in contemporary anthropology (with not only the contested culture concept, but the relative importance of values, beliefs and behaviors under argument), few anthropologists would be comfortable with the culture concept as sought out and embraced by Special Forces. For the military, the truth of the cultural claims made in the *Guide* are much less important than how it allows them to conceptualize culture in cartoonish ways that are already understood and embraced by those using the manual: in this context, the validity and reliability of the *Guide's* concept of culture are much less important than the unified simple culture paradigm that the *Guide* provides.

The Special Forces' view of culture resurrects psychological anthropology's state of the art back in the 1950s and 1960s drawing on bizarre notions of "culture and personality areas" that have not been seriously taught in anthropology classrooms for decades. These antiquated views present broad spectrums of cultural traits using metaphors often linked to simplified analysis of personality. These theories were largely rejected by anthropologists because their simplistic rendering of complex cultural phenomena glossed over vital complexities with simplistic stereo-types. This military predilection for the antique is not accidental: these are exactly the sort of culture notions the military seeks and selects for its own internal cultural reasons. These institutional notions of culture fit the military's desires to interpret and control environments where they operate. These crude culture characterizations likewise fit the military's desire for the categorical access of ethnographic data through uniform cultural databases. We should not expect military manuals to acknowl-edge more contemporary debates concerning the death of the culture concept; they need a living body of knowledge, and they will produce it… even if they must find it back in the 1950s.

The *Advisor Guide* argues: "the more that people understand about other people and places, the more they can enrich their own culture and the less likely they are to blunder into conflict. As the world becomes increasingly more accessible, [Special Operations] are becoming more dependent on the ability of the special advisor to demonstrate an under-standing of the rest of the world" (2-18). The *Guide* reduces this "rest of the world" into seven cultural regions consisting of: "North America and Europe (including Australia and New Zealand), Southwest Asia and North Africa, South and Central America (including Mexico), Sub-Saharan Africa, Pacific Rim (excluding the Americas), Russia and the Independent Republics, Oceania (the Pacific islands)" (2-17).

The 2008 *Guide* draws heavily on anthropologist Florence Kluckhohn's and social psychologist Fred Strodtbeck's Values Orientation Model to present cartoonish representations of regional cultural stereotypes. The Values Orientation Model was developed at Harvard's Laboratory of Social Relations during the 1950s, and it followed the premise that all cultures have "a central core of meaning—basic values," and using a series of standardized questions these core values are measured to understand the root values of a given culture (Kluckhohn & Strodtbeck 1961:2). Kluckhohn and Strodtbeck believed that, "value orientations are complex but definitely patterned (rank-ordered) principles, result-ing from the transactional interplay of three analytically distinguishable elements of the evaluative process-the cognitive, the affective, and the directive elements—which give order and direction to the ever-flowing stream of human acts and thoughts as these relate to the solution of "common human" problems" (Kluckhohn & Strodtbeck 1961:4).

The Values Orientation Model maintains that large cultural regions are dominated by easily characterized culture values that can be charted on a simple scale expressing tendencies related to five cultural elements with three possible responses for each of the five cultural elements. Kluckhohn and Strodtbeck believed that the following five cultural elements could be described with the three descriptors:

1. HUMAN NATURE (evil, mixed, good).
2. RELATIONSHIPS of people to nature (e.g. Subjugation-to-nature, harmony-with-nature, or mastery-over-nature).
3. TEMPORAL FOCUS (past, present, or future orientation).
4. HUMAN ACTIVITIES (being, becoming, doing).
5. SOCIAL RELATIONS between "men" (hierarchical, collateral, individual).

Under this Values Orientation Model's rubrics, a specific culture might have a collective outlook that conceived of human nature as either good, evil, or mixed, and so on. The combination of the three possible descriptors for each of the five cultural elements is supposed to combine to produce concise descriptors of culture groups (Kluckhohn Center 1995).

During the past century there have been numerous efforts by anthropologists to characterize or describe identifiable personality traits of entire cultures. In the early Twentieth Century (1934), Ruth Benedict's book *Patterns of Culture* used narrative descriptions of cultures. She poetically used Nietzsche's description of "Apollonian" and "Dionysian" to illustrate the power of enculturation by describing how individuals raised in Apollonian cultures (e.g. Zuni) grew to have subdued and restrained personality types, while those raised in Dionysian cultures (e.g. Kwakiutl) merged with these cultural values. Benedict believed that "a culture, like an individual, is a more or less consistent pattern of thought and action" (1934:46). During the Second World War and throughout the Cold War, anthropologists conducted national character studies designed to reduce the complexities and rationales of other nations down to overly simplified and often pseudo-psychological pro-files designed to help US forces understand their enemies. During the Second World War, Geoffrey Gorer theorized that Japanese military aggression was reducible to Freudian explanations of childhood toilet training, and during the Cold War Margaret Mead produced a RAND report describing what she believed to be uniform features of the Soviet national character (Price 2008a; Mead 1951).

With time, most anthropologists have come to see that efforts to identify national character, or broad culture and personality types were doomed to fail for several reasons. One significant reason was that when condensing broad cultural variations into simplistic characterizations anthropologists ignored more behaviors and beliefs than were ever explained, similarly, while statistical assessments of normative cultural values or behaviors were identified, there are significant variations among individuals in any society. Whatever "personality" is, it is not static, and just as individuals have broad ranges of responses to situa-tions, so do cultures. It's not even that *something* like identifiable traits for cultures don't exist; but today, anthropologists' debate not only the nature (and existence…) of culture, but there is greater acknowledge-ment of such a diversity of specific cultural traits, today few anthropolo-gists would be comfortable with the sort of vulgar generalizations that are the basis of Kluckhohn's work.

Today, the idea of reducing cultural characteristics to a small number (or even a large number) of identifiable elements that can be measured through simple questionnaires seems absurd to most anthropologists. Because this simplistic model has not aged well, it might be surprising to find it so prominently figuring in the ethos of the *Special Forces Guide*; but this is in fact the sort of mechanistic, interchangeable, conception of culture that we should expect various branches of the military to consume. It fits their dominant institutional cultural world views. The attraction of such "rank-order principles" models to the regimented structure of bureaucratized military culture is palpable, and it is easy to see why such an approach to cultural complexities would be structurally attractive to a culture so imbued with engineering.

When the firm cultural structures of the military want to embrace something as potentially soft as anthropology, it makes sense that it would be drawn to fantasies of hard science. Instead of reducing entire cultures to poetically rendered traits held by figures of classical Greek mythology such as Benedict's Apollonian and Dionysian, the military appears drawn to quantifiable, *scientistic* instruments that collect standardized data in ways to be analyzed and scaled in somewhat statistically sophisticated ways. These trappings of science, with complex graphs, data tables, equations and a multidimensional model give the appearance that values orientation does something more than express stereotypes; when at best all it can actually do is record self-imagined stereotypes of values that may or may not have any meaningful correlation with behaviors, and can shift radically over even short periods of time. To the methodologically unsophisticated, the camouflage of quantifications easily obscures the simplicity of what is being "measured."

The *Guide* downplays the problems of Kluckhohn and Strodtbeck's generalizations with a disclaimer that these summaries: "represent sweeping generalizations about very large regions. They are deliberate simplifications, intended only to capture some of the basic cultural differences and similarities among cultural regions" (2-19). But despite such warnings, an illustration abuts this disclaimer, stating that North Americans, Europeans and Australians all share: a human nature that is "basically good" and "changeable" with a "sense of time" that is "future-oriented" with social relationships that are "strongly individualistic" as if America's commitment to "future-oriented" outlooks could account for its blind commitment to living on credit beyond income production and its "basically good" human nature must account for American practices of rendition and torture. The following page assures readers that Central and South American cultures have human natures that are "unchangeable" and are a "mixture of good and evil" with "authoritarian social relationships." The sub-Saharan African summary declares that this vast and diverse region is governed by "human nature" that has a "mixture of good and evil", with "more evil than good" and a sense of time that is "past-oriented" with "authoritarian" social relations.

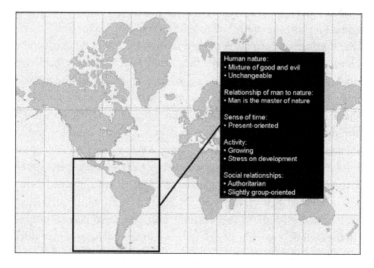

Figure 1, "Culture analysis—South America and Central America (to include Mexico)" *Special Forces Advisor Guide, Figure 2-2* (TC-31-73).

While these summaries are mindless in their over simplicity, it is a mindlessness of a specific sort that confirms simple institutional misunderstandings about culture by reinforcing stereotypes over vast regions of diversity. In this sense, the *Guide* is a relic of the military's institutional-cognitive view of the world that instructs us of the contours of its institutional imagination. The *Guide* codifies and affirms prevailing social facts of the values already institutionally believed to be governing actors around the globe. These stereotypes in the *Guide* are selected not because they educate; but because they tell the military what it already institutionally knows, and it allows it to frame the "others" of the world as imprisoned by the exotic belief systems summarized in the *Guide*.

In the *Guide's* section on negotiations and "relationship building" the essentialized representations of entire regions are used to suggest ways that the stereotypical personality traits dominating each region can be used to maximize the American advantage. For example:

When dealing with persons from Latin America, the Middle East, and the Pacific Rim, American negotiators should plan first to engage in small-talk. Subjects such as politics, race, religion, and gender issues should be avoided. These topics seldom help to build relationships between strangers. Instead, American negotiators should try discussing the foreign country's history, cultural heritage, traditions, beautiful countryside, contribution to the arts, economic successes, and popular sports. Questions about local restaurants are usually safe, neutral topics to begin a conversation. Negotiators must be prepared to discuss typical American traditions, sports, and cultural heritage; however, they must be careful not to go overboard with talk about America. It may come across as pompous and overbearing (4-23).

This is not rocket science and would be useful only to the extent that those reading it were truly culturally insensitive; though I would question the wisdom of recommending that representatives of US armed forces discuss "the foreign country's history" given the likelihood that the US presence in a given nation is part of a long history of foreign occupation or colonial occupation or neocolonial extraction of wealth or subversion of democratic self-rule.

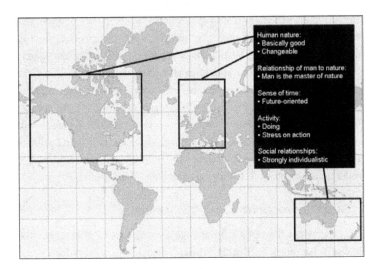

Figure 2. "Culture analysis—North America and Europe (including Australia and New Zealand)" *Special Forces Advisor Guide, Figure 2-1* (TC-31-73).

The *Guide* also informs us about widespread military desires for simplistic culture templates that the military can plug into interchangeable cultural data-sets. This military approach to culture dates back to the Second World War and George P. Murdock and the Institute of Human Relations' compilation of Cross Cultural Survey data for Naval Intelligence and Civil Affairs Handbooks (Price 2008:92-96). Today the military seeks these absurd reductions of culture and personality as part of a template they hope will allow them to quickly shift their theatre of operations effectively with little preparation.

Since the U.S. military is getting neither the levels of cooperation nor the types of "useful" theoretical applications they desire from civilian university anthropologists, the military has increasingly been developing the study of anthropology in its own higher education system. Special Forces are not the only branch of the military interested in pursuing Kluckhohn's values orientation model, Steven F. Burnett wrote a 2006 Naval Postgraduate School doctoral dissertation drawing on Kluckhohn's values orientation model in uncritical ways that would be rare in mainstream university anthropology programs (Burnett 2006). The recent growth of anthropology programs at US Air Force University, the US Naval Academy and other military universities is an effort to develop forms of social science that can produce the sort of knowledge that will better fit the military's cognitive understanding of culture. The contingencies driving the growth of these separate military universities cause their curriculum to list in ways that give the military with the sort of social science that many in mainstream academic settings are unwilling to provide for reasons of disciplinary histories, ethics and politics. These forces help us understand why the military is drawn to the sort of reductionistic approach to culture offered by Kluckhohn.

MILITARY-ANTHROPOLOGY TRAJECTORIES

Critiques of the poor scholarship, low-intellectual content, or the bad anthropology informing military doctrine inevitably lead some to argue that good anthropologists should work for the military to try and improve the military's poor state of anthropological knowledge. I reject these suggestions for political reasons (related to the neocolonial ends to which the U.S.'s military is engaged), and also because my institutional-structural orientation finds the military adopting inadequate culture models of the sort Kluckhohn devised, not because these models do a good job of explaining the world as it is; they are instead selected because they do a good job of explaining the military's institutional view of the world to itself. Arguments that the military's misapplications of anthropology demand better anthropological contributors ignore an increasingly well-documented history of anthropologists' serial-failures to get military bureaucrats to adopt anthropologically informed perspectives that went against the grain of widely held military-cultural views (Gordon 1988; Hickey 2003; Price 2008a).

My reading of the history of anthropological interactions with military organizations from the Second World War to the present finds a consistent structural history of cultural knowledge selection in which the large trends of independent academic research (e.g. at times stressing such crucial things as the importance of colonialism, neocolonialism, dependency and other means through which the core has dominated the periphery) have been categorically ignored for the sort of racially stereotyped just-so stories of the sort that Kluckhohn's Values Orientation Model represents. In this historical context: the Special Force's use of Kluckhohn's simplistic model is exactly the sort of theoretical orientation that we should expect the military to select for its manuals.

Even when the U.S. Department of Defense tries to fund independent academic research through programs like the Minerva Initiative, it inevitably funds ridiculous pseudo-science like psychologist David Matsumoto's almost $2-million Minerva project attempting to identify violent individuals by their face expressions. Anthropologists know that Matsumoto's efforts to study "video and transcripts from figures such as Osama bin Laden, Adolf Hitler, Benito Mussolini, Josef Stalin, Saddam Hussein and Ted Kaczynski, among many others" in a effort to find identifiable faces of evil is a high-priced fools-errand (Bohan 2009). But this is exactly the sort of neo-phrenological "science" that the military is institutionally drawn to seek and fund; despite the groans from critical academics who know that at best such efforts will quietly fail, and at worst, will be weaponized into new ways to harass minority populations. The military appears institutionally bound to reproduce its own blindness and shortcomings even as it flails to reach outside its institutional borders for "new" ideas.

Anthropologists working for military employers have been vocal in demanding the same academic respect as colleagues working for other organizations, but as I attend several academic conferences each year on panels with anthropologists working in these settings I find most of these papers lack the same level of detailed analysis showing the sort of academic rigor, and critique that I expect to find from anthropologists working in civilian university settings. Instead, I hear vague generalities about "minds changed," and "institutional cultures challenged" or the breakthroughs in getting the culture concept to military commanders; but the weak academic notions that appear in the military documents I am reading give serious reasons to question the quality of the social science being proffered to the military; and the structural dynamics governing military institutions appear to be limiting the possibility that anything but the most reductionistic forms of anthropology gets through the military's institutional conceptions of culture.

The *Special Forces Advisor Guide* and the larger trends in the U.S. military's supporting stunted forms of anthropology show us that while the military recognizes its own blindness and shortcomings in anthropological understandings of culture, its own institutional limitations (including deep *a priori* institutional assumptions about supporting neocolonial mission) hinder its ability to incorporate contemporary rigorous anthropological analyses. Instead, it seeks, adopts, and will now no doubt foster the growth of its own sub-parallel military university system designed to provide it with the forms of limited anthropology that mainstream universities are unwilling to offer. What will emerge from this military university system stands to develop in ways distinctly different from civilian universities, and while professors with anthropology degrees will increasingly teach within this system, it remains unclear if the body of knowledge that will emerge from this system will be recognized as anthropology as we understand the discipline today.

Finally, I suppose that my analysis opens me for criticism that my analysis of the rigidity of the military's social structure commits the same variety of totalizing over-simplifications that I accuse the military of undertaking. While I cannot entirely discount this possibility, I find the historical recurrence of these military approaches to foreign cultures, as well as the interdependency between America's military-industrial infrastructure and the military's internal structure and mediating military relationships with foreign cultures offers compelling support for the interpretations I offer here. I will be happy to revise this analysis should the US military begin producing widespread holistic accounts of cultures that are void of simplistic caricatures of cultural stereotypes, and have critical anthropological analysis of hegemonic power relations that include situating the military's roles in the creating the problems facing the cultures under consideration.

PART III COUTERINSURGENCY THEORIES, FANTASIES, AND HARSH REALITIES

CHAPTER NINE

HUMAN TERRAIN DISSENTER: INSIDE HUMAN TERRAIN TEAM TRAINING'S HEART OF DARKNESS

> All social research worthy of the name raises the question of who
> will use the results, and for what purposes. This is an old question
> among physical and biological scientists, and it will not [die] down.
> In the social sciences it carries more explosive implications, as
> when gangsters make use of studies of an American community to
> enrich themselves. This has happened more often that some social
> scientists realize.
>
> —Douglas G. Haring, 1951

I FIRST CAME INTO CONTACT WITH CULTURAL ANTHROPOLOGIST JOHN Allison in 2008 when he invited me to join a session of a global organization of archaeologists presenting innovative papers on themes related to military uses of anthropology and archaeology at the World Archaeology Congress in Dublin. I was unable to participate in the conference, but we corresponded occasionally after that. I had not heard from John in a while, and then in November 2009 I suddenly got an email from him telling me that he was writing me from inside the Human Terrain Systems training program in Leavenworth, Kansas.

My initial inclination was to wonder if this was a gag, or, having written several critiques of the Human Terrain Systems program describing why it is an ethical and practical anthropological disaster, I wondered if someone might be setting me up. While I've had several other Human Terrain social scientists write me with complaints about the program, it didn't seem likely that Human Terrain Systems (HTS) would hire someone with John's politically progressive views; but then again, the program has not been known for its competence in vetting employees. The email address was the same one John had used in the past, and John's story checked out and made sense, so I approached our correspondence along the lines of his initial request to help him organize his focus and to understand critiques of HTS; and as he undertook his HTS training, we corresponded and I passed along articles, and offered friendship and critiques of what he was learning in this training; not that John needed help with this critique, the flaws in the program were obvious to him.

John explained to me that a few weeks earlier he had lost his job working as a Cultural Resource Management archaeologist. He had been terminated for fulfilling his duties as a Program Manager, which led to him being accused of failing to follow the Chain of Command after having consulted with the California State Historic Preservation Officer. Within minutes of posting his resume on a job hunting website, he was contacted by a HTS contractor and recruited to begin training as a HTS social scientist. The contractor indicated John was just what they were looking for because he had conducted anthropological fieldwork in Afghanistan in 1969-70 while working towards a PhD in anthropology. The Human Terrain program recognized him as potentially a very valuable asset to the program. All this for a handsome salary during the pre-deployment training stage at a rate that was twice the salary I earn as a full professor.

Given the public claims that the Human Terrain program is saving lives of Afghan civilians, it made sense that John Allison would consider joining Human Terrain Systems (HTS). HTS proponents claim that it mixes ethnographic fieldwork and troop education in ways that will reduce violent interactions between troops and occupied/enemy populations. But the claims of what Human Terrain Teams (HTT) accomplish are far different from the reality; and anthropologists' ethical commitments to secure voluntary informed consent and to not harm studied populations creates insurmountable ethical problems for anthropologists in the HTS program. A 2009 detailed report written by a commission of the American Anthropological Association (of which I was a contributor) found that HTS was an ethical and practical failure that sloppily mixed education, research and intelligence gathering functions and had such poor safeguards that it inevitably contributes to targeting of populations (AAA 2009). This report concluded that, "when ethnographic investigation is determined by military missions, not subject to external review, where data collection occurs in the context of war, integrated into the goals of counterinsurgency, and in a potentially coercive environment—all characteristic factors of the HTS concept and its application—it can no longer be considered a legitimate professional exercise of anthropology" (AAA 2009:4). Yet, the well orchestrated PR campaigns pitching HTS to the public has made it an inviting program for many.

From the beginning, John was skeptical of the claims offered by the Human Terrain Systems program. While his research in Afghanistan, and Afghan friends who had died in the *Great Game* between the US, Russia and others interested in controlling Afghanistan made the possibility of reducing harm a personal issue; he was skeptical that the military could use anthropological knowledge in ways that would serve the Afghan people. Given the range of claims about the Human Terrain program and conflicting reports that its social scientists did or didn't engage in targeting or collect intelligence, he knew he was in a unique position to observe how the training program approached these issues; and the closed door reports from HTS team members reporting in from "down range" could provide a clear view of these and other issues.

Between mid-October 2009 and February 2010 I heard from John several times each week. Sometimes John wrote me emails requesting links to articles and sources on HTS; things like the American Anthropological Association's 2009 report on HTS, and articles written by Roberto González and other members of the Network of Concerned Anthropologists, other times he wrote with brief reports on the day's activities.

Early on, a lot of my correspondence with John consisted of just sending him journal articles, drafts of papers I was working on or the same news clips that I regularly sent to friends. A few days after his initial email, I sent John a link to a pretty typical, uncritical HTS story that had come out in *World Politics Review,* writing that I thought "it reads like the dozens of propaganda pieces that have come before it. Anything that you can gather on how the forty or fifty of these uncritical hegemonic press reports keep coming off the assembly line might be interesting--it isn't really a mystery how it works, it just might be interesting for you to watch how these reporters are corn-fed the party line from the inside" (DP to JA 11/25/09).

John replied that the function of these ongoing uncritical feature profiles on Human Terrain was clarified for him earlier that day when a retired Colonel had spoken to the group about the status of HTS, explaining that, "the program is still in the status of a Project. Projects are funded from year to year as non-recurring line items. They are trying to get the status of 'Program', which is a recurring budget line item. So, all these articles that are published in the military press and in public media, are attempting to influence both the military budget decision-makers and anyone in the civilian sector who might be able to influence the military decision-makers. That is what it is all about: budget turf wars" (JA to DP 11/25/09). Some of what is told to the media in these PR stories is simply not true. But the impossibility of Human Terrain Teams ever achieving most of the claimed outcomes, such as establishing local rapport and being the patient listening face of a harsh military occupation, so regularly fed to the American public, was made very clear to HTS trainees. In late November John wrote that, "one interesting fact that was revealed today is that *the time that an anthropologist or social scientist has to finish an interview before the probability of a sniper attack becomes drastically high, is about 7 minutes.* How deep an understanding, rapport or trust develops in 7 minutes? It seems that the 'data' sought is very limited to operationally tactically useful stuff. For anything deeper, they 'reach back' to the research centers for work from anthropologists that they will use without permission and without attribution" (JA to DP 11/25/09).

Classical ethnographic research usually takes a year or more of field-work before anthropologists begin figuring how things work; given HTS's difficulty in hiring culturally competent social scientists, seven minutes isn't even enough time for an ethnographer to get properly confused. John's reference to a "reach back" to Human Terrain research centers refers to the program's theoretical practice (theoretical, because the technology doesn't work as designed) of HTT field social scientists linking with US based HTT staff accessing published and unpublished social science data for use by HTT social scientists down range, with or without consulting with and getting permission of the researcher for using their data for this purpose.

Several emails from John detailed how the training used a classroom setting with a pretext of "teaching" and fostering "discussions" as a way to impart heavy-handed distortions about topics ranging from counterinsurgency, history, anthropological research methods and norms of ethical anthropological practice.

Some Human Terrain Team classroom training tried to address questions of ethics. But John wrote me that these classes were "strictly pro forma as, no doubt, required; but not much relevant discussion of the salient moral/ethical questions about what we would be required to do as integral part of a platoon" (JA to DP 1/18/10). But John wrote me that anthropological ethics conflict with HTS mission, and rather than focusing on ethics, the training focused on:

> the pressure to conform to the military mindset by the dominant and majority of the class that is military, either in uniform or in civilian clothes. If you don't join the lockstep notion that a US life is much more valuable than an Afghan life, then you will get marginalized and stigmatized in the class and down-graded during the peer review process. Most civilian 'social scientists' (which include historians, psychologists and industrial psychologists) have merged into that military mindset. The few who have not are being made to feel our separateness. If I was allowed to go downrange, those who would be my Team Leader would relish to opportunity to get rid of me at the first difference of opinion (JA to DP 1/18/10).

John explained that one of the training instructors, a Ph.D. anthropologist who worked mostly with statistical sociological methods as a public relations consultant was teaching the HTS class in "Ethnographic Field Methods"—a class that never touched on the central methods of ethnography—dismissed the ethical complication of HTS ethnography telling the class that, "consent is implied by the continued participation" of the "informant", and also, by those who join in the discussion without an invitation" (JA to DP 1/19/10). Not only is this a predatory standard of consent, but it runs counter to the Nuremberg Code, the Belmont Report, and US federal research consent guidelines.

Human Terrain Systems is desperate to hire anthropologists, but the ethical problems presented for anthropologists working on HTS counterinsurgency operations makes it difficult to keep actual anthropologists in the program. John had important insight into the program's failures to hire anthropologists or social scientists with pertinent cultural or linguistic experiences: "Though they want to have an anthropologist be the HTT Social Scientist, they are happy to get anyone with what could be remotely considered an 'advanced' degree in a social science. So, although we have five anthropologists, we also have several historians, an economist, an industrial psychologist, etc; and only one for the Iraq group and one (me) for the Afghanistan group has any previous experience in the region of their destination" (1/22/09 JA to DP). There are good historical reasons why anthropologists find HTS's practices to run counter to their disciplinary commitments to the people with whom they share their lives when doing fieldwork. Historians and industrial psychologists often approach the people they study, as "objects," or in ways that are more distant, or are fundamentally different than anthropologists.

After reading these observations about the program's difficulties in finding anthropologists, I wrote to John that, "though the HTS dream is to use anthropologists, it will have a next to impossible time hiring any (or at least any decent ones, esp. not ones with actual field research in the areas where HTS will work—today Afghanistan, tomorrow AFRICOM), so they will grab historians, religious studies, political science, accountants etc. to fill the gap, but these people won't come from disciplines that champion ethnographic fieldwork" (DP to JH 11/22/09). John wrote me that HTT personnel are given cursory lectures on research ethics, including information on the basics of the Nuremburg Code and ethical principles by professional organizations such as the American Anthropological Association, but that the specifics of how to negotiate ethical research in armed, occupied settings are not made clear to students. But such discussions are by far overshadowed by the demands of the larger military mission which HTT personnel exist to support. John wrote, "clearly [HTS] does not give its participants [the] luxury [to] consider whether the orders they comply with consider the ethical obligations to those they interview in the presence of their armed Team Leaders; some of whom have a deep dislike for 'the enemy' which includes most Muslims. And this is why they are hiring economists, historians and others as 'social scientists' who, initially, were intended to be cultural anthropologists" (JA to DP 12/1/09).

These issues have such significance to professionally trained anthropologists. The military is increasingly becoming aware that the unethical nature of the everyday procedures makes it difficult for them to hire Ph.D. anthropologists with normative understandings of ethical practices. One choice for the military facing this problem would be to halt a program that necessitates engaging in ethically problematic behaviors; the other choice for the military could be to start training their own "ethnographers" and "anthropologists," with a different standard of ethical behavior. According to John Allison, the military appears interested in the second of these two choices; in early December he wrote me that he concluded, "that the military is beginning to do an end run by producing its own anthropologists/social scientist PhDs at West Point, the Air Force Academy, the Naval Academy and other cooperating institutions; thus marginalizing the criticism" (JA to DP 12/8/09).

This makes a lot of sense. It fits with larger institutional moves in which the military (through programs like the Minerva Program, the Intelligence Community Scholars Program and the Pat Roberts Intelligence Scholars Program) is trying to bend independent scholarship in ways that will get scholars to more directly produce less-independent social science that will tell them what they want to hear or what they already believe.

This military university system can be used to produce social scientists operating with different ethical commitments, where military scholars can be trained to do the military's bidding without raising the sort of fundamental ethical questions that members of the American Anthropological Association (AAA) and other groups have raised. They can develop their own "ethics codes" that can warp ethical commitments in ways that will align with military missions. Allison wrote, "if military academies want to displace the AAA's ability to advise and sanction through resolutions, by providing degrees to career military officers who will not question the chain of command, then they will have their way ... for awhile. When the results of the HTTs in providing 'data' to the brigades are shown not to be what they had been anticipating, the 'HTT Project' will be denied 'Program' status, and the military will again turn to PsyOps, Provincial Reconstruction Teams, and the other standard military options for COIN. In the end, David, it is all really about profit and control" (JA to DP 12/8/09). Huge profits for the military contractors running the program (HTS training is managed by CLI contractors) and control for the army commanders directing HTS activities in the field. Promises of profit and control are the sort of desired outcomes that will keep HTS funded long after internal military evaluations show the program to be an abject failure.

John wrote me that in a class covering Information Operations (InfoOps) they were told that HTTs are used to "measure the change in the population's mental image after a PsyOps propaganda pamphlet drop." John wrote that "part of HTS's job is to devise such measures and make such an evaluation to be presented to the commander as a brief PowerPoint slide presentation" (JA to DP 1/12/10). Such mercenary acts transform anthropological sensitivities into mechanical instruments measuring the efficiency of military occupations.

Throughout our correspondence John's hopes for the program came and went. He began with hopes that HTS could shift the military's focus away from violent "kinetic engagements" towards engaging with the population without force. In early January he wrote me an enthusiastic email after engaging in some training role-playing where he had,

> asked one of the two Arabic-speaking HTT woman who where the interviewer and the interviewee, whether she would feel more safe if she were there with the woman alone, rather than accompanied by armed, uniformed soldiers. Her answer was "yes" (she has done fieldwork in Yemen for couple of years). I went on to make two suggestions that were well-received:
>
> 1. That HTT's job is as much to shift the 'Center of Gravity' (COG, in COIN-speak) of the military, including those military who are participating in HTTs, from the Kinetic to the COIN position. That is, to get them to see the world and their role in it differently. That they need to do that before they can effectively try to shift the COG

of how Afghans perceive them from negative to positive. In other words, their intent toward the Afghan people needs to become positive, not that of forceful occupiers.

2. That this would best be achieved by putting the HTT social scientist as resident with the local people, not embedded in the military and 'inside the wire.'

I was shocked at the response—quite positive, even from hardnosed career soldiers. Subversion, it may be; but for improving things so deeds match words (JA to DP 1/5/10).

I replied to John pointing out that the political issues raised by military-anthropologists embedding with villagers or the political and ethical issues raised by anthropologists becoming agents of occupation and counterinsurgency. I wrote him that this proposal sounded,

like the dream of panoptical control of the enemy: becoming the all seeing eye; surveillance ethnography brought to a new level. The counterinsurgency dream is to understand and control the other by shifting COG from the external shooting and threatening with harm by the military, to other means of cooption and control. The key is that the military still seeks to control local populations, not through hard power, but through soft power. The problem is found in what one means by 'become positive' in your sentence reading 'the intent toward the Afghan people needs to become positive, not that of forceful occupiers.' Notions of what would entail 'positive' would be measured not only by local standards (if this were the case, then 'positive' might include in some instances enabling insurgents to remove foreign occupiers by force) but by US military standards; in other words, if the US presence in Afghanistan, Iraq, (coming soon: Yemen, Nigeria, etc.) has anything to do with issues of empire (it does), then these issues remain elements of what a 'positive' outcome would be.

Moving HTT social scientists into local settings isn't some form of social work; it is a form of social control. The HTT project seeks to blur what COIN is, so that we internalize it as humanitarian assistance and cross-cultural understanding; but counterinsurgency remains counterinsurgency. Soft power in these circumstances remains military power. It leaves less obvious dead bodies in the streets, but it remains a tool of empire (DP to JA 1/6/10).

But even as John was working to keep his hopes for Human Terrain Systems alive, he—who had worked for five years as the Tribal Anthropologist for the Klamath Tribes—was engaging in some serious internal arguments with HTS personnel in which he openly compared the outcomes of HTS enterprises to other disastrous American campaigns. John wrote to HTS training personnel that this, "is not so different from what the European-Americans did to the Native Americans in the USA. Now, several generations later, the stories are passed on and are deep in the collective consciousness of those Indian peoples and colors their way of seeing the European-Americans today, having its effect on how they view 'government programs', attempts to change their view of work, alcohol & drugs, etc" (JA to DP 1/7/10). In January, John wrote that his HTT training group was undertaking intense role playing where Human Terrain social scientists advised commanders about whether or not the US military should undertake an airstrike on a specific northern Afghani village. John said the information used for these decisions, in the classroom and in Afghanistan, was mostly whatever they could muster from Google, but in one role-playing scenario assigned to him: the village under consideration in this instance was one he knew from his dissertation research. John wrote me that one team was asked to advise on a training scenario set in the Waigal Valley of Nuristan; the HTT social scientists assigned this case,

> based all his information on internet resources—as did everyone; and, as would be necessary for the real situation, since the air assault was necessary because the people there were not receptive to our occupation.
>
> Waigal Valley is the next valley east from the Ashkun area, where I did my doctoral research. When he finished, I gave a brief summary of the reality of Nuristan, told them that the suggestion of attacking them because they resisted invasion as they had against Islam, against the British and against the Russians, made me want to cry. I suggested that there has to be another function for the HTTs than simply to loyally and without direct knowledge of the people, subscribe to such an attack. I made it clear that I understood that the Air Assault would have to be followed by air support fire because the Nuristanis WILL RESIST. Afterward some of the career military folks and career CIA folks came over to try to explain the difference between an air assault and an air attack; and I told them that I understood the difference and also knew that the assault would be followed by air support if there was resistance; and that there would be resistance (JA to DP 1/9/10).

Insofar as Human Terrain seeks to connect hearts and minds, it is doomed to fail for all the dynamics played out in the above training scenario: the voice of anthropological knowledge and moderation was plowed under by the dominant military approach. If such failures were the rule in the classroom, there is no chance these views could hold sway in the battlefield.

John and a second anthropologist dissenter regularly raised questions about ethical and political issues related to HTS's mission in class. In the beginning this was welcomed as normal classroom discourse. With time these dissenters became increasingly marginalized within the cohort. Two months into the program John wrote me that the program was,

> getting tighter on those who don't buy into the military's version of what HTT should do. Now, it is becoming highly pressured to begin private lessons with firearms; and the image is that we will actually be soldiers who also do a little intel work as prescribed by the commander. The truth of the situation in the field is not quite that, as told by some who have recently returned, but the various career guys make it out that way: that you have to carry a weapon because you are bumping a soldier from the vehicle going on a mission that is exclusively military, and they are being so kind as to maybe allow you a few minutes to do some interviewing; but you better have a gun so as to be able to fill in for the soldier whose place you took in case of attack. The old Stockholm Syndrome pressures are increasing (JA to DP 1/15/10).

I replied that,

> from the outside, the timing of now introducing firearms lessons seems pretty smart: at this point you have all been indoctrinated with enough stories about what 'really happens down range' that whatever logical resistance to becoming armed members of a counterinsurgency team that would have naturally been vocalized by many in your class will have been pushed below the surface. The notion that you are all 'taking the seat of a soldier' on a mission where you may have to kill those you are trying to defeat with soft power is just another way of establishing how HTS social scientists *are* soldiers. I can only imagine how nasty the subtle and not so subtle group dynamics with all this can get (DP to JA 1/16/10).

During the following weeks, John's descriptions of his training increasingly presented a picture of an inflexible program that turned against, ridiculed, and isolated individuals offering advice aligned with perspectives outside the narrow limits of military doctrine. During the first week of February, John described how the range of acceptable views was rapidly narrowing and adherence to military doctrine became an objective unto itself, writing that the most important of:

> the targeting indoctrination presentation by the contractors, was that we all need to adopt the doctrinal language and viewpoint. Only by doing that can we successfully influence the tactical and strategic decisions of the commander and the planning team. When I tried to point out—again—that by being limited to talking and thinking like one of them the social scientist loses his own perspective and cannot really make the changes in perspective of the military—that is, to move the military's Center of Gravity toward a more human terrain, anthropology-focused viewpoint. Of course, then I had to put up with facing the usual solid wall of musk oxen telling me that I would be excluded from the Team if I tried to approach it with that suggestion (JA to DP 1/6/10).

John's last day of HTS training was the first day of MARDEX, a military role playing exercise designated as "Weston Resolve." For the exercise, the class was presented with a training scenario in which the fictional nation of "Lakeland" was located in an area to the northeast of Kansas City was the focus of operations. John wrote that,

> In the PowerPoint slide presentation laying out the background for the "operations", the Wargame role-playing is represented by staff as merging into the real world drug, crime, and environmental "contention" within the community. The whole mission is represented as bringing a military state control of the local population which has recently elected a local government that is a "permissive" (supportive) environment for US Army activities after the previous local government had withdrawn from the US as a sovereign society. Now the US military is taking over the area to reestablish public security (JA to DP 2/10/10).

The class was then told that the mission they were training to support was one in which the military was establishing order in a setting where environmentalist-separatists had taken over. John explained that in this hypothetical training scenario,

> IATAN, a coal-fired power plant on the Missouri side of the river is one of the main military foci due to "contention within the community" over the environmental pollution it is causing. Sierra Club and other, more radical groups have been active in this area: ELF is one such radical group. Even though there is an elected government and rule of law in Lakeland, there are some 'insurgents' who are opportunistic.' That is why the US Army has moved into this area that has broken away from US control.
>
> Staff Assignments to the several Human Terrain Teams that make up the class of the November Cycle were issued as follows: 1. 'Find out more details on the criminal activity.' 2. Find out the best conduits to pass 'information'(PsyOps and InfoOps) to the local population. 3. HTT is assigned to produce a 'Research Plan' to understand the situation at the IATAN power plant—people's concerns, desires, etc., and identify those who were 'problem-solvers' and those who were 'problem-causers,' and the rest of the population whom would be the target of the information operations to move their Center of Gravity toward that set of viewpoints and values which was the 'desired end-state' of the military's strategy.
>
> As I thought about what was being done in this activity, and the way it adapted COIN strategy for Afghanistan/Iraq to be applied by the US military in situations in the USA where the local population was seen from the military perspective as threatening the established balance of power and influence, and challenging law and order, I began to think back on stories that circulated among the ant-war movement in the 1960s-70s, about concentration camps being developed just for imprisoning such protestors an "problem-causers". And I wondered who would be working on the Human Terrain Teams to enable the US military's actions against unruly segments of their own countrymen; perhaps Afghan and Iraqi anthropologists who had specialized in US ethnography? (JA to DP 2/10/10)

Human Terrain Teams practicing training scenarios set in regions actually within the United States bring the very notion of "human terrain" back home to its domestic counterinsurgent roots. As anthropologist Roberto Gonzalez documents in his book, *American Counterinsurgency: Human Science and the Human Terrain*, the very phrase "human terrain" grew out of domestic counterinsurgency initiatives. Gonzalez describes how in 1968 the US House Un-American Activities Committee released a report entitled "Guerrilla Warfare Advocates in the United States" which warned that the Black Panthers and other militant groups threatened the country's political stability. HUAC warned that "irregular forces... possess the ability to seize and retain the initiative through a superior control of the human terrain" (González 2010:113-114). The clear implication was that the control of civilians in America's cities was vital to winning the counterinsurgency struggle at home.

When John resigned from the program on February 10, 2010, he submitted a summary critique of HTS to those directing the program. John's words convey his hopes and disappointments for the Human Terrain Systems program, and clarify the deep systemic problems with this flawed program. Below is the critique he submitted upon his resignation:

SUMMARY CRITIQUE OF HUMAN TERRAIN SYSTEMS
FROM A TRAINEE'S PERSPECTIVE

John Allison, Cultural Anthropologist. (Resigned from the Human Terrain System Training Program, November 2009 Cycle, effective February 10, 2010)

I volunteered for the HTS program because I had done my doctoral research in the Hindu Kush area of Afghanistan known as Nuristan long before the train of disasters, caused by foreign forces over the past 35 years, ran through this land of diverse peoples, historic sites and monuments, and ecosystems. I had hope that I could help to save the loss of any more innocent Afghan lives. Several of my Afghan friends had died, some having been executed because of their associations with US agents there.

After beginning training in the HTS program, I was shocked when I first mentioned that this was my purpose and one of my classmates expressed contempt for that motive and said that he was only there because he didn't want to see one more US soldier's life lost; didn't want to have to take the US flag to the door of an US mother and tell her that her son was killed. And, when I asked about Afghan mothers whose sons were killed by US errors of judgment causing "collateral damage" in their kinetic warfare, he responded that he didn't '... give a fuck about those people. I would just drive through their village in my Humvee and throw money at those mothers.' This was a Colonel who is a doctoral candidate in a military history program at a military-funded university; a Team Leader. Although this man was more outspoken than most of his military colleagues, my impression now is that he expressed what almost all of them think and feel.

My experience in the program included both instruction in such things as military culture, military language, military decision-making process, Counter-Insurgency doctrine, and many other topics intended to socialize the trainees into the world as seen by the military. During this time, more than once, the majority of the class—who were either current or retired career military or those with former military service who were hoping to convert into an intelligence role such as CIA—would speak about the 'Stockholm Syndrome'. This refers to how the majority in a group can shape the values and perception of the minority. Apparently, in most 'cycles' (six-month long training group schedules up to deployment), the majority of the HTT candidates are such military personnel as were in our November 2009 Cycle, which actually began mid-October. It became clear that the majority saw their job as to expedite the acculturation of the rest of us—those who had the skills and credential that were needed to support the 'soft' warfare image that HTS advertises—an image of winning the hearts and minds of the peoples of Afghanistan and Iraq—to win the anthropologists over to their military culture's world view and values; or to marginalize and force the non-compliant to resign.

In addition there were a couple weeks of 'Introduction to Anthropology' and three weeks of 'Ethnographic Method'. The Introduction to Anthropology was cursory and quick. Some important terms were introduced—e.g. 'emic' and 'etic'—but not taken to enough depth in examples to drive home the deeper implications. Holt, who served on an HTT in Afghanistan and wants to return, is a cultural materialist, and limited his perspective to mostly the etic. He was the dominant voice. He soon transitioned into a scenario in which he assigned the several class teams to provide a 5-slide PowerPoint presentation (with a maximum of 5 bullet 'points' on each slide) to the Commander to advise him on what to do when he has troops on the ground in a village area that he has heard is 'hostile', based on HTT research. Of the seven teams, only one dared to suggest that the commander should wait until the HTT had done further field research before launching the assault. This was clearly the Stockholm effect of the Team Leader and others forming the behavior of the Social Scientist.

There were several weeks of 'Ethnographic Method', in which there was no introduction to real participant-observer methods or anything really related to ethnographic method. Instead, this was a rapid fire, cursory presentation of a myriad of methods used in sociological statistics; but not in enough depth in any one of them to really become functional if the student did not already have a strong background. It was also rooted in computer software that might not be available 'downrange'. It gave colorful, simplistic representation of complex social facts—in US society—that fit well into the PowerPoint presentations of five slides, each with a few bullets or a single, simple graphic.

On the one hand, HTS contractors make a concerted effort to recruit and hire cultural anthropologists because these are the obviously most qualified professionals to participate as social scientists on the HTTs in the theaters in Afghanistan and Iraq, and for the anticipated expansion of COIN to sub-Saharan Africa, Indonesia, Malaysia and other places in the Islamic world. In the November cycle, I was the only social scientist on 5 teams who had previous experience in Afghanistan. Among those teams scheduled for Iraq, there was also only one social scientist who had such experience.

Yet, on the other hand, the prevailing military culture, and the nature of the operations at the Brigade and lower unit levels at which HTT's are assigned, subordinate the judgment of these anthropologists and other 'social scientists' (which include such as historians, psychologists, and economists who have absolutely no training in cross-cultural field research) to the dictates of the Brigade or Battalion command.

The command is dominated by the military (specifically US Army) culture and the related inclination to use the HTT to aid in gathering intelligence useful for supporting kinetic operations; which is strictly forbidden in the surface representation of the HTS. Yet, it is made clear in training that this is the fact of life on the Team. Since the Team Leaders are part of the military culture, the social scientist has no recourse. One presenter from the Reachback Research Center (RRC) estimated that 30% of the HTTs become tools for such intel needs of the Brigade rather than to provide needed information for moving the population's Center of Gravity from favoring the resistance forces' agenda to favoring the occupying 'Coalition' forces and their agenda, as represented in the public representation of HTS.

There is a great distance, an effective separation, between the HTS 'Directorate' and the training staff and the trainees. This was emphasized in my exit interview with my Seminar Leader, ████████. When I told him that I had only one other possibility other than entirely resigning, he told me in so many words, 'forget it'; explaining that there was not a lot of interest at the Directorate level in talking with trainees about such things. ████████ clearly regrets this fact.

This was reinforced in my telephone conversation with my CLI supervisor ████████ when I told her of this conversation with ████████. She reciprocated with a story from a returning social scientist who had served a tour in Afghanistan. He told her that he had many suggestions for improving the program that he hoped to communicate to the HTS Social Science Directorate. However, when he got to his debriefing interview and attempted to relate his thoughts and suggestions to the upper echelons, the interviewer (either Montgomery McFate or Jennifer Clark) simply blew him off and cut him short, not allowing him to really express himself in less than ten minutes allotted to him after a year of service.

You, yourself, Mark, told me that this was consistent with your impressions: there is not a lot of receptiveness to feedback from the rank and file if it runs against the grain of military culture—especially US Army culture, as contrasted with US Navy, Air Force or even US Marine culture, that still is the dominant kinetic perception of the purpose of deployment. Even though Generals McCrystal and Petraeus have made the transition to the "soft" strategy of modern COIN, the predominant US Army mindset is still deeply set into the kinetic approach.

Until the Center of Gravity of the brains of the US military's 'boots on the ground' is moved to understand the value of a cultural anthropologist's in-depth research to really helping the US military and civilian assistance to enable a nation such as Afghanistan to achieve self-determined stability and sovereignty, the money spent on HTS will be greatly a waste of US taxpayer money. This includes the need for the military as well as the US Department of State to understand the reasons behind the ethical concerns of anthropologists regarding this program (JA to DP 2/12/10).

The significance of John Allison's insider account of HTS training is found in the details he provides about the program's inability to address basic ethical or functional issues. John was open to the possibility of reforming a program with so many structural shortcomings, but I remain convinced that the program's flaws are too fundamental for a course correction; the ethical problems alone will make it impossible for the program to recruit competent anthropologists.

The fate of Human Terrain as a program is uncertain, the 2010 Defense Budget withheld funds from the program until it demonstrates measures of its effectiveness and demonstrates it is complying with normal research ethics standards. As a recent House Armed Services Committee investigation gathered reports of serious problems ranging from fundamental incompetence and ineffectiveness to reports of financial waste, the historical trajectory of recurrent military desires to try and solve military problems with promises of culture magic indicates that the abject failures of Human Terrain Systems may matter little in a world where Pentagon desires trump human needs and obvious measurable outcomes.

CHAPTER TEN

GOING NATIVE: HOLLYWOOD'S HUMAN TERRAIN AVATARS

> Anthropology since its inception has contained a dual but contradictory heritage. On the one hand it derives from a humanistic tradition of concern with people. On the other hand, anthropology is a discipline developed alongside and within the growth of the colonial and imperial powers. By what they have studied (and what they have not studied) anthropologists have assisted in, or at least acquiesced to, the goals of imperialist policy.
>
> —Radical Caucus of the American Anthropological Association, 1969

At the end of 2009 James Cameron's 3D cinematic science fiction saga dominated the American box office, and even as tie-in products permeated fast food franchises and toy stores, one could not escape an interesting bit of cultural leakage tying America's own real militarized state to Cameron's virtual world of *Avatar*.

Avatar is set in a world where the needs of corporate military units align against the interests of indigenous blue humanoids long inhabiting a planet with mineral resources desired by the high tech militarized invaders. The exploitation of native peoples to capture valuable resources is a story obviously older than Hollywood, and much older than the discipline of anthropology itself; though the last century and a half has found anthropologists' field research used in recurrent instances to make indigenous populations vulnerable to exploitation in ways reminiscent of *Avatar*.

Avatar draws on classic sci-fi themes in which individuals break through barriers of exoticness, to accept alien others in their own terms as equals, not as species to be conquered and exploited, and to turn against the exploitive mission of their own culture. These sorts of relationships, where invaders learn about those they'd conquer and come to understand them in ways that shake their loyalties permeate fiction, history and anthropology. Films like *Local Hero, Little Big Man, Pocahontas, Dances with Wolves, Dersu Uzala,* or even the musical *The Music Man* use themes where outsider exploitive adventurists trying to abuse local customs are seduced by their contact with these cultures. These are themes of a sort of boomeranging cultural relativism gone wild.

Avatar drew plenty of criticism from some anthropologists for its stereotypical portrayals of ecologically balanced natives unable to organize an effective military resistance without the gallant assistance of a heroic white male outsider. While I wouldn't dismiss these obvious criticisms, I also found the film to be exploring themes of domination and subjugation in ways that resonated with American audiences that are deeply immersed in a culture of militarization and expansion. Fans of *Avatar* were moved by the story's romantic anthropological message favoring the rights of people to not have their culture weaponized against them by would be foreign conquerors, occupiers and betrayers. It is worth noting some of the obvious parallels between these elements in this virtual film world, and those found in our world of real bullets and anthropologists in Iraq and Afghanistan.

Since 2007, the occupying U.S. military in Iraq and Afghanistan have deployed Human Terrain Teams (HTT), complete with HTT "social scientists" using anthropological-ish methods and theories to ease the conquest and occupation of these lands. HTT has no avatared-humans; just supposed "social scientists" who embed with battalions working to reduce friction so that the military can get on with its mission without interference from local populations. For most anthropologists these HTT programs are an outrageous abuse of anthropology, and in November 2009, a lengthy report by a commission of the American Anthropological Association concluded that the Human Terrain program crossed all sorts of ethical, political and methodological lines, finding that, "when ethnographic investigation is determined by military missions, not subject to external review, where data collection occurs in the context of war, integrated into the goals of counterinsurgency, and in a potentially coercive environment—all characteristic factors of the HTT concept and its application—it can no longer be considered a legitimate professional exercise of anthropology" (AAA 2009:4). The

American Anthropological Association's executive board found Human Terrain to be a "mistaken form of anthropology" (AAA 2009 Executive Board on receipt of CEAUSSIC HTS Report). But even with these harsh findings, the Obama administration's call for increased counterinsurgency will increase demands for such non-anthropological uses of ethnography for pacification.

There are other anthropological connections to *Avatar*. James Cameron used University of Southern California anthropologist, Nancy Lutkehaus, as a consultant on the film. In December 2009 I wrote Lutkehaus to see if her role in consulting for Cameron had included adding information on how anthropologists have historically, or presently, aided the suppression of native uprisings; but Lutkehaus wrote me that her consultation had nothing to do with these plot elements, her expertise drew upon her fieldwork in Papua New Guinea to consult with choreographer, Lula Washington, who designed scenes depicting a coming-of-age-ritual in the film (NL2DP 12/14/09).

Among the more interesting parallels between *Avatar* and Human Terrain Systems is the way that the video logs that the avatar-ethnographers were required to record were quietly sifted-through by military strategists interested in finding vulnerability to exploit among the local populous. A December 2009 story in *Time* magazine quoted Human Terrain Team social scientist in training Ben Wintersteen admitting that in battlefield situations "there's definitely an intense pressure on the brigade staff to encourage anthropologists to give up the subject.... There's no way to know when people are violating ethical guidelines in the field;" and the AAA's report found that "Reports from HTTs are circulated to all elements of the military, including intelligence assets, both in the field and stateside" (Shay 2009:1; AAA 2009:34). Like their HTT counterparts, the avatar teams openly talked about trying to win the "hearts, mind, and trust" of the local population (a population that the military derisively called "blue monkeys") that the military was simply interested in moving or killing. And most significantly, the members of the *Avatar* unit had a naive understanding of the role they could conceivably play in directing the sort of military action that would inevitably occur. Sigourney Weaver's character, the chain-smoking, tough talking

Avatar Terrain Team chief social scientist, Grace Augustine, displayed the same sort of unrealistic understanding of what would be done with her research that appears in the seemingly endless Human Terrain friendly features appearing in newspapers and magazines.

Past wars found anthropologists working much more successfully as insurgents, rather than counterinsurgents: in World War II it was Edmund Leach leading an armed insurgent gang in Burma, Charlton Coon training terrorists in North Africa, Tom Harrisson arming native insurgents in Sarawak (Price 2008:55–59). These episodes found anthropologists aligned with the (momentary) interests of the people they studied (but also aligned with the interests of their own nation states), not subjugating them in occupation and suppressing their efforts for liberation as misshapen forms of ethnography like Human Terrain.

Anthropologically informed counterinsurgency efforts like the Human Terrain program are fundamentally flawed for several reasons. One measure of the extent that these programs come to understand and empathize with the culture and motivations of the people they study might be the occurrence of militarized ethnographers "going native" in ways parallel to the plot of *Avatar*. If Human Terrain Teams employed anthropologists who came to live with and freely interact with and empathize with occupied populations, I suppose you would eventually find some rogue anthropologists standing up to their masters in the field. But so far mostly what we find with the Human Terrain "social scientists" is a revolving cadre of well paid misfits with marginal training in the social sciences who either do not understand or reject normative anthropological notions of research ethics, who rotate out and come home with misgivings about the program and what they accomplished.

On the big screen the transformation of fictional counterinsurgent avatar-anthropologists into insurgents siding with the blue skinned Na'vi endears the avatars to the audience, yet off the screen in our world, this same audience is regularly bombarded by media campaigns designed to endear HTT social scientists embedded with the military to an audience of the American people. The engineered inversions of audience sympathies for anthropologists resisting a military invasion in fiction, and pro-military-anthropologists in nonfiction is easily accomplished because the fictional world of a distant future is not pollinated with the forces of nationalism and jingoistic patriotism that permeate our world; a world where anything aligned with militarism is championed over the understanding of others.

CHAPTER ELEVEN

PROBLEMS WITH COUNTERINSURGENT ANTHROPOLOGICAL THEORY: OR, BY THE TIME A MILITARY RELIES ON COUNTERINSURGENCY FOR FOREIGN VICTORIES IT HAS ALREADY LOST

> The secret of being a top-notch con man is being able to know what the mark wants, and how to make him think he's getting it.
>
> —Ken Kesey, *One Flew Over the Cuckoo's Nest*

CULTURALLY INFORMED COUNTERINSURGENCY CATEGORICALLY PRESents three types of problems for anthropology, these categories are: ethical, political, and theoretical. The ethical problems concern voluntary informed consent, transparency, manipulation of studied populations, and the likelihood of harm befalling those researched; while the political problems most obviously concern using anthropology to support neo-colonial projects of conquest, occupation and domination.

The ethical and political problems associated with using anthropology for counterinsurgency operations are significant enough to prevent most anthropologists from applying their disciplinary knowledge to support American counterinsurgency efforts. Most anthropologists are justifiably concerned enough by the prospect that counterinsurgency operations violate basic anthropological ethics standards; but these reactions can change quickly, especially as military operations give way to counterinsurgency operations (such as building hospitals, schools, micro loan programs, etc.) that can easily be confused with humanitarian aid operations. Likewise, many anthropologists have strong political objections to supporting the military occupations of foreign nations.

Thinking beyond the vital political and ethical questions raised by using anthropological methods and theories for counterinsurgency, I want to consider how militarized counterinsurgency operations are imagined to work within the universe of anthropological theory. While no single strain of anthropological theory provides a basis for today's counterinsurgency theory, the contradictory range of latent and manifest assumptions and claims about how culture works informs us not only of the poor intellectual base underlying these efforts, but of the apparent impossibility of counterinsurgency programs ever working in the ways they are being sold to the military. I want to consider very basic questions of how counterinsurgency in foreign cultures is supposed to actually work given the claims of the statements made in the *Counterinsurgency Field Manual* and a broad range of anthropological theoretical understandings of culture.

In this chapter I use two different means to identify the epistemology expressed in US counterinsurgency theory: the first method examines a draft document that makes unusually manifest links to anthropology's theoretical literature; the second method examines the latent assumptions and principles expressed in the writings and statements of American counterinsurgency doctrine.

How to Make Occupations and Influence People

It is clear that some simple forms of counterinsurgency are not only possible, but are common military practice. These forms are exemplified by the minor ways in which occupying military forces succeed in reducing conflict by adapting their policies to create less friction by such practices as acknowledging local cultural practices/beliefs, or delivering government services and enforcing laws (and there are other more economically coercive means through the sort of USAID-type development schemes that I have discussed elsewhere (Price 2010)). The importance of recognizing local culture has long been taught to troops by military Cultural Affairs Officers, and generally is part of training for local theatres. These forms of counterinsurgency can be just thought of as "simple counterinsurgency".

I do not find the claims for "simple counterinsurgency" to be controversial, but I reject the more remarkable claims made by Counterinsurgency's anthropology aggressive public salesmen and women. The most visible of these public salespeople are militarized social scientists like Montgomery McFate and David Kilcullen, who are thrust forth in the media making extraordinary claims that counterinsurgency (COIN) can be used to accomplish military victory in Afghanistan. McFate, Killcullen and others on this American "COIN Team" are trying to sell the military on the possibility that regionally-competent cultural specialists can coordinate forms of cultural engineering designed to exploit local cultural features not just to reduce conflict, but to *defeat* insurgents.

The COIN Team's theory asserts that cultural manipulation is something that cleaver people can undertake through a certain level of attentive understanding of the beliefs and practices of the culture one wants to control. They claim that well informed, culture savvy operators can *play* culture—pulling the cultural strings in a given cultural setting to move and drive the culture in ways advantageous to Occupiers. But these claims are at odds with most past and present anthropological notions of culture. I don't expect the military to have the social science expertise to question the social theory behind the COIN Team's extraordinary claims, but anthropologists, sociologists and other social scientists do—and social scientists need to publicly demand answers.

Method One: Manifest Expressions in the COIN Manual

A brief examination of some of the *manifest,* explicit theories found in the *Field Manual* demonstrates a damagingly inconsistent mixture of social theories being paraded about to justify counterinsurgency tactics. After I published a November 2007 *CounterPunch* article documenting the extent of the sourcing problems in the *Counterinsurgency Field Manual*, some unidentified person provided the *Small Wars* website with a document reporting to be the first draft of sections of the COIN manual from which many of the problematic sections appeared (see: COIN Draft n.d.). This document answers none of my indentified concerns, but it likely is, as claimed, an original draft of theoretical sections of what would become the final manual (complete with extensive citations and quotes), and as such it provides an invaluable glimpse at the raw theory informing those cooking-up anthropologized counterinsurgency theory (COIN Draft n.d.).

In just a few pages, this draft manuscript cites and quotes from such diverse sources as: Evans-Pritchard's 1940 definition of "social structure" from *The Nuer* (COIN Draft n.d.:1, n3), Gramschi's 1930s *Prison Notebooks* on dominant hegemonic culture (COIN Draft n.d.:1, n2), Raymond Firth's 1955 "Principles of Social Organization" (COIN Draft n.d.:1, n4), A.R. Radcliffe-Brown's 1952 vision of social structure (COIN Draft n.d.:1, n5), Ralph Linton's 1940 conception of social organization (COIN Draft n.d.:2, n8 & 9), Anthony Giddens on ethnicity, ca. 1993 (COIN Draft n.d.:2, n18), Malinowski on social institutions, 1945 (COIN Draft n.d.:3, n23), Geertz on cultural interpretations, 1973, (COIN Draft n.d.:5, n26), Chagnon on cross-cousin marriage (COIN Draft n.d.:6, n29), Paul Ricoeur on cultural narratives, 1991 (COIN Draft n.d.:7, n41), Victor Turner, 1968, on rituals and symbols (COIN Draft n.d.:7,n44-47), Pierre Bourdieu on social capital (COIN Draft n.d.:9, n48), and Max Weber on traditional power and authority (COIN Draft n.d.:10, n51).

The resulting mishmash of inconsistent social theory conjured by this swampwater version of culture supporting the *Counterinsurgency Field Manual* is instructive. The clumsy surgical joining of such divergent works creates something misshapenly Frankenstinean. The *Field Manual's* quick conjoinings produce unlikely grafts where we find: Evans-Pritchard's segmentary view of social structure stressing idioms of alliances combined with Gramsci's hegemonic cultures and sub-societies struggling for contested meanings (meanings that COIN operators dream they can manipulate like puppet strings). Firth and Radcliffe-Brown's attention to the structural articulations of these groups reveals limits to the ways that meanings and behaviors can be negotiated. Linton's notion of "status" alerts COIN operators to specific roles that can be manipulated to COIN's advantage, just as Gidden's distinctions between ethnic groups can be played against one another. Ricoeur's attention to subtleties of cultural narrative combines with Turner's grasp of rituals and symbols promising an ability to read and hijack local meanings for counterinsurgent ends. Bourdieu's cultural, social and economic capital combine with Weber's understanding of Traditional Authority to reveal hidden power alliances that can be manipulated. This contradictory conjoining of seriously divergent theories betrays not only an amateurish and uncritical approach to social theory, but it betrays a sloppy effort to sell the military claims of cultural manipulation that would not survive ten minutes of scrutiny in an undergraduate anthropological theory seminar.

While the COIN Team glossed over the profound epistemological differences inherent in these cannibalized theoreticians work, it behooves anyone interested in thinking through just how these vague counterinsurgency plans are supposed to work to stop and consider, before awakening with a quagmire hangover, just how incompatible the different elements of this hastily concocted cocktail is. Obviously, the military doesn't get why it is problematic to indiscriminately mix Evans-Pritchard, Gramsci, Riceur, Bourieu, Geertz, Radcliffe-Brown and the rest of these folks together. Given the historical problems between two the most theoretically similar from this mix (e.g., the hyphenates: Radcliffe-Brown & Evans-Pritchard), it is an inconsistent, incoherent, theory that mixes say, Clifford Geertz and Napoleon Chagnon together as if they were theoretical kindred brethren whose world views were separated only by differences in vocabulary.

To understand the ends to which the *Manual* imagines applying this amalgamation of culture theory, consider this brief passage that appears in a *Manual* section following this sampling of theory. The Manual observes that, "tribal and religious forms of organization rely heavily on traditional authority. Traditional authority figures often wield enough power, especially in rural areas, to single-handedly drive an insurgency. Understanding the types of authority at work in the formal and informal political system…will help counterinsurgency forces identify the agents of influence who can help or hinder the completion of objectives"(COIN

Manual 3-64). Through such logic Max Weber's distinctions of authority types can be used to select tactics and targets. The logic of counterinsurgency is that those who "hinder" occupations are eliminated, while those who "help" are supported. And in theatres of operation dominated by over 14,000 drones, anthropologists are increasingly needed at ground level to sort the "hinderers" from the "helpers" and to divine the landscape of culture and symbols that the drones cannot decipher.

There are other forms of intellectual bankruptcy underlying the theoretical (dis)orientation of the COIN Manual: the mental world of "culture" is disarticulated from the physical world so that culture does not include learned behaviors; while anthropologists have argued for decades over definitions of culture (and sometimes over the existence of it), choosing a definition of culture that excludes behaviors creates more problems for counterinsurgency theory. But without differentiating between ideas and practices, there is little hope of accounting for the physical-behavioral and ideational components of occupation, subjugation and resistance.

Despite fundamental claims to the contrary, counterinsurgency theory confuses the controlling of bodies with the capturing of spirits—believing that cultural nuance will get the occupied to render unto Caesar not just that which is Caesar's, but *loyalties*. The COIN Team disarticulates culture into non-constituent pieces (as imagined variables) in simplistic ways that misses that anthropology's holistic understanding that culture necessarily exists in time and place within a physical world: and that time, place, and the physical world are themselves elements of culture in ways that are not easily played by would-be culture-engineers.

As the graveside Engels reminds us, Marx cut through that hitherto concealing "overgrowth of ideology" and observed "that mankind must first of all eat, drink, have shelter and clothing, before it can pursue politics;" in the context of occupation, I would add that these physical conditions have as much to do with the conditions in which one wages Counterinsurgency as does knowledge of cross-cousin marriage practices. An environment marked by the slaughtered remains of dead bodies, broken buildings, sewer systems, roads and power grids (and twelve years of sanctions) is not easily shrouded by the sort of growths of ideology that the COIN Team promises to cultivate as part of its central plan. The *Manual* admits that in order for counterinsurgency to succeed, an open acknowledgement of, and corrective action towards fundamental problems must occur (3-24: I-14), but the *Manual* does not say what is to be done if the fundamental causes to be addressed are neo-colonialism, the installation of illegitimate governments, and illegal invasions. Counterinsurgency cannot talk its way out of this dilemma—but if you can believe the *Counterinsurgency Field Manual*, that's the plan.

The *Manual* hides behind the elusive mumbo-jumbo of anthropology's theoretical Tachyon Particles, but the stark physical conditions of occupation weakens the possibility that culturally appropriate propaganda messages, or targeting key individuals can defeat an insurgency.

Method Two: Latent Expressions in the COIN Manual

Let me switch my analysis from manifest themes to consider some of the latent themes in this work: while the new *Counterinsurgency Field Manual*, and the published writings of anthropologically informed counterinsurgency advocates like McFate and Kilcullen show a fond reliance on mechanistic forms of structural-functional anthropology used by anthropologists linked to British colonialism, the *Manual* expresses no single manifest or latent paradigm of how culture works. If one reads the *Manual* it is impossible to divine a consistent model of culture, much less of how one "controls" culture. The latent culture paradigm of the *Counterinsurgency Field Manual* finds inconsistently jumbled culture theories of a sort that play well with the non-social scientists consuming this work in the Pentagon, but appear sophomoric to anthropologists familiar with the lineages of this work.

In the *Manual*, "culture" is neither strictly an atavistic force of symbols or meanings beyond the awareness and control of individuals; nor is it the outcome of an infrastructural base, hidden structural forces, or political economy. Instead: the *Manual's* latent notion of culture is that it is whatever it is needed to be. While it is clear that the culture of occupied peoples is something that soldiers ignore at their peril, in the "zen like" world of the *Manual*, the culture of occupied peoples is conceived as simultaneously being an independent and dependent variable—though most often represented as an independent variable that can be understood by savvy occupiers intent on engineering the occupied's culture.

The *Counterinsurgency Field Manual's* conception of culture views it as an isolatable variable in a larger human and environmental equation. Culture is presented as a variable that is to be understood and manipulated:

> 1-124: "Successful conduct of COIN operations depends on thoroughly understanding the society and culture within which they are being conducted. Soldiers and Marines must understand the following about the population in the [Area of Operations]:
> · Organization of key groups in the society.
> · Relationships and tensions among groups.
> · Ideologies and narratives that resonate with groups
> · Values of groups (including tribes), interests, and motivations.
> · Means by which groups (including tribes) communicate.
> · The society's leadership system." (FM-3-24: 1-124)

These six elements are thus seen as independent variables to be added to the military's master domination equation. Most of these six elements are structural or ideational cultural elements. The *Manual* also identifies "six sociocultural factors" to be analyzed in counterinsurgency operations, these are: Society, Social structure, Culture, Language, Power and Authority, & Interests (FM-3-24: 3-19). The *Manual* instructs that "once the social structure has been thoroughly mapped out, staffs should identify and analyze the culture of a society as a whole and of each major group within the society" (3-36). This absurdly glib statement is akin to having a NASA technical manual that instructs: "add wings to space shuttle, glue on ceramic tiles; reenter earths atmosphere at correct angle". The *Manual* brushes aside the difficulties of conceptualizing social structure; instead, just one quick "yadda-yadda-yadda" and presto: the "staffs" have mastered these vital independent variables for manipulation. Anthropologists can devote years to studying and then struggling to represent the social structure of a single village, yet our counterinsurgency theorists cavalierly rush past the complexities of such small scale undertakings and pretend that such operations can meaningfully and quickly occur on a societal level. That no one within the military challenges this as nonsense reveals the low level of critical analysis and skepticism within these military circles as those hawking outlandish claims of cultural engineering are heralded as making revolutionary contributions.

The *Manual's* focus on Max Weber's writings on modern legal-rational authority reveals the COIN Team's awareness of the central problems of legitimacy (3-63); but the Manual does not examine how historically difficult it is for external occupiers to acquire the forms of legitimacy that Weber recognized. It is the centrality of legitimacy that makes domestic counterinsurgencies operations (like the FBI's COINTELPRO campaigns against the Black Panthers, American Indian Movement, socialists, communists, anarchists etc.—in these campaigns the FBI already had legitimacy with the bulk of the domestic population) so much more successful than the foreign-occupier scenarios of the *Manual.* The *Manual* argues that "Political power is the central issue in insurgencies and counterinsurgencies; each side aims to get the people to accept its governance or authority as legitimate." But anthropologists know the difficulties for outsiders to achieve legitimacy, and the *Manual* has no magic answers to this problem. As William Polk bluntly concluded in his book *Violent Politics*' review of two centuries of insurgencies: "*the single absolutely necessary ingredient in counterinsurgency is extremely unlikely ever to be available to foreigners*"—*that ingredient being: legitimacy* (Polk 2007:209-210). The Manual's focus on the writings of Antonio Gramsci betray the authors' worried interest in how occupying forces can learn to hijack hegemonic narratives to aid in full spectrum domination.

Three macro latent themes emerge in the *Counterinsurgency Field Manual.* The first is that, the military specific definitions of "culture" view's culture exclusively as structural and meaning based systems of knowledge (ignoring material and behavioral components). Second, culture has identifiable structural components that not only determine the nature of social life, but these can be identified, and controlled to one's advantage. Third, crudely mechanical views of culture are presented in ways consistent with structural-functionalist anthropology's historic links to colonial management. One implication of these three themes is that culture, or elements of specific cultures are seen as consisting of interchangeable data-units that can be managed in databases—a point linking counterinsurgency theory with Human Terrain's plans for handheld field access to HRAF databases for interchangeable theatres of operation.

It is worth briefly mentioning some of what is *not* represented in the *Counterinsurgency Field Manual's* latent culture theory: most prominent is the absence of any systemic discussion of how difficult it is to bring about engineered culture change, there is no mention of applied anthropologists failures to get people to do simple things (like recycling, losing weight, reducing behaviors associated with the spread of HIV, etc.) basic things that are arguably in their own self-interest. The *Manual* does not address the fact that no amount of cultural shinola can hid from occupied people the brutal facts of their situation—yet this is just what Complex Counterinsurgency seeks to do. The COIN Team thinks they can leverage social structure and hegemonic narratives so that the occupied will internalize their own captivity as "freedom".

Sock Puppets Dreaming of Being John Malkovich

The COIN Team's representations of anthropology to their Pentagon customers remind me of Borat's representations of Kazakhstan. Both accentuate and exploit preexisting stereotypes held by their target audiences. Borat's shtick depends on extant notions of Steppe peasants who might really bring live chickens in their suitcases onto a New York Subway; the COIN Team's shtick depends upon notions of near-magical anthropological levels of knowledge of the mysteries of culture and local customs. Borat's joke is on the unsuspecting Americans who think they are interacting with a confused but kindly foreigner; the COIN Team's joke is on Pentagon-customers who think they're buying the real magic beans of culture. But anthropologists know better. Even when anthropologists can agree that culture itself actually exists, anthropologists know that culture doesn't work that way: it doesn't matter where you side between Culture or Practical Reason: culture can't be hacked in the simple ways the military is being told it can (cf. Sahlins 1978, Harris 1979).

I suppose this leaves anthropology in the same position as the actual nation of Kazakhstan—and while the Kazakh Embassy's public miss-reactions to Sasha Baron Cohen's satire have easily been funnier than Borat himself (with the Embassy taking out full-page ads in the *Washington Post* and *New York Times* basically explaining that Kazakh cars have engines and are not pulled by yoked men), but anthropology's response to McFate and Kilcullen's claims for anthropology has appeared to many in the public as similarly odd—with some voices condemning the politics or ethics of the project, others supporting it, but few outright rejecting the theoretical possibility that this project being hawked to the military could ever work as advertised.

In an essay on "The Martialization of South African Anthropology" Robert J. Gordon documents how South African ethnographers once contributed anthropological knowledge to the South African Defense Force's (SADF) brutal control of South Africa's indigenous populations. While the lower ranks within the SADF were skeptical of the value of this ethnographic information, many SADF officers came to fetishize this knowledge, and with time SADF anthropologists became highly cherished experts. Some of these successful SADF ethnographers plagiarized the ethnographic writings of other scholars; others legitimated common folk knowledge about tribal populations (Gordon 1988:448). Gordon establishes that much of the "ethnographic" knowledge was little more than racist stereotypes repackaged with endorsements of anthropological legitimacy in ways that left SADF ethnographers reinforcing what SADF officers already believed. Gordon insightfully observed how the elevation of South African ethnographers as possessing unique, invaluable cultural knowledge for use in counterinsurgency operations "bolsters the status of the ethnologist as a ritual 'expert' since other White personnel have little chance of challenging his or her magical knowledge" (Gordon 1988:446). The hokum of claims of special "magical" knowledge of the inner workings of culture thematically connects this past South African reliance on anthropological knowledge with the current COIN Team, as both present unexamined claims about special cultural knowledge that are uncritically embraced by military personnel desperately seeking answers but who are unequipped to evaluate the veracity of remarkable claims.

The *Counterinsurgency Field Manual*'s approach to anthropological theory was not selected because it "works" or is intellectually cohesive: it was selected because it offers an engineering friendly false promise of "managing" the complexities of culture as if increased sensitivities, greater knowledge, panoptical legibility could be used in a linear fashion to engineer domination. It fits the military's structural view of the world. It is the false promise of "culture" as a controllable, linear product that drives the COIN Team's particular construction of "culture." Within the military, the COIN Team is not alone in this folly: this is reminiscent of the absurd forms of analysis discussed in Chapter Eight's analysis of the *Special Forces Advisor Guide* where military clients are drawn to simplistic, dated anthropological notions of culture and personality theories which produce essentialized reductions of entire continents as having a limited set of uniform cultural traits—a feat that finds the military embracing a form of anthropology that quantitatively tells it the world is a lot like it already understood it to be.

I'm not surprised, but remain outraged that the social scientists advising the military have been allowed to push counterinsurgency within military circles while avoiding explaining to anthropologist colleagues how counterinsurgency is even supposed to theoretically work—and without having to face up to the paucity of successful historical examples of armed foreign counterinsurgency campaigns. McFate and Kilcullen do not answer the critiques of academics; they know that the military is not concerned with the noises coming from the academy because they have cultural engineers telling them what they want to hear. The COIN Team downplays the failures of counterinsurgency's history in a hyped cloak of "theory," but upon closer inspection this cloak appears to be not much more than tattered scraps selectively sewn together providing little cover.

One thing this cloak is hiding is the likelihood that once a nation finds itself relying on counterinsurgency for military success in a foreign setting it has already lost. I am not arguing that insurgencies are always successful, I am instead following military strategist and historian, Edward Luttwak's observation that: "insurgents do not always win, actually they usually lose. But their defeats can rarely be attributed to counterinsurgency" (Luttwak 2007:34). Even Kilcullen admits that counterinsurgency victories have been rare in the last half century; he just has the hubris to think that he has built a better mousetrap, a claim thwarting millennium of historical, structural, and material trends. The insurmountable problem that the COIN Team faces is that expressed by a senior French commander who told journalist Eric Walberg that: "We do not believe in counterinsurgency" because "if you find yourself needing to use counterinsurgency, it means the entire population has become the subject of your war, and you either will have to stay there forever or you have lost" (Walberg 2008). Hiding behind a mess of unarticulated bits of anthropological and sociological theories doesn't change this situation. It is a problem of history, cultural contingencies and limits of possible forms of cultural engineering. The jumbled amalgamations of anthropological theory that the COIN Team is hiding behind shows how weak are the theoretical foundation underlying the empty promises that Kilkullen and McFate are making for their Emperor's-New-Clothes-counterinsurgency-ensemble. The inconsistencies and internal structural failures of their own articulated theory betray the improbability that the product they're selling could ever work as advertised.

CHAPTER TWELVE

WORKING FOR ROBOTS: HUMAN TERRAIN, ANTHROPOLOGISTS AND THE WAR IN AFGHANISTAN

War in the age of intelligent machines depends primarily on machines, rather than human beings, for the production, analysis and distribution of death. Decentralization of command and control schemes, the development of 'smart' weapons, video combat simulation, and other technological manifestations increasingly remove human beings from the lethality of war.

—Montgomery Carlough [McFate], 1994

AS ANTHROPOLOGIST MONTGOMERY MCFATE BECAME THE PUBLIC spokesperson for Human Terrain Systems, she increasingly pulled back from public discussions of the workings and implications of Human Terrain. But in her early writings on British counterinsurgency operations against the IRA, we find a model of how she (and, it appears, her military sponsors) view anthropology as a tool for military conquest.

While working on her doctorate in anthropology at Yale in the early 1990s, Montgomery McFate undertook fieldwork and library research focusing on the resistance of the Provisional Irish Republican Army and British military counterinsurgency campaigns in Northern Ireland. She was not yet married to stability operations specialist and retired army officer, Sean McFate, and her dissertation appears under her maiden name, Montgomery Carlough. She focused on the 1969-1982 period, and British army changes away from strictly tactical military responses to more culturally calibrated counterinsurgency campaigns during those years. McFate's research was supported by a mix of fellowships including the National Science Foundation, Mellon, and several Yale-based fellowships directed toward international security issues.

McFate explained that her dissertation examined "how cultural narratives, handed down from generation to generation, contributed to war," and "how people justify violence" (Kamps 2008:310). This resume might lead one to assume her research was balanced between the positions of the Irish insurgents and British counterinsurgents. Such an impression would be false. Her dissertation reads as a guide for militaries wanting to stop indigenous insurgent movements.

McFate's doctoral dissertation (written under her maiden name, Montgomery Carlough) was an exercise in sympathetically understanding the internal meaning of the Irish resistance. This was not a cultural study designed to give voice to the concerns of an oppressed people so that others might come to see their internal narrative as valid; it was designed to make those she studied vulnerable to co-optation and defeat (Carlough 1994).

For her dissertation fieldwork, McFate made multiple trips to Ireland and met with members of the occupying British military and of the Provisional IRA, but when she wrote her dissertation, she made a conscious decision not only not to identify whom she had spoken with, but also not to directly quote from these interactions (Carlough 1994:iii). In her dissertation, McFate claimed that her decision to not quote from these fieldwork experiences was done for disciplinary ethical reasons.

McFate's proclaimed concern in 1994 over the ethical protection of research participants is admirable, and stands in stark contrast to Human Terrain's later disregard of such ethical protections. It remains unknown what happened to her notes and other records from interviews with IRA members, but given McFate's later work in environments requiring security clearances, such past contacts and records would have raised many questions when she applied for her security clearance. It would be standard operating procedure during a security clearance background investigation to ask about the identity of her 1990s contacts with the Provisional IRA and other groups, as it would be normal to ask such a clearance applicant for field notes and other such material.

McFate's early counterinsurgency years provide a significantly less guarded glimpse at her (then) understanding of the promise of anthropology's role in counterinsurgency. This younger, less prudent McFate avoided soft language: she now calls her "mercenaries" of yesteryear "independent military subcontractors" (Carlough 1994:iv). While she now avoids linking militarized anthropology with killing, in her dissertation days she more openly asked if "one could conclude that ethnocentrism—bad anthropology—interferes with the conduct of war. But does good anthropology contribute to better killing?" (Carlough 1994:13-14). Though an affirmative answer to this rhetorical question is implied, McFate left this question unanswered. McFate today categorically rejects claims that Human Terrain Teams are involved in using anthropology for what she referred to in 1994 as "better killing." But one of McFate's own Human Terrain social scientists told the press that she was comfortable with HTS data being used by the military when "looking for bad guys to kill" (Landers 2009).

McFate's dissertation identified two counterinsurgency elements requiring anthropological skills. The first involved psychological warfare operations, where cultural readings could be used for defining perceptions of one's enemy because "creating a mask for the enemy to wear is essential for psychological warfare" (Carlough 1994:86). The second argued that "knowledge of the enemy leads to a refinement in knowledge of how best to kill the enemy" (Carlough 1994:110).

The desire to understand and re-humanize an enemy and the rationalizations of the enemy's motivations is at the heart of counterinsurgency operations, and McFate argued these goals hold vital roles for anthropology: "the fundamental contradiction between 'knowing' your enemy in order to develop effective strategy, and de-humanizing him in order to kill efficiently is a theme to which we will return. Suffice to say, that the dogs of war do have a pedigree, which is often 'anthropological' and that counterinsurgency strategy depends not just on practical experience on the battlefield, but on historically derived analogical models of prior conflict. Paraphrasing Lévi-Strauss, enemies are not only good to kill, enemies are good to think" (Carlough 1994:114). Here McFate expressed a desire for PSYOP anthropologists to use anthropological conceptions of cultural relativism to understand how enemies view the world and to use this information to better understand how one's own actions or use of symbols will be interpreted by enemies. McFate insists on ethnographies of enemies in order to out-think them, because "understanding the possible intentions of the enemy entails being able to think like the enemy; in other words, successful pre-emptive counter moves depend on simulating the strategy of the opponents" (Carlough 1994).

McFate wanted military forces to understand how their actions have undesired consequences that they cannot understand unless they learn to see things from within the enemy's mindset. This approach is often spun by McFate and her supporters as being a desire to use anthropology so that less violence will be used by U.S. forces. But McFate and HTS supporters desire minimal force because they believe it leads to a more efficient occupation, cooption and conquest of enemies, not because they object to occupation, cooption and conquest. This presents serious political problems for most anthropologists, and given anthropology's often odious past role as a handmaiden to colonialism, these issues easily move from the realm of individual politics to disciplinary politics, and properly raise the attentions of disciplinary professional associations.

DRONES AND HUMAN INTELLIGENCE

Today, reliance on military robotics and drones in Iraq and Afghanistan progresses at a startling rate. In the span of the past eight years, the robotic presence in these theaters has increased from a state when there were no military robotic units to today's total of over 12,000 robotic devices in use, with over 5,000 flying drones in use. Unmanned aerial vehicles (UAV) like the *Predator*, with a flight range of over 2,000 miles, an ability to remain airborne at high elevations for over 24 hours at a time, advanced optical surveillance capabilities with the remote pilots linked by satellite half the world away, can track and kill humans on the ground. Other earthbound robots like the *PackBot* and *Talon* detonate landmines or roadside bombs, while some like Special Weapons Observation Reconnaissance Detection System have options of being armed with M-16s and other weapons (Singer 2009).

The impact of this tactical shift has radically changed the U.S. military's ability to track and control occupied and enemy populations. As P.W. Singer shows in *Wired For War: The Robotics Revolution and Conflict in the 21st Century*, battlefields and occupations are being revolutionized in ways that are quickly progressing beyond strategists' ability to understand how these increases in remote tracking, controlling and killing are impacting the cultures they are physically dominating. Unsurprisingly, increases in robotic-panoptical monitoring and control have negative consequences for American interests, as mechanical manipulation reveals deep divisions between the worlds of machines and humans (Singer 2009). To her credit, a decade and a half ago, McFate understood how such dynamics would play out, though her "practical" solution to such dilemmas is mired in irresolvable political and ethical problems for the anthropologists that would become the sensors for the machines dominating these battlefields.

Early-McFate's most insightful statements concerning military needs for anthropological knowledge focus on high-tech warfare's inability to decipher or address the human reactions and problems created by warfare. McFate understood that, "global positioning systems and cruise missiles won't pay for your ammunition in Kurdistan. Low-intensity conflict requires human generated intelligence, local knowledge, and mission-oriented tactics. Atavistic modes of intelligence collection—espionage, infiltration—take precedence over more sophisticated techniques in these conditions. Thus, an interesting inversion occurs: as the technological sophistication of the enemy declines, reliance on intelligence derived from human sources (HUMINT) increases" (Carlough 1994:216).

McFate was correct. While battlefields become increasingly dominated by high-tech gadgetry and panoptical drones, iris-scanners and computer tracking software, something like the currently attempted Human Terrain Teams will be needed to gather human knowledge on the ground. McFate's early writings clarify why those designing counterinsurgency campaigns crave anthropological knowledge—and given the economic collapse's impact on the anthropological job market, I would not preclude the likelihood of some measure of success, especially as these calls for anthropological assistance are increasingly framed in under false flags of "humanitarian assistance" or as reducing lethal engagements.

Obama's illegal drone war in Pakistan raises the scorn of American counterinsurgency masterminds like David Kilcullen and Andrew McDonald Exum who publicly criticize the Bush and Obama administrations' use of remote robotic killing from above as effective (in terms of killing desired "targets") but counterproductive. In the pages of the *New York Times* they asked readers to, "imagine, for example, that burglars move into a neighborhood. If the police were to start blowing up people's houses from the air, would this convince homeowners to rise up against the burglars? Wouldn't it be more likely to turn the whole population against the police? And if their neighbors wanted to turn the burglars in, how would they do that, exactly? Yet this is the same basic logic underlying the drone war" (Kilcullen and Exum 2009). Kilcullen and Exum do not object to the hunting and killing of enemies. They object to the robotic limitations of killing from above divorced to sensitivities to the human meanings on the ground.

These war machines need human input. The machines need not so much anthropologists' eyes and ears (they see and hear better than we ever will), but they need our *spirits*—our ability to symbolically and humanly process the human environments these machines dominate. The war-machines are technically efficient but humanly stupid. They can track and control the movement of human bodies, but they cannot understand the webs of cultural meanings of those they physically dominate. They cannot sense their own effectiveness on the lives they control: this is one of the reasons why something like human terrain teams are needed to function as nerves, feeling and reporting the cultural-emotional responses of occupied peoples so that the machines of war can more exactly manipulate and dominate them. It is useful to metaphorically consider themes of *The Matrix* when considering the ways that humans (anthropologists) are needed to be the interface with and serve the machines of high tech-warfare.

Nabokov riddles his novel *Lolita* with references to a form of destiny referred to as "McFate," which are cruel turns of apparent coincidence that set characters upon paths linking their destinies with larger themes. In Nabokov's world, the "synchronizing phantom" of McFate arranges what might have been chance events into patterns revealing if not providence, then at least a recurrence of trajectories (Nabokov 1959:103). In only a partial Nabokovian sense, anthropology's McFate merges old anthropological and military themes together in ways revealing new uses for anthropology that the core of the discipline will be increasingly unable to control regardless of how offensive these uses are to core anthropological values.

It's not that anthropology and warfare haven't merged before; they have fatefully merged in all sorts of ways that have been historically documented. One stark difference is that today's counterinsurgent abuses of anthropological knowledge occur after the discipline of anthropology has clearly identified such activities as betraying basic ethical standards for protecting the interests and well-being of studied populations. Anthropologists' professional activities in the Second World War occurred without the existence of professional ethical codes of conduct, and it was a direct result of anthropological misconduct during the Vietnam War that the American Anthropological Association developed its first formalized Code of Ethics in 1971. It insisted that anthropologists' primary loyalties be to those studied and that research not lead to events harming research participants. There was to be no secret research. There were mandates for voluntary informed consent. That HTS throws up weak sophistic arguments claiming that their involvement in warfare reduces harm changes nothing.

The notion of using anthropologists and other social scientists to gather information, probe and soothe the feelings of those living in these environments, increasingly monitored and controlled by machines, strikes me as an anthropological abomination. Given what we know anthropologically about the complexities of *how* culture works, it also seems doomed to failure.

Simple notions of mechanical, disarticulated representations of culture can be found in the Army's new *Counterinsurgency Field Manual*, in which particular forms of anthropological theory were selected not because they "work" or are intellectually cohesive but because they offer the promise of "managing" the complexities of culture, as if increased sensitivities, greater knowledge, panoptical legibility could be used in a linear fashion to engineer domination. Such notions of culture fit the military's structural view of the world. It is the false promise of "culture" as a controllable, linear equation that drives the COIN Team's particular construction of "culture."

What McFate's writings and those of fellow-counterinsurgency supporters do not address is just how difficult it is for anthropologists, or anyone else, to successfully pull off the sort of massive cultural engineering project, needed for a counterinsurgency-based victory in Afghanistan. Those advocating anthropologically informed counterinsurgency are remarkably silent concerning just how difficult it is to bring about engineered culture change.

Beyond Human Terrain Systems, the Pentagon and the State Department can come up with other counterinsurgent uses for anthropologists, many of which will not alarm anthropologists in the ways that HTS, with its armed presence, does. But given the manipulative forms of cultural engineering goals behind these projects, many of the same ethical and political issues are raised by anthropologists' participation in this work. Anthropologists and others being recruited to try and enact these counterinsurgency dreams risk confusing a supportive role in the wake of military decimation with engaging in humanitarian work. Reliance on "soft power" for the building hospitals, schools, supplying microloans and other agents of apparent gentle persuasions will help bring many liberals into the counterinsurgency fold, but it doesn't resolve the problems of the larger project, even if the machines seeking our help are armed not with bombs and bullets but with the dolling out of needed loans, food, water, health and infrastructure (see Price 2010).

REFERENCES CITED

Ackerman, Spencer. 2010. "Hundreds in Army Social Science Unqualified, Former Boss Says." *Danger Room* 12/21/10. http://www.wired.com/dangerroom/2010/12/human-terrain-unqualified/

Agee, Philip. 1976 *Inside the Company: CIA Diary*. New York: Bantam.

AAA. 2007. "American Anthropological Association Executive Board Statement on the Human Terrain System Project." October 31, 2007.

AAA. 2009. Authors: Robert Albro (chair), James Peacock, Carolyn Fluehr-Lobban, Kerry Fosher, Laura McNamara, George Marcus, Laurie Rush, Jean Jackson, David Price, Monica Schoch-Spana and Setha Low] "AAA Commission on the Engagement of Anthropology with the US Security and Intelligence Communities (CEAUSSIC). Final Report on The Army's Human Terrain System Proof of Concept Program." Submitted to the American Anthropological Association Executive Board, October 2009.

Asad, Talal, ed. 1973. *Anthropology and the Colonial Encounter*. New York: Humanities Press.

Bateman, Robert. 2007. "How to Make War: Unusual U.S. Military Field Manual Had an Unusual Provenance" *Chicago Tribune* 9/8/07. P. 3.

Bender, Bryan. 2007. "Efforts to Aid US Roil Anthropology." *Boston Globe* 10/8/07.

Beyerstein, Lindsay. 2007. "Anthropologists on the Front Lines." *In These Times* 11/30/07.

Bohan, Suzanne. 2009. "Research Wins Grant to Study How Violence Can Be Seen in Expressions." *Oakland Tribune* 2/22/09

Brown, Kenneth. 2001. "A Few Reflections on the 'Tribe' and 'State' in Twentieth-Century Morocco." In F. Abdul-Jabar & H. Dawod, eds., *Tribes and Power*. Pp 205-214. Saqi Books.

Burleigh, Nina. 2007. "McFate's Mission." *MORE*, Sept. 2007, 122-128.

Burnett, Steven F. 2006 "Modeling Macro-Cognitive Influence on Information Sharing Between Members of a Joint Team." Naval Postgraduate School, Monterey, California. Doctoral Thesis.

Cardinalli, AnnaMaria.2009. "Pashtun Sexuality." Human Terrain Team (HTT) AF-6 Research Update and Findings, no. (2009): 18.

Carlough, Montgomery Cybele. 1994. "Pax Britannica: British Counterinsurgency in Northern Ireland, 1969-1982." Doctoral dissertation, Yale University.

Chomsky, Noam. 1991. *Deterring Democracy*. New Yok: Hill & Wang.

Church Committee. 1976 see: Final Report of the Select Committee to Study Governmental Operations with Respect to Intelligence Activities (Church Report), Senate Report, 94 Cong. 2 SESS., no. 94-755. Washington, DC: Government Printing Office.

CFALL (Center for Army Lessons Learned). 2004. "Initial Impressions Report: Operations in Mosul, Iraq." Stryker Brigade Combat Team 1, 3rd Brigade, 2nd Infantry. December 21, 2004.

Condominas, Georges. 1977. *We Have Eaten the Forest*. Farrar, Straus & Giroux, Inc.

Condominas, George, 1973, "AAA Distinguished Lecture 1972: Ethics and Comfort: An Ethnographer's View of His Profession," *AAA Annual Report 1972*, pp. 1-17.

COIN Draft. n.d. "Claimed COIN Manual Draft Section." http://smallwarsjournal.com/documents/coin-draft-excerpt.pdf

Connable, Ben. 2009. "All Our Eggs in a Broken Basket: How the Human Terrain System is Undermining Sustainable Military Cultural Competence." *Military Review* March-April 2009:57-64.

Coon, Carleton 1980. *A North Africa Story: The Anthropologist as OSS Agent, 1941-1943*. Ipswich, MA: Gambit.

Democracy Now. 2007. "Anthropologists Up in Arms Over Pentagon's 'Human Terrain System.'" *Democracy Now* 12/13/07.

Eickelman, Dale F. 1986. "Anthropology and International Relations." in *Anthropology and Public Policy, A Dialogue.*, Walter Goldschmidt ed., 34-44. Washington, D.C.: AAA Special Publication, No. 21.

Encyclopedia Britannica. 1974. "Race." 1974, vol. 15.)

Ephron, Dan. 2006. "The Book on Iraq: The Pentagon Issues a Guidebook on Fighting a Counterinsurgency." *Newsweek* 12/15/06.

Ephron, Dan and Silvia Spring. 2008. "A gun in one hand, a pen in the other." *Newsweek*, 4/12/08.

Eveland, Wilbur. 1980. *Ropes of Sand*. New York: Norton.

Featherstone, Steve. 2008. "Human Quicksand for the U.S. Army, A Crash Course in Cultural Studies." *Harper's Magazine*, September, 2008, p 60-68.

Fluehr-Lobban, Carolyn (ed.). 2002 *Ethics and the Profession of Anthropology*. Second edition. Walnut Creek, CA: AltaMira Press.

Field, Kelly. 2005. "Small College Wins No-Bid Contract From Homeland Security Department, Prompting Cries of Favoritism." *Chronicle of Higher Education* 3/18/05.

Finney, Nathan (Captain). 2008a. *Human Terrain Team Handbook*. (Sept. 2008) Ft. Leavenworth, Kansas.

Finney, Nathan K. 2008b. "The Military and Anthropology." *Newsletter of the Society for Applied Anthropology* 19(1):7-8., Feb. 2008.

Frank, Adam. 2001. "Letter: Coming of Age in the NSA?" *The Nation*." Feb. 12, 2001. P2 & 23.

Gates, Robert M. 2008. "Address Delivered, Association of American Universities." Washington, D.C., 4/14/08.

Gezari, Vanessa M. 2009. "Rough Terrain". *Washington Post*, Sunday Magazine, 830/09.

Giroux, Henry. 2007. *The University in Chains: Confronting the Military-Industrial Academic Complex*. Boulder, CO: Paradigm.

Gates, Robert M. 2008. "Speech Delivered to the Association of American Universities." (Washington, D.C.)." *Monday, April 14, 2008*. http://www.defense.gov/speeches/speech.aspx?speechid=1228 .

Glenn, David. 2005a "Cloak and Classroom" *Chronicle of Higher Education* April 25, 2005.

Glenn, David. 2005b Cloak and Classroom: Colloquy Live. Chronicle of Higher Education Wednesday, March 23, 2005.

Gentile Gian. 2007. Comments posted at *Small Wars Journal* blog, October, 27, 2007.

Giddens, Anthony. 2006. *Sociology*. London: Polity Press.

González, Roberto & David Price. 2007. "When Anthropologists Become Counterinsurgents." *CounterPunch 9/28/07.*

González, Roberto J. 2007 "Towards Mercenary Anthropology?" *Anthropology Today 23(3):14-19)*

González, Roberto J. 2009. *American Counterinsurgency: Human Science and the Human Terrain*. Chicago: Prickly Paradigm Press.

González, Roberto. 2010 *Militarizing Culture*. Walnut Creek: Left Coast Press.

Gordon, Robert J. 1988. "'Ethnological Knowledge is of Vital Importance': The Martialization of South African Anthropology." *Dialectical Anthropology* 12:443-448.

Gusterson, Hugh. 2008. "The U.S. Military's Question to Weaponize Culture." *Bulletin of Atomic Scientists* 6/20/08.

Gusterson, Hugh & Catherine Lutz. 2007. "An Open Letter to Richard Shweder."

Harris, Marvin. 1979. *Cultural Materialism*. New York: Random House.

Hayden, Tom. 2007. "The New Counterinsurgency" *The Nation* 9/6/07.

Hickey, Gerald. 2003. *Window on a War: An Anthropologist in the Vietnam Conflict.* Texas Tech University Press.

Higman, Howard. 1998. *Higman, A Collection.* Lafayette, CA: Thomas Berryhill Press.

Jamail, Dahr. 2010. "When Scholars Join the Slaughter" *Truthout* 12/26/10.

Kamps, Louisa. 2008. Army Brat: How did the child of peace-loving Bay Area parents become the new superstar of national security circles? *Elle*, April, 309-311, 360-362.

Kansas University Radio. 2003. "Felix Moos sound bites." Kansas University Radio Archive. 9/10/03.

Kaplan, Fred. 2007. "Challenging the Generals" *New York Times Magazine.* 8/26/07.

Kerley, David 2006. "How to Beat Insurgents: Military Updates Playbook." ABC News. 12/15/06.

Kilcullen, David & Andrew McDonald Exum. 2009. "Death from Above, Outrage Down Below" *New York Times* 4/16/09.

Kilcullen, David 2009. *The Accidental Guerrilla: Fighting Small Wars in the Midst of a Big One.* New York: Oxford University Press.

Kinzie, Susan & Stan Horwitz. 2005. "Colleges' Hottest New Major: Terror." *Washington Post* 4/30/05 A01.

Kluckhohn Center. 1995. *User's Manual for the Value Orientation Method.* Kluckhohn Center for the Study of Values, Bellingham, WA.

Kluckhohn, F. R., & F. L. Strodtbeck. 1961. *Variations in Value Orientations.* Evanston, IL: Row, Peterson.

Kurtz, Stanley. 2005. "Who Will Defend the Defenders? The Academy Takes Aim at the Pat Roberts Intelligence Scholars Program." *National Review* March 31, 2005.

Landers, Jim. 2009. "Anthropologist from Plano Maps Afghanistan's Human Terrain for Army" *Dallas Morning News* 4/8/09.

Lazarsfeld, Paul & Wagner Thielens, Jr. 1958 *The Academic Mind: Social Scientists in a Time of Crisis.* New York: Free Press.

Low, Setha to J. Nussel 5/28/08, http://www.aaanet.org/issues/policy-advocacy/upload/Minerva-Letter.pdf

Luttwak, Edward. 2007. "Dead End: Counterinsurgency Warfare as Military Malpractice." *Harper's* Feb. 2007: 33-42.

Lutz, Catherine 2008. "The Perils of Pentagon Funding for Anthropology and the Other Social Sciences." SSRC papers on the Minerva Controversy. Nov. 8, 2008. http://essays.ssrc.org/minerva/

McCuin, Tom. 2007. "Army Response to Counterpunch." *Small Wars Journal* Nov. 1, 2007.

McFate, Montgomery. 2005. "Anthropology and Counterinsurgency: The Strange Story of Their Curious Relationship." *Military Review* March-April 2005:24-38.

Marks, John. 1979. *The Search for the "Manchurian Candidate."* New York: Times Books.

Marlowe, Ann. 2007. "Anthropology Goes to War: There Are Some Things the Army Needs in Afghanistan, But More Academics Are Not at the Top of the List." *The Weekly Standard*, 13 (11), Nov. 26.

Mead, Margaret. 1932. *The Changing Culture of an Indian Tribe*. New York: Columbia University Press.

Mead, Margaret, et al. 1949. "Report of the Committee on Ethics." *Human Organization* Spring:20-21.

Mead, Margaret. 1951 *Soviet Attitudes Toward Authority*. New York: RAND/McGraw-Hill.

Mills, Ami Chen. 1991. *CIA Off Campus*. Cambridge, MA: South End Press.

Mitchell, Richard G., Jr. 1993. *Secrecy and Fieldwork*. Qualitative Research Methods, Volume 29. Newbury Park: Sage.

Moos, Felix. 1995. "Anthropological Ethics and the Military." *Anthropology Newsletter* Dec. 1995, p 34.

Moses, Lester. 1984. *The Indian Man: A Biography of James Mooney*. Urbana: University of Illinois Press.

Nabokov, V. 1959. *Lolita*.

Nader, Laura. 1997. "The Phantom Factor: Impact of the Cold War on Anthropology." In *The Cold War and the University*. pp. 107-146. New York: New Press.

Nagl, John. 2007. "'Desperate People with Limited Skills:' Writing and Employing the Army/Marine Corps Counterinsurgency Field Manual." *Small Wars Journal* Nov. 1, 2007.

Nature. 2008a. "A Social Contract: Efforts to Inform US Military Policy with Insights from the Social Sciences Could be a Win-Win Approach." (Editorial) *Nature* 454, 138 (10 July 2008).

Nature. 2008b. "Failure in the Field: The US Military's Human-Terrain Programme Needs to be Brought to a Swift Close." (Editorial) *Nature* 456, 676 (11 December 2008).

NCA (Network of Concerned Anthropologists). 2009. *The Counter-Counterinsurgency Manual*. Chicago: Prickly Paradigm Press.

Newsweek. 2010. "Louisiana Suspect's Academic Program was Designed to Attract and recruit Potential Female Spies. 1/28/10. http://www.newsweek.com/blogs/declassified/2010/01/28/louisiana-suspect-s-academic-program-was-designed-to-attract-and-recruit-potential-female-spies.html

NPR (National Public Radio). 2002. "Anthropology and Warfare." Morning Edition 8/14/02

NPR. 2007. "Army Unveils Counter-Insurgency Manual." Day to Day 12/15/2006.

Newman, David. 2006. *Sociology*. 6th ed. Newbury Park, CA: Pine Forge Press.

Packer, George. 2006. Knowing the Enemy: Can Social Scientists Redefine the "War on Terror?" *The New Yorker* 12/18/06.

Packer, George. 2008. "Kilcullen on Afghanistan: 'It's Still Winnable, But Only Just.'" *The New Yorker*, November 14, 2009.

Patai, Raphael. 1973. *The Arab Mind*. Hatherleigh Press.

Polk, William. 2007. *Violent Politics*. New York: Harper Collins.

Plog, Fred and Daniel Bates. 1988. *Cultural Anthropology*. Random House. 2nd ed.

Preston, Douglas. 1995. "The Mystery of Sandia Cave." *The New Yorker* June 12, 1995, pp 66-83.

Price, David H. 2000. "Anthropologists as Spies" *The Nation* 271(16):24-27.

2001. "Letters, 'Price Replies.'" *The Nation* Feb. 12, 2001. Pp23.

2003. "Cloak and Trowel: Should Archaeologists Double as Spies?" *Archaeology* Sept. 2003:30-35.

2004. *Threatening Anthropology: The FBI's Surveillance and Repression of Activist Anthropologists*. Durham: Duke University Press.

2007. "Buying a Piece of Anthropology" Parts One and Two *Anthropology Today* 23(3):8-13 & 23(5):17-22.

2008. *Anthropological Intelligence: the Deployment and Neglect of American Anthropology in the Second World War*. Durham: Duke University Press

2010. "Soft Power, Hard Power and the Anthropological 'Leveraging' of Cultural 'Assets.'" In John Kelly, et al eds., *Anthropology and Global Counterinsurgency* Chicago: University of Chicago Press.

Priest, Dana & William Arkin. 2010. "National Security Inc." *Washington Post* (special investigation series) A1. 7/20/10.

Ransom, David. 1975. "Ford Country." In *The Trojan Horse*. S. Weissman et al. eds, pp 93-116, San Francisco: Ramparts.

Rehm, Daine. 2007. "Anthropologists and War" *The Diane Rehm Show* 10/10/07.

Ridgeway, James, Daniel Schulman & David Corn. 2008. "There's Something About Mary: Unmasking a Gun Lobby Mole." *Mother Jones* July 30, 2008.

Rohde, David. 2007. "Army Enlists Anthropology in War Zones." *The New York Times.* 10/5/07, pA1.

Rokeach, Milton. 1973. *The Nature of Human Values.* New York: Free Press.

Rose, Charlie. 2007. "Sarah Sewall and Montgomery McFate." *The Charlie Rose Show,* 12/24/07.

Rubin, Amy. 1996. "National Security Education Program May Halt Grant Awards." *Chronicle of Higher Education* 5/17/96 42(36):A45.

Rubinstein, Robert. 2009. "Ethics, Engagement and Experience: Anthropological Excursions in Culture and the Military" Paper presented at the Society for Applied Anthropology annual meetings, Santa Fe, NM.

Sahlins, Marshall. 1966 "The Destruction of Conscience in Vietnam." Originally published in *Dissent* (Jan.-Feb. 1966) *Reprinted in Culture and Practice: Selected Essay.* Pp 229-260. Zone Book, MIT Press.

Sahlins, Marshall. 1967. "The Established Order: Do Not Fold, Spindle or Mutilate." in I. L. Horowitz ed., *The Rise and Fall of Project Camelot.*, pp 71-79, Cambridge: MIT Press.

Sahlins, Marshall. 1978. *Culture and Practical Reason.* Chicago: University of Chicago Press.

Schafft, Gretchen. 2007. *From Racism to Genocide: Anthropology in the Third Reich.* Urbana: University of Illinois Press.

Scott, James. 1999. *Seeing Like a State.* New Haven: Yale University Press.

Shachtman, Noah. 2007. "How Technology Almost Lost the War: In Iraq, the Critical Networks are Social—Not Electronic." *WIRED* 15, 12, November 27.

Shachtman, Noah. 2009. "Mass Exodus from 'Human Terrain' Program: At Least One-Third Quits" *Danger Room* 4/6/09.

Shay, Christopher. 2009. "Should Anthropologists Go to War?" *Time* Dec. 13, 2009.

Shweder, Richard A. 2007. "A True Culture War." *New York Times* 10/27/2007.

Silbey, Susan. 2002. "Sociology study notes." http://ocw.mit.edu/NR/rdonlyres/Anthropology/

Simons, Dolph C. 2003. "Intelligence Training Plan Could Provide Vital Insight to U.S." *Lawrence Journal World and News* 11/29/2003.

Singer, P.W. 2009. *Wired For War.* New York: Penguin.

Spancenthal-Lee, Jonah. 2008. "Spook School." *The Stranger,* 7/22/08, www.thestranger.com/seattle/Content?oid=626734 .

Stanton, John. 2009. *General Petraeus' Favorite Mushroom: Inside the US Army's Human Terrain System*. Wiseman Publishing.

Stanton, John 2008. "US Army Human Terrain System in Disarray." *Online Journal* August 15, 2008.

Stier, Ken. 2007. "Anthropologists on the front lines." *Time*, 12/11/07.

Stockwell, John. 1979. *In Search of Enemies*. New York: Norton

Sutherland, J.J. 2008. "New Army Field Manual is Road Mad to Stabilization." NPR's Morning Edition. 10/7/08.

Thompson, Laura. 1944. "Some Perspectives on Applied Anthropology" *Applied Anthropology* 3:12-16.

Turner, Victor. W. 1977. "Symbols in African Ritual." In J. Dolgin, et al., eds., *Symbolic Anthropology*. 183-194, Columbia Univ. Press.

Turner, Victor. 1967. *The Forest of Symbols*. Cornell University Press.

U.S. Army & Marine Corp. 2007. *Counterinsurgency Field Manual*. University of Chicago Press.

U.S. Army 2008. TC-31-73 *Special Forces Advisor Guide*. Headquarters, Department of the Army. (July 2008), http://www.wikileaks.com/wiki/US_Special_Forces_Advisor_Guide%2C_2_July_2008.

U.S. Congress. 2004. "Intelligence Reform and Terrorism Prevention Act of 2004." Public Law 108-458—Dec. 17, 2004.

UW Faculty Senate Minutes, 12/4/08, http://www.washington.edu/faculty/facsen/senate_minutes/08-09/senate_120408.pdf.

UW Faculty Senate 1/29/09, P 3, http://www.washington.edu/faculty/facsen/senate_minutes/08-09/senate_012909.pdf.

Wakin, Eric. 1998. *Anthropology Goes to War: Professional Ethics and Counterinsurgency in Thailand*. Madison: University of Wisconsin Press.

Walberg, Eric. 2008. "Heart of Darkness: Princess Patricia and the Taliban" *CounterPunch* June 4, 2008.

Wasinki, Chrisophe. 2007. "CounterPunch contre Counterinsurgency. Plagiat et contestation anthropologique à propos du nouveau manuel contre-insurrectionnel des forces armées américaines." Paru dans Cultures & Conflits,71:133-149.

Wax, Murray. 2002. "On Deconstructing Patriotism." Paper presented at the 2002 annual meetings of the American Anthropological Association. New Orleans.

Wax, Murray & Felix Moos. 2004. "Anthropology: Vital or Irrelevant." *Human Organization* 63(2):246-247.

Weber, Max. 1922 [1978] *Economy and Society*. Univ. Calif. Press.

Willing, Richard. 2006. "Intelligence Agencies Invest in College Education." *USA Today* 11/28/06.

Winks, Robin. 1996 *Cloak and Gown: Scholars in the Secret War, 1939-1961. 2nd edition.* New York: Morrow.

Wolf, Eric R. and Jorgensen, Joseph G. 1970. "Anthropology on the Warpath in Thailand." *New York Review of Books*, 19 November: 27.

Vergano, Dan, and Weise, Elizabeth. 2008. "Should anthropologists work alongside soldiers?" *USA Today*, 12/8/08.

Vonnegut, Kurt. 2005. *Man Without a Country*. New York: Random House.

Zwerling, Philip. 2009. "The CIA on my Campus...and Yours." *Nebula* 6.4: 238-263. December 2009.

INDEX

82nd Airborne Division, US Army 96
ABC News 114
Academia, and CIA 33–57, 67–90
Academic freedom 56, 67–69, 76, 87–90, 122
Academic Mind, The (Thielen) 87–8
Ackerman, Spencer 97, 110–1
Acoma Pueblo 19
Afghanistan 5–6, 12, 27, 98, 115, 122, 130–1, 157–8, 160–1, 163, 167–71, 174, 181, 193–200
African Studies Association 34, 49
AfriCom 109, 160
Agee, Philip 44
Agency for International Development (USAID) 24, 180–1
Agriculture Department (USDA) 70
Air Force (USAF) 148, 161, 171
Air Force Academy 148, 161
Al Qaeda 104–5
Alexander of Macedon (the Great) 12
Allison, John 6, 106–8, 155–72
Al-Mohammed, Hayder 6
Alternative media 98
Amazon.com 127
American Anthropological Association (AAA) 18, 22–3, 24–5, 29–30, 37, 39, 57, 62–3, 80, 96, 101, 136, 156–7, 160–1, 174–5, 199
American Anthropologist 25
American Association of University Professors (AAUP) 57, 76, 77
American Council of Learned Societies 34
American Counterinsurgency (González) 109–10, 167
American Indian Movement (AIM) 187

American Psychological Association (APA) 57
Amos, Lt. Gen. James 113
Analyst Notebook 105
Anson, Thomas 6
Answers.com 121
Anthrax 47
AntrhoPac 105
Anthropological Theory 11, 62, 108, 125–127, 140–151, 179–191, 193–200; Culture and personality, 2, 139–151, 190
Applied Anthropology 22
Arab Bulletin 117
Arab Bureau (UK) 117
Arabic language 35, 40, 42, 162
ArcGIS 105
Archaeology 20, 106
Area Study Centers 22, 44, 61, 69
Arizona State University (ASU)64
Arkin, William 55
Armed Services Committee (US House) 111, 171
Arms sales, by US 1, 71
Army War College 114
Army, US 15–6, 23–4, 96, 102, 109–10, 113–31, 133–7, 139–51, 166–7
Asad, Talal 15
Assange, Julian 6, 100–1
Assassination, by US government 1, 28, 105, 129–30
Association of American Universities (AAU) 60
Asymmetrical warfare 2–3, 38
Avatar (Cameron) 173–7
Ayala, Don 101
BAE Systems 110–1
Basque language 42
Bateman, Robert 114
Bates, David 117, 120
Beals, Ralph 24
Beggins, Michael 84
Belmont Report 159–60
Bender, Brian 129–30
Benedict, Ruth 17, 143–5, 148
Berman, Eli 65
Bernard, H. Russell 105–6
Besteman, Catherine 6
Beyerstein, Lindsay 70, 98–9

Beyoghlow, Kamal 65
Bickford, Andy 6
Bin Laden, Osama 149
Biological weapons 21, 35
Bioterrorism 35
Birkenstein, Jeff 6
Black colleges, and CIA 74–75
Black Panthers 75, 168, 187
Blair, Dennis 56
Boas, Franz 17–9, 20, 37
Boggs, Rep. Hale 70
Borat 188–9
Boren Scholarship Program 45–55
Boren, Sen. David 45–6
Boston Globe 129–30
Bourdieu, Pierre 125, 182
Brown, Kenneth 117, 120
Bulletin of the Atomic Scientists 63–4
Bureau of American Ethnology 15–6
Burnett, Stephen 148
Bush Doctrine 64
Bush, George Herbert Walker 50
Bush, George W. 1–2, 27, 38, 42, 55, 68, 127, 198
California State Historic Preservation Office 156
Cambodia 82
Cameron, James 173–7
Carnegie Mellon University 73
Center for Academic Excellence in National Security Studies (CAE-NSIS) 74
Center for Army Lessons Learned 133, 136–7
Central Intelligence Agency (CIA) 1–2, 22–4, 26, 139, 169
Church Hearings and 22–3, 67–8 CIA Coups, 28 and universities 33–57, 67–90, and social science funding 61–2, and Death Squads Death squads 28, and NGOs 85–6, 164–5
Chagnon, Napoleon 125, 182–3
Charlie Rose Show (PBS) 131
Chicago Tribune 114
Chile 23
China 23, 35, 61, 63, 64–5, 126

Chinese language 35
Chomsky, Noam 67
Christian fundamentalists 54
Chronicle of Higher Education, The 38, 43
Church Committee Hearings, on CIA 22–3, 67–8
Church, Sen. Frank 22–3, 67–8
CIA Day 70
CIA Off Campus (Mills) 42, 67
Citations, and COIN manual 116–25, 128–30, 182–3
Clackamas Community College 54
Clancy, Tom 37
Clark Atlanta University 72–4
Clark, Jennifer 171
Clark, William 12–4
Classified research 3, 39–40, 48, 63–64,
Clemson University 73
Cloak & Gown (Winks) 39–40
Cockburn, Alexander 6, 71–2
Cohen, Sasha Baron 189
COINTELPRO (FBI) 187
Colbert, Stephen 38
Cold War 22–4, 55, 63–4, 69, 82, 87, 107–8, 143–4
Collins, Jason 6
Colonialism 1, 14, 126, 130, 149, 185, 196
Columbia University 17
Commerce Department 128–9
Condominas, Georges 129
Congo 24
Conklin, Harold 25
Conquest, military 11–2, 14, 16–7, 31, 96, 110, 130, 174, 179, 196
Coon, Carleton 128, 176
Copyright, and COIN manual 122–5
Cortes, Tony 6
Counter-insurgency 1–2, 12, 16–7, 23–7, 105–11, 113–31, 132–137, 155–172, 173–177, 179–91, 199–200
Counter-Insurgency Field Manual 3–4, 100, 113–31, 180–2, 193–200

Counter-Insurgency Information Analysis (CINFAC) 24
CounterPunch 6, 38, 43, 100, 121, 122–3, 125, 181–2
Counter-terrorism 35–6
Covert actions, by CIA 24–5, 28, 41, 82–3
Crane, Conrad 114, 123
Crenshaw, Martha 65
Culture and personality, 2, 139–151, 190
Cultural Anthropology (Plog) 117, 120
Cultural engineering 22, 103, 106–8, 113–31, 144–5, 200
Cultural relativism 17, 174, 195
Cultural stereotyping 139–51, 174, 188–9
Cultural traits 106–8, 141–147, 190
Culture, definition of 14, 117, 1141–142, 184, 187–8,
Customs, study of 19, 120, 130, 135, 174–5, 188
Dai, Stan 70
Daily Show, The 113–4
Dances With Wolves (Costner) 174
Danger Room (*Wired*)97. 98, 115
Dari language 35
Defense Advanced Research Project Activities (DARPA) 36
Darwin, Charles 59
David, Steven R. 55
Davies, Robertson 59
Death squads, and CIA 28
Defense Intelligence Agency (DIA) 33, 41, 51, 72, 73
Democracy Now 43, 98
Department of Defense (Pentagon) 1–2, 26, 28, 36–7, 46, 50, 60–6, 68, 87, 98, 114–5, 116, 127, 129–30, 140, 149, 171–2, 185
Dersu Uzala (Kurosawa) 174
Detention camps, of Japanese-Americans 20, 22
Dhavan, Purnima 83
Diane Rehm Show (WAMU) 98

Dick, Philip K. 57
Disclosure of sponsorship 18, 25, 50–2, 56
Doctors Without Borders 96
Domscheit-Berg, Daniel 6
Earth Liberation Front 167
East Asian Studies Department (UC) 60–1
Economy & Society (Weber) 117, 121
Education Department 45
Egypt (Ptolemaic) 12
Eisenhower, Pres. Dwight D. 41
Electronic intelligence 47–8
Elle 97, 115
Encyclopedia Britannica 116–7, 119
Engels, Frederick 184
Erie, Penn. 55
Espionage, by scientists 18–9
Ethical Code, of AAA 25–6, 39, 51, 80–1, 96, 199
Ethical standards, in anthropology 4–5, 11, 31, 21–4, 39–42, 51, 56, 74, 80–1, 96, 139–40, 156, 159–61, 179–81; Informed consent, 18, 19, 21, 30, 51, 101, 109, 139, 156, 159–60, 179, 199; Disclosure 18, 25, 50–2, 56; "Do no harm" 25, 90, 100, 105, 139, 156–7, 179, 199
Ethics Committee (AAA) 25–6
Ethiopia 24
Ethnogeographic Board 20
Ethnography 14–6, 28, 101, 120, 158–9, 168–70, 175–6, 189, 196
Eugenics 20
Evans–Pritchard, E.E. 125, 182–3
Exum, Andrew M. 198
Fair use, and COIN manual 122–5
Farm collectivization, in USSR 59
Farsi language 42
FBI files, on American academics 41–2, 87–8
Federal Bureau of Investigation (FBI) 33, 41,

43–5, 47–8, 54, 73–5, 87–90, 187

Feldman, Greg 6

Finney, Cpt. Nathan 102–5

Firth, Raymond 125, 182

Flattes, Nicolas 45–9, 52–3

Florida A&M University 73

Fondacaro, Steve 99, 110

Food security 21, 45–6

Fort Leavenworth 36, 98–9, 103, 114, 133, 135, 155–172

Forte, Maximillian 6

Fortune, Reo 18

Foster, Sharon 42

Foundations, and CIA 22–3

Fox News 28

France 191

Frank, Adam 49–51

Freedom of Information Act (FOIA) 1, 41, 87, 89, 96–7

Fried, Mort 25

From Racism to Genocide (Schafft) 20

Front organizations, for CIA 22–3

Fulbright Scholarships 33, 49–50, 53, 62, 70, 85

Funding of anthropological research, by US government 22–3, 33, 49–50, 53, 61–6, 70, 85

Galtung, Johan 23

Galula, David 12

Gates, Robert 53, 60–6

Geertz, Clifford 125, 182–3

Gender studies 38, 45–6

Gentile, Lt. Col. Gian 108–9, 123–4

Geographical knowledge, by native populations 19–20

Georgian language 35

Geo-spatial analysis 105–6

Ghost Dance 16

Giddens, Anthony 117–8, 119, 182

Giebel, Christoph 76, 78, 83

Giroux, Henry 33, 68

Glakas, Tommy 35–6

Glenn, David 38–39

Global War on Terrorism (GWOT) 1, 6, 27–8, 31, 37–8, 42

González, Roberto 6, 73–4, 95, 99, 104–5, 109–10, 117, 157, 167

Goodman, Alan 80

Goodman, Amy 98

Gordon, Robert 189–90

Gorer, Geoffrey 144

Gramsci, Antonio 125, 182, 187

Grave robbing, by anthropologists 17, 19

Greece (classical) 12

Green Beret (US Army) 129

Green, Linda 6

Griffin, Marcus 109

Group think 42–3

Guantanamo Prison 81

Guerilla Warfare Advocates in the United States (HUAC Report) 168

Gun control groups, spying on 100

Gusterson, Hugh 6, 37, 63–4, 126

Hale Boggs Federal Building 70

Hampton, Fred 75

Haring, Douglas 155

Harrisson, Tom 176

Harper's 97, 115

Harrington, John Peabody 19

Harris, Marvin 25, 188

Harvard University 54, 113, 142–143

Hayden, Tom 125–6

Henchy, Judith 83

Herodotus 128

Hibbin, Frank 23

Higman, Howard 41

Hindu Kush Mountains 168

Hitler, Adolf 149

Hodge, David 79

Homeland Security Department 33, 48, 54, 73, 87–8

Hoover, J. Edgar 41, 43, 75, 89

House UnAmerican Activities Committee (HUAC) 167–8

Houtman, Gustaaf 6

Howard University 74–5

Human Ecology Fund 23

Human rights 30

Human Terrain Systems (HTS) 2–3, 6, 27–30,

95–112, 115, 122, 126, 129–30, 134–6, 155–72, 174–5, 188–9, 193–200

Human Terrain Systems Handbook 100–12

Humphrey, Norman 41

Hunt, E. Howard 70–1

Huntington, Samuel 37

Hussein, Saddam 149

Hymes, Dell 25

Hypothermia studies 21

In Search of Enemies (Stockwell) 44

In These Times 98–9

India 45–6

Indigenous cultures 25–6

Indonesia 82, 170

Infinite Jest (Wallace) 11

Information Operations (InfoOps) 162, 167

Informed consent, of research subjects 18, 19, 21, 30, 51, 101, 109, 139, 156, 159–60, 179, 199

Inside the Company (Agee) 44

Institute of Human Relations 106–7, 148

Institute for National Security Education and Research (INSER) 74, 76–9, 83

Institutional Review Boards 41, 51–2, 80, 99, 108–109

Intelligence Advanced Research Projects Activity (IARPA) 69–72

Intelligence Authorization Act (2004) 34

Intelligence Committee (Senate) 43

Intelligence Community Centers of Academic Excellence (ICCAE) 5, 42, 54–5, 67–90

Intelligence Community Scholars Program (ICSP) 44–5, 53–4, 60, 69, 161

Intelligence Reform and Terrorism Prevention Act (2004) 44

Intelligence Studies Fund Group Librarians 84–5

Intelligencecareers.com 35

Interior Department 15–16

International Committee of the Red Cross 96
International Trade Office 50
Interrogation manuals 85
Interrogation techniques 23, 85, 104–5
Iraq 5–6, 27, 30, 61, 65, 98, 109–10, 113, 122, 127, 129–30, 133–7, 163, 167, 170, 174, 196
Ireland 193–4
Irish Republican Army (IRA) 193–4
Islam 35, 61, 63, 64–5, 164, 170
Jackson, Jean 6
Jackson, Sen. Henry "Scoop" 81
Jamail, Dahr 98
Japan 20–3, 126, 144
Jaurequi, Bea 6
Jefferson, Thomas 12–4, 24
Jewel, Timothy 84
Johns Hopkins University 55
Jordan, William 84
Junior Statesmen of America 70
Kaczynski, Theodore 149
Kansas University Radio 37
Kazakhstan 188–9
Kelly, John 6
Kent, Sherwood 40
Kesey, Ken 179
Kilcullen, David 117, 181, 185, 189–91, 198
Kim, Jeffrey 76
Kinetic engagements 95–6, 111, 162, 168–170
Klamath Nation 163–4
Kluckhohn Center 143
Kluckhohn, Florence 142–3, 145, 148–9
Korea 35
Korean language 35
Kroeber, Alfred 17, 19
KUBARK, CIA interrogation manual 23
Kurdistan 197
Kurtz, Stanley 43
Kwakiutl Nation 143
Lakota Nation (Sioux) 15–6
Lamarkian biology 59
Landrieu, Sen. Mary 70

Language studies 2, 12, 19–20, 22–3, 29, 33–6, 39, 41, 42, 61, 69, 74
Lansdale, Edward 12
Laos 36
Latin American Studies Association 34, 49
Lawrence Journal World 35
Lawrence, T.E. (of Arabia) 117, 124
Lazarfeld, Paul 87–8
Leach, Edmund 176
Leighton, Alexander 130
Lethal Effects Targeting 104–5
Lévi-Strauss, Claude 133, 195
Lewis & Clark Expedition 12–4
Lewis, Meriwether 12–4
Liberals, support of COIN 56–7, 115–6, 200
Liddy, G. Gordon 71
Linguistics 3, 17, 19, 33–4
Linton, Ralph 125, 182
Little Big Man 174
Local Hero 174
Logan, Susan 65
Lolita (Nabokov) 198–9
Looting, by anthropologists 17–9
Loschiano, Brian 6
Low, Setha 62–3
Lutkehaus, Nancy 175
Luttwak, Edward 191
Lutz, Catherine 6, 61–2, 71
Lysenko, Trofim 59–61
M–16 rifle 196
Machiavelli, Niccolo 139
Macy, Neb. 18
Malaysia 170
Malinowski, Bronsilaw 125, 182
Mardex 166–7
Marine Corps, US (USMC) 65, 113–31
Marx, Karl 2, 184
Marxism 2, 43
Massachusetts Institute of Technology (MIT) 54
Matrix, The 198
Matsumoto, David 64–5
McCarthy, Sen. Joseph 1, 41, 43, 87
McCarthyism 1, 41, 43, 87

McChrystal, Gen. Stanley 171
McCuin, Maj. Tom 122
McFate, Montgomery 27–8, 39, 98–100, 123–6, 171, 181, 185, 189–90, 193–200
Mead Committee Report, for AAA 26
Mead, Margaret 17–8, 20, 26, 144
Mead, Stephen 6
Medial research, on humans 21–2
Mellon Foundation 193
Mendel, Gregor 59
Mengele, Dr. Josef 20–1
Mercenaries 12
Mercyhurst College 54–5
Middle East Studies Association 34, 49
Miles College 73, 75
Militarizing Culture (Gonzalez) 73
Military spending, by US 71
Mills, Ami Chen 67
Mills, C. Wright 125
Minerva Consortium 2, 5, 53, 60–6, 86, 149–50, 161
Mitchell, Sean 6
Modernization programs (USAID) 14, 24, 62, 180
Moerman, Michael 25–6
Montagnards 129
Montagu, Ashley 17
Mooney, James 15–6
Moos, Felix 36–7, 38–9
More 97, 115
Morocco 128
Mosul, Iraq 133–7
M–Project 20
Murdock, George Peter 107, 148
Murphy, Robert 25
Museums, and cultural looting 19
Music Man, The 174
Nabokov, Vladimir 198–9
Nader, Laura 6, 23, 37–8
Nagl, Lt. Gen. John 113–4, 123–6, 131
NASA 186
Nash, June 133
Nation, The 17, 49–50, 125–6

National Academic Consortium for Homeland Security (NACHoS)54–5
National Defense Education Act (1958) 69
National Endowment for the Humanities (NEH) 63
National Ground Intelligence Center 35
National Institute of Health (NIH) 61, 63
National Public Radio (NPR) 43, 113
National Review 43
National Science Foundation (NSF) 45, 61–3, 65, 70, 85, 193
National Security Agency (NSA) 33, 36, 41, 45, 48, 50, 73, 88
National Security Education Program (NSEP) 33–4, 44–53, 60
Native American Indians 12–6, 125–6, 163–4
Natural resources, indigenous knowledge of 19–20, 106–7
Nature 97, 101
Naval Academy (Annapolis) 148, 161
Naval Postgraduate School 148
Naval War College 36, 65
Navy, US 36, 47–8, 65, 148, 161, 171
Nazi, anthropologists 20–1
NBC News 114
Neo–colonialism 30, 95–6, 139, 149, 185
Neoconservatives 43
NetDraw 105
Network of Concerned Anthropologists 29–30, 111–2, 157
New Disciplines Project 63
New York Times (NYT) 96–7, 114, 126, 189, 198
New Yorker, The 97, 115
Newman, David 116–7, 119
Newsweek 70, 114
Nietzsche, Friedrich 143
Nigeria 163
Nike, Inc. 85

Niva, Steve 6
Non–Governmental Organizations (NGO) 46, 86
Northern Ireland 193–4
Nous Avons Mangé la Fôret (Condominas) 129
Nuclear bomb testing 23
Nuremberg Code 21, 41, 159–60
Nuremberg Tribunals 21
Nuristan 164–5, 168–9
Nussle, Jim 63
O'Keefe, James 69–70
Obama, Barack 2, 29–31, 55–6, 175, 198
Occupation, military 12–3, 96, 109–10
Office of Director of National Intelligence (ODNI) 44, 56, 73, 81–2
Office of Naval Intelligence (ONI) 18, 36, 148
Office of Strategic Services (OSS) 21–22, 128
Omaha Nation 18
One Flew Over the Cuckoo's Nest (Kesey) 179
Open source research 39–40, 60
Opium 12–3
PackBot 196
Pakistan 43, 198
Papua New Guinea 175
Paracelsus 59
Pashto language 35
Pat Roberts Intelligence Scholars Program (PRISP) 2, 5, 33–42, 53–4, 60, 69, 86, 161
Patrick Henry College 54
Patriot Act 43, 88–9
Pattern analysis 105–6
Patterns of Culture (Benedict) 143
Patton, David 6
Pauley, Ann 70
Payback agreements, for scholarships 33–57, 61–2
Pearl Harbor, attack on 19
Penn State University 73
Persian language 35
Peru 20

Petraeus, Gen. David 113–4, 115–6, 127, 133, 135, 171
Peyote, as Native American sacrament 16
Philippines 82
Phoenix Program 105, 126
Plog, Fred 117, 120
Pochahontas 174
Polk, William 187
Poppy (opium) cultivation 12–3
Population control & manipulation 5, 12, 14–5, 16–7, 21, 102–3, 106–7, 163, 166, 174, 196–197
Powell, Maj. John Wesley 15
Powers, Christopher 46–8
Predator drones 196–8
Price, Midge 6
Price, Milo 6
Price, Nora 6
Priest, Dana 55
Principles of Anthropology (Coon) 128
Principles of Professional Responsibility, (AAA) 25–30, 39, 80–1
Prison Notebooks (Gramsci) 182
Project Camelot 23–4
Project Themis 36
Propaganda 20, 111, 126–8, 131, 157, 162–3, 185
Provincial Reconstruction Teams 162
Psychological Operations (PSYOPS) 16, 25, 162, 167, 195–6
Queen, Lisa 6
Racial equality 30
Racial identity 17, 116–7, 121
Radcliffe–Brown, A.R. 125, 182
Radical Caucus, of AAA 25–6, 173
RAND, Corp. 24, 37, 144
Reach–Back Analysis 103, 135–6, 170
Reach–Back Research Center 103, 170
Rebel Angels, The (Davies) 59
Recruiting, by CIA 67–9
Redford, Robert 72
Rehm, Diane 98

Reidhead, Van 76
Relocation, of war refugees 20
Reservations, for Native American Indians 13–4, 125–6
Reserve Officer Training Corps. (ROTC) 35, 56–7
Ricoeur, Paul 182–3
Ridge, Gov. Tom 55
Ridgeway, James 100
Ritual 115–7, 120–1, 182
Roberts, Sen. Pat 2, 34, 43–4
Robertson, Cliff 72
Rohde, David 96–7
Rose, Charlie 131
Ross, Eric 6
Royal British Army 193–4
Rubenstein, Robert 37
Russia 35, 142, 157
Russian language 35, 69
Sahlins, Marshall 6, 23–4, 140, 188
San Francisco State University 64–5
Sarawak 176
Shachtman, Noah 97–8, 115
Schafft, Gretchen 20
Schild, Schuyler 6
Scholarship, and COIN manual 113–131, 182–3
Schwarzenegger, Gov. Arnold 60
Schweitzer, Col. Martin 96–7
Scott, James 65, 103, 190
Secrecy, problems of 27, 29–30, 39–41, 52, 67–8, 89
Seeing Like a State (Scott) 103
Segal, Daniel 6
September 11, 2001, attacks of 27, 33–4, 36, 46, 63, 68, 77
Seventh Cavalry (US Army) 15
Sewell, Sarah 113–4, 131
Shell-Duncan, Bettina 79–81
Shirk, Susan 64–5
Shweder, Richard 126
Sierra Club 167
Simons, Anna 37
Singer, P.W. 197
Sioux Nation (Lakota) 15–6
Small Wars Journal 122–3, 125, 182
Smithsonian Institution 20

Snider, Roger 6
Social control 5, 15, 24, 103, 106–7, 157, 163, 166, 168, 181, 184–87, 189, 190, 196–200
Social Science Research Council 34
Social structures 117–8, 122
Society for Applied Linguistics 21–2
Sociology (Giddens) 118–9
Sociology (Newman) 116
South Africa 189–90
South African Defense Forces (SADF) 189–90
Spain, William 65
Special Forces (Army) 139–51
Special Forces Advisor Guide 139–51, 190
Special Operations Research Office (SORO) 24, 107–8
Special Weapons Observation Reconnaissance System (SWORS) 196–7
Spradley, James 105–6
Spying, on academics 41–2, 87–8
St. Clair, Jeffrey 6
Staff & Command College 36
Stalin, Josef 149
Stanford University 65, 123–4
Stanton, John 98, 103
Star Trek 107
State Department 2, 68, 140, 171
Stewart, Jon 114
Stockholm Syndrome 169
Stockwell, John 44
Strategic Hamlets Program (Vietnam) 12, 24
Stress studies 23
Strodtbeck, Fred 142–3, 145
Stryker Brigades 133–7
Stryker Report on Iraqi Failures 5, 133–7
Student Mobilizer, The 25–6
Subjugation 61, 102–5, 109, 174, 184
Sun Dance 16
Sun Tzu 12, 37
Sustainable agriculture 45–6
Tajik language 35
Taliban 104–5
Talon 196

Taylor, Janelle 79–80
Tennessee State University 73
Terrorism 1, 6, 21, 31, 35, 38, 63, 176
Thailand 25, 36, 82
Thielen, Wagner 87–8
Thompson, Linda 21
Thompson, Sir Richard 12
Threatening Anthropology (Price) 87
Three Days of the Condor 72
Thucydides 128
Time 97, 175
Title VI, funding under 33, 53
Torture 1, 85, 104–5
Torture manuals 85
Transparency, in government contracts 57–8
Treasury Department 47, 50
Trinity Washington University 54, 70, 72–3
Truthout.org 98
Tryneski, John 127
Turkish language 35
Turcoman language 35
Turner, Adm. Stansfield 36
Turner, Terence 29
Turner, Victor 116–7, 121, 182–3
UCINet 105
Union of Soviet Socialist Republics (USSR) 59–60, 65, 69, 87, 144, 157
Universities, and intelligence agencies 1–2, 5, 33–57, 59–66, 67–90
University in Chains (Giroux) 68
University of California at Berkeley 19–20
University of California at Los Angeles (UCLA) 25
University of California at San Bernardino 72
University of California at San Diego (UCSD) 64–5
University of California at Santa Barbara (UCSB) 38
University of Chicago 54
University of Chicago Press 113–4, 124–5, 126–8
University of Hawaii 45–6
University of Kansas 36

University of Maryland 73
University of Nebraska 73
University of New Mexico 73
University of North Carolina
   at Wilmington 73
University of Southern
   California (USC) 175
University of Texas at El Paso
   (UTEP) 73
University of Texas Pan
   American 73, 76
University of Washington
   73–4, 76–83
Urdu language 35
USA Today 97
Uzbek language 35
Values Orientation Model
   142–4
Van Derbur, Marilyn 41
Viet Cong 105, 129–30
Vietnam War 5, 12, 24–6, 30,
   36, 105, 126, 129–30, 199
Vine, David 6
Violent Politics (Polk) 187
Virginia Polytechnical
   University 73, 75
Vonnegut, Kurt 137
Waigal Valley 164–5
Walberg, Eric 191
Wallace, David Foster 11
Walton, Jeremy 6
War Relocation Authority 20
Warren, Adam 83
Warren, Jonathan 81–2
Washington Post 55, 75–6,
   97, 189
Washington, Lula 175
Wax, Murray 19, 37
Wayne State University 73–4
Weaver, Sigourney 175
Weber, Max 117, 121, 182–4, 187
Weekly Standard, The 115
Weisler, Michele 6
Weltfish, Gene 41
Wenner-Gren Foundation 62
West Point Academy 161
Weston Resolve 166–7
White, Leslie 19
Wichita Eagle 43
Wikileaks 100–1, 140
Wilson, Cathy 6
Wilson, Edward 71
Winks, Robin 39–40

Wintersteen, Ben 175
Wired 97, 115
Wired for War (Singer) 197
Wiretapping 69–70
Wise, Phyllis 80, 85
Wolf, Eric 25–6
Woodward, Mark 64
World Archaeology Congress
   155
World Bank 36
World Politics Review 157–8
World Trade Center, attacks
   on 27, 33–4, 36, 46, 63
World War One 2, 17
World War Two 2, 5, 18–9,
   21–2, 30, 42, 61, 72, 107–8,
   115, 143–4, 148, 176, 199
Wounded Knee, Battle of 15
Yale Report, on classified
   research (Kent) 39–40
Yale University 38, 40, 54, 193
Yaphe, Judith 65
Yemen 163
Zuni Pueblo 143
Zwerling, Philip 90